The Zong

The Zong

A MASSACRE, THE LAW AND THE END OF SLAVERY

JAMES WALVIN

YALE UNIVERSITY PRESS
NEW HAVEN AND LONDON

For information about this and other Yale University Press publications, please contact:

U.S. Office sales.press@yale.edu   www.yalebooks.com
Europe Office: sales@yaleup.co.uk   www.yalebooks.co.uk

Set in Adobe Caslon by IDSUK (DataConnection) Ltd

Library of Congress Cataloging-in-Publication Data

Walvin, James.
    The Zong : a massacre, the law and the end of slavery / James Walvin.
        p. cm.
    ISBN 978-0-300-25388-7
    Includes bibliographical references and index.
    1. Zong (Slave ship) 2. Slave-trade—England—Liverpool—History—
18th century. 3. Slave-trade—Jamaica—History—18th century. 4. Slaves—
Violence against—History—18th century. 5. Mass murder—History—18th
century. 6. Seafaring life—History—18th century. 7. Trials—England—
London—History—18th century. 8. Marine insurance—Great Britain—
History. 9. Slavery—Law and legislation—Great Britain—History. 10.
Antislavery movements—Great Britain—History.   I. Title.
    HT1164.L5W35 2011
    306.3'62094275309033—dc22
                                                                        2011001489

A catalogue record for this book is available from the British Library.

For Michael Craton

Contents

List of Illustrations

Acknowledgments

I COULD NOT HAVE WRITTEN THIS BOOK WITHOUT THE HELP and encouragement of a number of colleagues and friends. My warmest thanks go to Heather McCallum of Yale University Press, who not only commissioned the book, but stuck with it through thick and thin. Rachael Lonsdale's editing greatly improved my early draft. And Judith Wardman proved an exemplary copy-editor. Thanks also to Charles Walker for his efforts on my behalf.

I also owe a great deal to Yale University. Colleagues at the Yale Center for British Art made my stay there both congenial and productive. Among colleagues at Yale I would like to single out Gillian Forrester, Hazel Carby, David Blight and Dana Schaffer. Caryl Phillips in particular has listened with great interest to my preoccupation with the *Zong*, in locations as far afield as Ilkley and Sydney. He also made it possible for me to make my first visit to Ghana's slave forts. David Richardson, exemplary scholar and friend, answered my regular queries promptly and with great patience. Avner Offer, always generous with his time and thoughts, steered me towards literature and ideas I had not previously considered.

I benefited greatly from discussing the *Zong* at different academic venues. At Yale (thanks to the Gilder Lehrman Center and the Department of African-American Studies), at the University of Freiburg (courtesy of Frans Bruggemeier), at the University of Nottingham (thanks to Dick Geary). Simon Lewis was my host at the College of Charleston. At Monticello, I would like to thank Mary Scott-Fleming and Andrew O'Shaughnessy.

Research for this book has been greatly helped by the hospitality of a number of friends, especially Byron Criddle in London and Fred Croton and Selma Holo in Los Angeles. In Jamaica, old friends again made me welcome and at home, and I thank Joan and Peter McConnell, Robert and Billie Clarke, and David and Andrea Hopwood. My greatest academic debt, however, is to the anonymous reviewer of my initial draft. That long, detailed and perceptive criticism enabled me to write the book which follows.

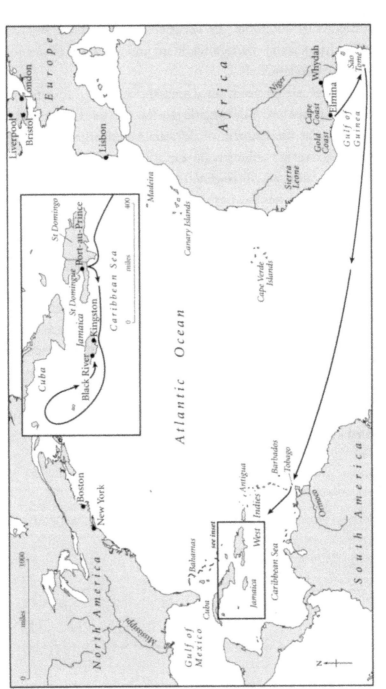

The route taken by the *Zong*, 18 August–22 December 1781.

CHAPTER I

A painting and a slave ship

On 19 March 1783 Granville Sharp, a humble clerk in the Ordnance Office, but already well-known to England's black community for his indefatigable efforts on their behalf, noted in his diary: 'Gustavas Vasa a Negro called on me with an account of 130 Negroes being thrown Alive into the sea from on Board an English Slave Ship.'[1] Thanks mainly to a detailed report in a London newspaper, the news of the killings quickly spread. To many, even the bare details seemed scarcely credible. In the last weeks of 1781, the crew of the *Zong*, a Liverpool-registered slave ship, had thrown 132 Africans overboard to their death. The ship was *en route* from Africa to Black River in Jamaica, had overshot its destination and was running short of water. It was reported that the ship's captain, Luke Collingwood, had ordered the Africans killed, in three batches, in order to reduce the demand for water and to ensure that 'marketable' slaves would survive to landfall in Jamaica.[2]

The atrocity might have passed virtually unnoticed but for one extraordinary fact: the syndicate of Liverpool businessmen who owned the *Zong* took their insurers to court to secure payment for the loss of the dead Africans.[3] The shipowners were pursuing their claim under well-established protocols of maritime insurance which accepted that enslaved Africans on board the Atlantic ships were insured *as cargo*. Moreover, under certain circumstances, the loss of those Africans could be claimed on the ship's insurance.[4] In 1783, however, Granville Sharp and his African informant, Gustavus Vassa (better-known today as Olaudah Equiano), saw the story in an utterly different light. To them (and, as the news spread, to an expanding army of outraged British critics) the *Zong's* owners were demanding money for over a hundred human lives brutally and purposefully cut short.

The resulting legal dispute between the shipowners (Gregson) and the insurers (Gilbert) ensured that the story of the *Zong* was transformed from a murderous secret among the small handful of sailors who carried out the killings, and their employers in Liverpool, into a highly visible political and legal issue. The consequences of the *Zong* affair were enormous. The very name – the *Zong* – quickly entered the demonology of Atlantic slavery, and came to represent the depravity and heartless violence of the entire slave system. The legal and political arguments about the *Zong* inevitably spawned an abundance of contemporary paperwork: legal documents, press coverage, contemporary commentaries, shipping records, correspondence. But we have no surviving picture of that ship. One painting, however, has, over the years, come to be closely associated with the *Zong*. Indeed scholars from various disciplines have, mistakenly, accepted that the painting was directly inspired by that tragic ship. Today, if anyone wishes to use a visual representation of the *Zong*, they are very likely to turn to

J.M.W. Turner's masterpiece *The Slave Ship*, with its haunting portrayal of black bodies drowning beside a ship threatened by a looming storm.[5]

Turner's painting, first exhibited in London in 1840, poses troubling questions about what it depicts, as well as why it was painted. Why kill Africans at sea when the sole aim of the slave trade was to sell them for a profit in the markets of the Americas? Why did Turner decide to paint this picture thirty-three years *after* the British had abolished the slave trade in 1807, when by all rights it should have been a fading memory? And further, why do scholars and others continue to regard this picture as representative of the slave trade itself, when in fact it portrays, not a profitable commerce in humanity, but its very opposite: the calculated killing of Africans at sea?

For all that, *The Slave Ship* remains an astonishing artistic achievement, and to scrutinise the painting at close hand is to be confronted by the realities of the Atlantic slave ships. Legions of people must have seen copies of Turner's painting in one form or another, and even in a poor reproduction it remains a remarkable image. But to study the original painting, in Boston's Museum of Fine Arts, came as something of a shock. For a start, it is small, measuring only three feet by four feet, and on the day I spent in its company, it was sharing an exhibition wall with another painting. I had fully expected it to have a wall of its own, to offer an uncluttered assertion of Turner's genius, as well as to testify to the appalling importance of its subject matter. I had wanted it to hang alone, if only to confirm its centrality in my own imagination. During the time I had been working this book, I had turned time and again to this particular painting. Like many others I assumed – and was led to believe by what I read – that

The Slave Ship was indeed the *Zong* itself. I even had a post-card of the painting on my desk as I wrote this book. But my mind's eye had always conjured forth a very different image from the reality facing me in Boston. I had expected – *hoped* – to see an immense painting, primarily (I suspect) because of the enormity of the subject matter. If ever there was a subject that demanded a significant physical presence, this was it. *The Slave Ship* was not at all what I wanted.

Still, nothing could minimise the painting's impressiveness and impact – notwithstanding its size. I stood before it much longer than I had for any other painting, occasionally moving left and right, closer or further away, all the while negotiating the crowds flowing through the astonishing treasures housed in the gallery. I broke away to visit other exhibits, then returned, later in the day, to look at it again, and to renew acquaintance with what had become a horrible fascination. It is, after all, a painting which tells a terrible story.

Turner's *Slavers Throwing Overboard the Dead and Dying* (better known as *The Slave Ship*) is one of his finest, perhaps even *the* finest of his paintings. It is a dazzling picture, filled with mesmeric confusions, images and colours. The painting is a mosaic of perplexing issues. At times it is hard to see what Turner is trying to convey, though the picture's basic compo-nents seem clear enough. There is a sailing ship in the distance, about to be engulfed by a typhoon. In the foreground, black people are drowning in a turbulent ocean. In one corner there is a confusion of fish, birds, limbs – and chains. The whole seems a clutter of almost surreal confusion, with shackles and chains appearing to defy physical laws, rising above the waves instead of sinking to the ocean bed. And what are those outstretched arms and hands? A final despairing wave from wretches doomed to a terrible fate? The fishes' staring eyes seem to gawp at the viewer, as they home in to feast on a fettered leg, while hungry seagulls flap above the human and watery mayhem, ready to pounce on whatever scraps of flesh the fish might miss.

Dominating everything – almost splitting the painting down the middle – is a dazzling sunset which ignites the entire ghastly scene. It is a vista of oceanic suffering; of dying humanity, unseen except for beseeching hands and one severed leg, soon to be devoured. This is a world of grotesque imagination, so vile in its detail that it almost beggars belief. Yet Turner's portrayal is far from imaginary. Africans had indeed been thrown to their deaths from Atlantic slave ships, most infamously (but, as we shall see, not only) in 1781 from the Liverpool-registered *Zong*. Turner's painting of 1840 is also a reminder of another, less well-known issue: that the Atlantic slave trade continued despite the Anglo-American abolitions of 1807 and 1808, and that enslaved Africans remained victim to periodic acts of atrocity on those later clandestine foreign vessels.

At the time when Turner was working on *The Slave Ship*, it had become clear that a number of such killings had recently taken place on Atlantic slave ships (mainly under Spanish and Portuguese flags). Accounts of those killings – all of them harrowing, some scarcely credible in their extreme horror – were widely publicised in parliament, in the press and in abolitionist literature, where they were used as part of the ever more aggressive drive against the continuing Atlantic slave trade.[6]

Despite the barbarity of these incidents, and despite the urgency they brought to the anti-slave-trade arguments in the 1820s and 1830s, they formed only one theme in a British abolition campaign whose prime aim was the ending of slavery in the British colonies. When full emancipation was finally achieved in 1838 (at a staggering cost of £20 million in compensation paid to the slave-owners) it prompted celebrations on both sides of the Atlantic. American abolitionists took great heart from British emancipation: it showed that slavery *could* be brought down, however severe the obstacles. The Americans thought the time was now ripe for abolitionists worldwide to come together to show their resolve and strength, and they proposed an international anti-slavery convention.

Thus, on 1 June 1840 the first World Anti-Slavery Convention opened in London's Exeter Hall. Appropriately, the opening address was given by Thomas Clarkson, who had been the indefatigable foot soldier of the abolitionist movement since its foundation in 1787. The convention was packed with an extraordinary collection of delegates: 250 from around Britain, and others from as far afield as Canada, the USA, Mauritius, Haiti and Sierra Leone. There was also a sizeable female presence (although an argument ensued about whether women should have full delegate status – it was refused).[7]

The convention met in Exeter Hall, a large new building, capable of providing a public meeting place for thousands of people, and located opposite the current Savoy Hotel on the Strand. Had the 1,840 delegates been so inclined, they could have walked down the Strand, past the building work then taking place to construct Nelson's Column, and on to the Royal Academy in Trafalgar Square. There they would have found the Academy's annual exhibition of paintings.

On Monday, 4 May 1840, precisely one month before the Anti-Slavery Convention began, the Royal Academy had opened its seventy-second annual exhibition to the public. Two days later *The Times*'s review of the exhibition made plain its dislike of item 203: J.M.W. Turner's painting *Slavers Throwing Overboard the Dead and Dying*. It is, said the reviewer,

> irksome to find fault with so admirable an artist as Mr. Turner has been, but it is impossible to look at this picture without mingled feelings of pity and contempt. Such a mass of heterogeneous atoms were never brought together to complete a whole before. Amidst a regiment of fish and fowl of all shapes, colours, sizes, and proportions, is seen the leg of a negro, which is about to afford a nibble to a John Dory, a pair of soles and a shoal of whitebait.[8]

Many others disliked the painting – indeed, criticism was general and widespread. Reviewers in a number of the major newspapers and journals ridiculed its subject matter (suggesting that drowning slaves was horrific and unsuitable for depiction in paint) while others denounced its use of colour. *The Slave Ship* was a picture which provoked extreme and conflicting reactions. The *Art Union* of 15 May published perhaps the most caustic of comments on the painting: 'Who will not grieve at the talent wasted upon the gross outrage on nature, No. 203'.[9] Even people who liked certain aspects of the picture remained confused by it. Thackeray, for example, 'treated Turner's painting with a mixture of admiration and contempt'. He praised the aesthetics of its colour, but denounced it for its treatment of the drowning slaves. He wrote of the 'huge, slimy, poached eggs in which the hapless niggers plunge and disappear. Ye Gods what a "middle-passage" '.[10]

One man, however, admired it intensely. In the New Year of 1844, John Ruskin was given the painting by his father (who had bought it for 250 guineas). It was, Ruskin believed, Turner's great masterpiece: 'if I were reduced to rest Turner's immortality upon any single work, I would choose this'. Yet even Ruskin was uneasy with this troubling painting, and throughout the twenty-eight years he owned it, he remained perplexed by its content and by its connotations. He never really found a suitable place for it in his home, hanging it in various rooms: in his bedroom, in the hall, and even propping it on his bed before he finally decided that he simply could not live with it. He later explained that he had sold the painting, 'because as I grow old, I grow sad, and cannot endure anything near me, either melancholy or violently pessimistic'.[11] Ruskin finally sold it, and, like a slave ship, the painting crossed the Atlantic to its present home.

When it was first exhibited in Boston in 1875, it was again heavily criticised. Mark Twain, for example, described it in *A Tramp Abroad* (1880) as 'a manifest impossibility – that is to say, a lie', and as reminding a Boston newspaper reporter of 'a tortoise-shell cat having a fit in a platter of tomatoes'. Twain's derision recurred time and again in his notebooks, and he clearly could not shake the picture from his thoughts. In Europe, whenever he looked at other Turner paintings, *The Slave Ship* immediately sprang to mind. It was a picture which made Twain feel sick – long after he set eyes on it.[12]

The visceral distaste expressed by Mark Twain and other critics towards *The Slave Ship* tended to be on aesthetic grounds. But would they have felt such physical revulsion had they pondered the historical realities represented by the painting? In his unique fashion, Turner was confronting an issue which, then as now, cannot be treated or discussed with any degree of comfort. *The Slave Ship* was, at heart, a memorial: it is claimed by an eminent art critic to be the only 'indisputably great work of Western art ever made to commemorate the Atlantic slave trade'.[13] It effectively commemorates the millions who disappeared into the maws of the Atlantic slave trade. It was – and remains – a deeply troubling, discomforting painting, though nothing like as troubling as the history which lurks behind it.

What prompted Turner to attend to this dark subject matter? Turner scholars accept that he was greatly influenced, throughout much of his work, by the eighteenth-century poetry of James Thomson, more specifically by Thomson's poem 'Summer' (published between 1726 and 1730).[14] That poem includes a description of a slave ship caught up in a typhoon (itself symbolising the destruction of the slave trade), and of a 'direful shark' devouring the limbs of hapless slaves – though Thomson's aquatic agent of justice metes out the same fate to the crew members tossed by the storm into the water:

Lured by the scent
Of steaming crowds, of rank disease, and death,
Behold! he rushing cuts the briny flood,
Swift as the gale can bear the ship along;
And from the partners of that cruel trade
Which spoils unhappy Guinea of her sons
Demands his share of prey – demands themselves.
The stormy fates descend: one death involves
Tyrants and slaves; when straight, their mangled limbs
Crashing at once, he dyes the purple seas
With gore, and riots in the vengeful meal.[15]

But there were other, more immediate influences which may have edged Turner towards thinking about slave ships. There was, most obviously, a charged political atmosphere in Britain during the 1820s and 1830s and the campaign against slavery, culminating in emancipation in 1838.[16] Two major books published in 1838–40 – a biography of the great reformer Wilberforce by his sons, and a reprint of Thomas Clarkson's history of abolition – looked back over the fifty-year campaign against the slave trade and slavery.[17] There was, in addition, a mounting concern that the British Abolition Act of 1807 was not totally effective: it had *not* managed to stop the flow and abuse of enslaved Africans across the Atlantic. And in this restless milieu, the most infamous atrocity, committed a full fifty-eight years earlier, was reprised by Thomas Clarkson in his 1839 *History of the Rise, Progress, and Accomplishment of the Abolition of the African Slave Trade*. The *Zong* continues to cast a long shadow.

Along with many other historians of slavery, I have found it impossible to escape that shadow. The story of the *Zong* has insinuated itself into much of what I have written about the slave trade, from a book I wrote in 1973 through to one published in 2007.[18] More recently, I have become convinced that the story of the *Zong* is too central (and too instructive) to be left simply as a marginal story, tangential to other historical narratives. What follows then is an attempt to tackle the *Zong* directly: to confront many of the complex issues and difficulties it poses and which, so far, I have only skirted. The *Zong*, as we shall see, was not only a horrific occurrence, but a nascent step in the origins of the campaign to bring the British slave trade to an end. It struck a chord, then as now, finding a niche in popular memory, and maintaining a resonance right down to the present day.

Today, it may seem obvious that a mass killing such as that on the *Zong* would cause outrage when exposed. Yet why *should* people have felt so outraged in 1783, in a British society which had, since time out of mind, routinely shipped millions of Africans as items of trade, in thousands of British ships, to the slave colonies? After all, in the process of enslavement and transportation, and long before the *Zong*, untold numbers of Africans had died, in Africa, on the slave ships, and soon after landing in the Americas, victims of the dangerous, diseased and violent world of Atlantic slavery. What makes the *Zong* different from what had gone before?

The story of the *Zong* is also an exploration of changing sensibility among the British – their rejection of a lucrative habit. The *Zong* helped prompt a growing revulsion against the bleak inhumanities which formed the basis of the Atlantic slave trade. The account which follows is, at once, a simple story of one slave ship, and an account of a confusing and troubling enigma at the heart of British trade and empire in the late eighteenth century.

The *Zong* was registered in Liverpool, and the subsequent legal dispute involved a group of businessmen from that city. By 1783, when the story broke, Liverpool had established itself as the undisputed boom port of the Atlantic slave trade. Like so many aspects of the British slave trade, what follows begins in Liverpool.

CHAPTER 2

The city built on slavery

W HEN THE *ZONG* WAS PURCHASED BY A GROUP OF
Liverpool merchants in 1781, that city was the dominant
force in the Atlantic slave trade: by the time the British slave
trade ceased in 1807, one in six or seven Africans who had
crossed the Atlantic had done so in a Liverpool-registered
ship. By that point, Liverpool had become synonymous with
the slave trade, but its inexorable rise had come on the back of
a flourishing maritime business in many different cargoes, not
solely human. The city's coastal trade remained *the* dominant
form of Liverpool's trade throughout the eighteenth century,
and brought great wealth to the city.[1]

Liverpool boomed. It was a place which buzzed with
energy, with armies of people bustling around the river front
and docks, or working to build and expand the fabric of that
thriving port. Here was a prosperity which had grown quite
recently out of the city's seaborne trade. The *Annual Register*
said of Liverpool, as early as 1764, that '. . . within these fifty
years it hath increased prodigiously in trade, and is now the

greatest seaport in England, except London and Bristol'.[2] There was hardly an inch to spare at the water's edge, as vessels jostled from all corners of European and Atlantic trade for berths. The city's ships, and the myriad industries they spawned and relied on, were served by an expanding population of working people who flocked to Liverpool from a wide hinterland of Britain, and from across the Irish Sea. These migrants settled down as best they could into already crowded quarters, or spilled out into the 'long, narrow streets of poor housing' springing up to the north of the city. As poor migrants moved in, the better-off moved out to the city's new suburbs, or even further afield.

Time and again visitors were struck by the tide of humanity crowding the city's streets. At the beginning of the eighteenth century, Liverpool's population had been a mere 5,145. At mid-century that had swelled to 18,400. By the time of the first census in 1801, it had shot up to 77,653.[3] The engine, the cause and occasion behind this human growth, was the massive expansion of Liverpool's seaborne commerce. The men who dominated that commerce also dominated the politics of Liverpool throughout the eighteenth century, and masterminded the transformation of Liverpool from a small coastal trading port into a city of global significance.

Though the city developed a reputation as a flinty, unsophisticated place, there was plenty of evidence to the contrary. There was much more to the city of Liverpool than its docks, shipping and the dynamism of its commercial life. Liverpool's city fathers ensured that the city that emerged from this hive of commerce was not only an economic power-house, but was also a city to be admired. Visitors were impressed by what they saw. Edward Daniel Clarke, mineralogist, tutor and consummate traveller, stopped off in Liverpool during his tour of England in 1791: 'Hackney coaches ply in the streets; the shops are uncommonly elegant; the town is well paved and lighted, and, in short, offers a pleasing epitome of the metropolis. [. . .] The principal street is very fine, and makes an appearance inferior to few in London.'[4] Liverpool's political and commercial elite crafted the urban fabric of the city to suit their own interests and standing, as well as to reflect their wealth.

By the late eighteenth century, Liverpool had become a sophisticated city, with rows of elegant town houses, secluded city squares and a host of new urban institutions, from hospitals to churches, from gentlemen's clubs to theatres. Like many English provincial towns, Liverpool enjoyed a remarkable Georgian renaissance, with a proliferation of cultural buildings and societies, though not on the scale of the spa towns and fashionable watering places. This was a city which had a mercantile gloss to its urban culture. Still, Liverpool offered bowling greens, sea-baths and a tree-lined 'Ladies' Walk'. Fringing the edge of the city were splendid new homes and parklands, built for the pleasure and comfort of wealthier merchants – men who took their seats in the city's more fashionable churches, and who showed no sense of conflict between their sabbath worship and their workaday business of buying and selling Africans. There were parks and open-air pleasure gardens, in addition to an array of men's dining and drinking clubs. Later they were joined by debating societies and by coffee houses.[5]

Coffee houses were of course more than places for leisure: they were important centres of business and commerce. The one in Liverpool 'in the Hotel, at the bottom of Lord-street', offered not only a range of newspapers and magazines but also 'a book in which is entered the name, cargo, and place sailed from, of every vessel that arrives in the port. It has a list of about three hundred annual subscribers, at a guinea and a half each.' Although the 'Merchants' Coffee House' in Old Church Yard was much smaller than other coffee houses in the city, it had a unique advantage: 'a view of the river and signal poles, it is conveniently situated for attending to the movement of the shipping'.[6] Thus, even in a place of relaxation and leisure, the city's merchants kept one eye on the Mersey's traffic.

Liverpool boasted a theatrical culture, though the early theatre was rough and ready (little more than a pit and gallery). After 1772, however, the city could claim that the Theatre Royal was one of the largest theatres outside London. Originally open only in summer (when London theatres closed, allowing their players to travel to the provinces), by the end of the century it opened throughout the year, 'from the increase of theatrical rage'.[7] The new Music Hall (opened in 1786) could hold 1,400 people, its audiences treated to that remarkable mix of musical entertainments, high to low, from Handel to 'Bacchanalian Songs', which was to become the staple diet of the music halls in the nineteenth century.[8]

For the more literary-minded, there were at least three gentlemen's subscription libraries. When for instance the Athenaeum was founded in 1799, it made ample provision for 'News-Papers, Reviews, Magazines, Pamphlets, and other periodical works', with any surplus cash to be spent on 'the purchase of books in the foreign and learned languages; and the balance shall be expended in purchasing books in our own language'.[9] The bulk of subscribers to these ventures were merchants who saw the practical (and hidden) benefits to be had from investments in civic amenities. And nowhere was this more striking than in the Exchange.

Of all the new buildings which transformed the skyline of eighteenth-century Liverpool, the most striking, and certainly the most emblematic, was the Exchange. Designed by John Wood of Bath, one of the country's most fashionable architects, and built between 1745 and 1754 at an enormous cost of £30,000, the Exchange was to be, at once, town hall, exchange and assembly rooms. It was, wrote T.H.B. Oldfield in 1792, 'a grand edifice of white stone, built in the form of a square, round which are piazzas for merchants to walk in'. While the ground floor was for commercial business, the upper floor housed the mayor's office, court rooms, council chambers 'and two elegant ballrooms'. Its opening in 1754 was celebrated with a series of fashionable balls, concerts, public breakfasts, and boat races on the Mersey. Like the building itself, these opening ceremonies formed a lavish display both of civic pride and of new-found wealth. Indeed the two came together in an impressive and utilitarian structure: a home for local political power, commercial dealings and an opportunity to put profit to pleasurable use. Yet perhaps *the* most significant feature of the Exchange was less obvious, but no less important: the frieze chosen to decorate the exterior of the Exchange included images of African heads.[10]

Liverpool at mid-century had become a major port whose ships traded to all corners of the Atlantic. It had all the advantages of geography. The 1740s proved a turning point for Liverpool's slave merchants, offering them opportunities denied to established traders in London and Bristol (as well as the other ports dotted around the east and southern coasts of Britain which dabbled in slave trading: who, today, would associate Lyme Regis, Preston, Workington or Lancaster with the wretched business?[11]). During the war of the Austrian Succession (1740–48), for example, ships from those southern ports, which sailed into the Atlantic via the English Channel, were permanently exposed to French enemy warships. Liverpool, by contrast, was described in a book of 1752 as 'being situated so near the Mouth of the North Channel between Ireland and Scotland, (a passage very little known to, or frequented by the Enemy) afforded many Conveniences to the Merchants here untasted by those of other ports'.[12] This accident of geography was again to prove useful when later wars also disadvantaged ports in the south of England. During the period of the Seven Years' War (1756–63) a visitor to Liverpool remarked: 'By coming north-about, their ships have a good chance of escaping the many privateers belonging to the enemy which cruise to the southward.'

But what enabled the city's ambitious merchants to develop their oceanic reach were humbler changes in its immediate geographic hinterland. It handled growing volumes of bulky goods from Lancashire, Yorkshire, Cheshire and the Midlands, all transported to Liverpool for onward shipping. Those goods travelled along a spider's web of new turnpike roads, but more especially along new inland waterways. Rivers were made navigable for trade into Cheshire (in 1721), and a string of new canals constructed after 1757 linked Liverpool to inland coalfields. The Sankey Canal (constructed in the 1750s), financed by Liverpool Corporation, brought coal in flat-bottom barges to heat the city, and to fuel its important salt works. In the 1770s the Bridgewater, Trent and Mersey canals linked the city to the expanding industries of Manchester and the Midlands. The Wigan coalfield was linked to Liverpool by canal in 1774.

The new canals, nosing their way into interior industrial regions, and tapping into England's major river systems, were the key to Liverpool's growing prosperity. They made it possible for goods to be transported to Liverpool from across Lancashire, from Yorkshire, the Midlands and north Wales, and even from the Thames Valley. There were even ambitious plans, as early as 1765, to construct a canal linking England's east and west coasts, from Hull to Liverpool.[13] By 1795 a map of the region's canals and rivers showed the entire north-west and Midlands apparently draining towards the port of Liverpool, and thence onward and outward to the ocean.[14]

Goods and commodities flowed in increasing volumes to the city, and from there were shipped to other parts of England, to Ireland, to northern Europe – and to Africa and the Americas.[15] Liverpool's proximity to the linen and cotton industries of south Lancashire, expanding after 1750, was crucial. Light textiles, which Africans found ideal for local use, formed the largest item of goods shipped to West Africa, on outbound slave ships. This humble English material came to play an important role in the trade for African captives.[16]

But Liverpool's prosperity was based not solely on the regional cotton trade. In addition to textiles, William Moss's 1796 guide to the city declared: 'the earthen wares of Staffordshire, can no where be shipped abroad to great advantage as from here. The same may be said of the hard wares of Sheffield'.[17] So too slate and salts from Wales and Cheshire, coals from the Midlands, salt and foodstuffs of every variety (beef, pork, oats and barley in particular) all arrived in Liverpool bound for distant destinations.[18] Although by far the largest single trade was to Ireland, and remained so throughout the eighteenth century, a vast array of goods also found their way to Africa to be exchanged for slaves. When Captain Crow from Liverpool bought slaves in Bonny in the Bight of Biafra (modern Nigeria) in the 1790s, he offered in return textiles, handkerchiefs, a brass pan, muskets, powder, flints, shot, knives, iron pots, hats, caps, cutlasses, beads and brandy.[19]

Liverpool's eighteenth-century boom is made plain in its shipping data. In 1701 the city had 102 registered vessels; a century later the figure stood at 796. In 1709 Liverpool handled only 14,600 tons of shipping, but that had doubled by mid-century, and by 1800 had risen to 450,000 tons. The only Liverpool ship trading to Africa in 1709 was a mere 30 tons, but in the last year of the century 134 ships, with a total tonnage of 34,966 tons, were destined for Africa.[20]

This massive and growing movement of goods in and out of Liverpool required a revolution in the way the port handled its shipping. Above all it required the construction of new docks where ships could be loaded and unloaded free from the Mersey's powerful tidal flows. The first dock, the Old Dock, was built in 1715; there followed the Salthouse Dock (1738), George's Dock (1762), Duke's Dock (1773) and the King's and Queen's docks in 1788 and 1796. All were owned (until 1825) by the Liverpool Corporation.[21] It was there, at the heart of the city's urban politics, that we can begin to see how Liverpool's city fathers promoted their own commercial interests by shrewd investment in the city's port and infrastructure.

Liverpool was steered towards its commercial prosperity by an elite of merchants who dominated local politics. They saw their own personal wellbeing inextricably linked with the physical development of the city itself, and they governed with an eye to enhancing their own, and the city's, prosperity. The city's merchants had dominated Liverpool's politics from the late seventeenth century, and by the last years of the eighteenth century, the great majority of men on Liverpool's common council were merchants.[22] They enjoyed significant advantages over their rivals, notably in Bristol and Whitehaven: a thriving industrial and commercial hinterland which provided them with both a market for imported goods *and* a source of major exports; new communications, notably canals; and a freedom from the restrictions of old guilds. In effect, the way was open for ambitious and energetic men – sailors, small-scale manufacturers, humble traders – to transform themselves, in a generation, into major merchants with flourishing contacts around the Atlantic.

Men attracted to Liverpool's trade came from a variety of social backgrounds. The sons of gentry went to work as apprentices in the merchant houses and workplaces which sprang up around the city's docks and offices. William Davenport, for instance, son of a gentry family in London, was apprenticed to a Liverpool slave trader in 1741. He thrived remarkably and between 1754 and 1789 had invested in no fewer than 150 slave voyages. William Gregson, later owner, with others, of the *Zong*, began his working life in Liverpool as a humble rope-maker. By the end of his life, he had invested in at least 152 slave voyages. John Earle, the son of a Warrington brewer, was initially apprenticed to a Liverpool merchant house, later becoming a trader in wines, with a side interest in iron, tobacco and sugar. His son was a timber merchant, with a partnership in a local sugar refinery and in slave trading, and his brother-in-law, John Copeland, captained the ship *Calypso*, which traded to Africa.[23]

Such men, the 'mariner-merchants', were crucial figures in Liverpool's rise. They were men who moved easily (and successfully) from one form of business to another: from investing in industry to speculation in property, to ship-ownership (often in partnerships with others) and to commercial voyages to Europe and, increasingly, across the Atlantic. Such men made the most of new opportunities to trade to and from Africa.

The continent had long been an attraction – as early as 1709, along with a string of other ports, the Liverpool Corporation petitioned parliament against the monopoly of the Royal African Company on African trade. When that monopoly was ended and trade to Africa expanded in the early eighteenth century, Liverpool merchants established important trading positions at particular points on the African coast. By the late century it was clear enough that, despite Liverpool's extensive and diverse overseas trade in many commodities, for the city's merchants the 'most beneficial trade is to Guinea and the West-Indies, by which many have raised great fortunes'[24] – in other words, transporting slaves. Few thought about the morality of that 'beneficial' business – it was yet another opportunity to engage in profitable oceanic trade.[25] In the words of a guide to the city, 'As a simple moral question, considered in the abstract, it can meet with no countenance. In a political point of view, every thing favours it.'[26]

The first evidence of a slave voyage from Liverpool was in the 1690s. Thirty years later there were fifteen slave traders in the city. When, in 1753, the Company of Merchants Trading to Africa was created (to take over the functions of the old Royal African Company) Liverpool had three delegates on the Board of Governors, securing parity with London and Bristol. By then, the city boasted 101 merchants trading to Africa, and almost half of all British slave ships originated there.[27] Fifty years later it was universally recognised that 'The African trade forms no inconsiderable part of the commerce of Liverpool.'[28] Over the preceding century, some 5,000 slave voyages had sailed from its docks.[29]

Liverpool rose to be the dominant British slave port by pushing aside its rival, Bristol. One critical factor seems to have been where the Liverpudlians chose to do business in Africa. They concentrated their efforts on the Bight of Biafra and West Central Africa (and to a lesser extent on Sierra Leone and the Windward Coast), where they forged durable and lucrative commercial (and personal) links with African traders. The stretch of African coastline between the Niger Delta and Gabon became 'the cornerstone of Liverpool's slaving activity from 1725 through to 1807'. In addition, Liverpool's merchants developed their own orderly financial system, which made much more effective use of bills of credit than merchants from elsewhere. They also exploited financial links between Liverpool and the money and expertise of the City of London (first forged in the late seventeenth century).[30] Liverpool's burgeoning African and colonial trade in the eighteenth century was thus facilitated by London money and commercial experience.

The end result was that Liverpool's captains were able to embark for Africa and the Americas armed with bills of credit, ample cash, with specific and clear instructions from the shipowners, and with a list of good, reliable contacts, on both sides of the Atlantic. They were, quite simply, much better placed for trading, both on the African coast and in the Americas, than rivals from other ports.

The particular process of slave trading on the African coast depended on local geography. But it thrived best when there were good, proven relations – trust – between slave captains and local Africans. Here, Liverpool merchants excelled, developing steady personal and commercial links with African elites. Indeed relations were so firm, so mutually beneficial, notably at the ports of Bonny and Old Calabar, that African traders were granted unsecured credit for supplying their slaves (just as planters in the colonies were allowed credit for the purchase of the slaves).

The trading conducted by Liverpool's merchants was mutually beneficial.[31]

There were of course other factors in Liverpool's favour. Her ships charged lower rates, and they tended, crucially, to be faster in completing their protracted three-legged voyages (England–Africa, Africa–America, and back to England) in less time than their rivals. And as more and more Liverpool ships moved into the slave trade, their owners and captains developed an intimate knowledge of the trade, its quirks, dangers and opportunities. Along with their personal contacts on the African coast and in the Americas, there evolved a shared and communal source of trans-Atlantic information available to all.

Liverpool's trade to Africa and thence to the Americas was managed by syndicates of local businessmen who pooled their capital and expertise, shared their trading contacts, and covered their risks by spreading the expense of the insurance cover on their ships and cargoes. Spreading the commercial jeopardy, they divided the spoils. They proved themselves commercially nimble and adaptable, and were not encumbered, like Bristol merchants, by guild restrictions. Liverpool's merchants also fully exploited a number of the city's local advantages in the course of the eighteenth century, especially a thriving local ship-building industry. That industry geared itself to building slave ships, employing 3,000 local shipwrights who constructed vessels which were, typically, of 300 tons, with distinctive 'lodging of slaves for African vessels'.[32] Of the 8,087 British ships engaged in the slave trade between 1701 and 1810, 2,120 (26 per cent) had been built in Liverpool, with a staggering 82 per cent of them constructed in the second half of the eighteenth century when Liverpool dominated the British trade.[33] In the last twenty years of the trade (1787–1807) ship-builders on the Mersey turned out no fewer than 469 ships. These 'Guinea men' were bigger and faster (on the Atlantic leg), thus increasing their efficiency (and profitability) and enabling them to outrun enemy warships. All the ships, of course, required provisioning, manning, and more. Like Bristol before it, Liverpool's local manufacturing base became inextricably linked to the slave trade, with a related growth in local artisan trades and industries. The city even developed its own gun-making industry, with most of its weapons sold to the slave ships[34] – a stark reminder for the people at home of the trade's perils. It was, quite simply, impossible to escape from the shadow of the slave trade in late-eighteenth-century Liverpool. The city had become a veritable cornucopia, disgorging goods to Africa in return for slaves and profits.

The African slave coast became a much sought-after area of trade among all the major European maritime powers. Inevitably, they clashed. The Atlantic slave trade became an issue of international dispute, diplomatic wrangles, strategic bargaining and outright war, in which slave ships sometimes found themselves caught up.[35] Here was an oceanic trade with plenty of its own dangers, without the added risks of naval warfare and the threat of seizure by enemy vessels. No one doubted, by the mid-eighteenth century, that Britain needed a strong navy: 'The Kingdom of Great-Britain being on all Sides surrounded by the Sea, there will always be a Necessity of Maritime Forces; and as Neighbours grow more potent at Sea, the Kings of this Nation will be necessitated to augment their Maritime Forces proportionately.'[36] As British commerce became ever more global, her commercial security required military support.[37] The ships of the Royal Navy provided protection for British traders and merchants – in return, often taking men from the crews to supplement their own ranks.

On land, in distant locations, Europeans tried to secure their positions by defences and fortifications – against other Europeans. On the African coast, for example, the European presence is, to this day, remembered by a string of forts designed both to protect their trade and military presence, and to secure the flow of goods and people to and from the African coastline. Concentrated mainly along what was then known as the Gold Coast, the forts became as much a costly burden as a strategic advantage. Perhaps the most impressive was the remarkable British stronghold at Cape Coast, a massive castle-like fortress which commanded the coastal reaches and dominated its immediate African hinterland. It still offers an impressive vista of European power and ambition on the Slave Coast. Some eighteenth-century European visitors even found it pleasing to the eye: 'The prospect of this fortress is extremely beautiful towards the sea, the fortifications are happily imagined, and all the assistance that art could give is added to nature.'[38] Generations of African captives, spending their last days on the continent incarcerated in its dank, gloomy cellars, would not have concurred.[39]

Once the headquarters of the old Royal African Company, Cape Coast Castle remained the focal point for British slaving along a stretch of coast which became a favourite hunting ground for slave ships, especially from London. Slave traders were attracted especially to Cape Coast and Anomabu, the latter being constructed with two million bricks imported from Britain.[40] It was on that stretch in 1781, close to the two forts, that the Liverpool slave ship, the *William*, owned by a syndicate led by one of the city's major slave traders, William Gregson, arrived to buy and barter for its human cargo. It seemed just another unexceptional slave voyage out of Liverpool. By a quirk of wartime circumstance – the British were at war with the American colonies and their European supporters – the Liverpool captain was presented with an opportunity to buy a Dutch slave ship, the *Zorgue*, recently impounded elsewhere on the coast. He promptly bought it on behalf of the Gregson syndicate. This was precisely the sort of transaction that Liverpool's slave industry enabled and encouraged, and one of the reasons that Liverpool merchants had thrived in recent years: a captain with initiative, with finance to hand, making the most of an unexpected opportunity on distant shores, and opening another stream of revenue for his employers and backers at home.

Before the new ship began to trade on its own behalf, it was renamed: the *Zong*. An apparently unexceptional, enterprising venture was soon to become a notorious episode in history.

CHAPTER 3

Crews and captives

GREGSON'S NEWLY ACQUIRED SLAVE SHIP, THE *ZONG*, WAS an unusual vessel for the 1780s. At 110 tons, she was relatively small, and when she finally set out on her Atlantic crossing, on 6 September 1781, she was carrying 459 people. Though the economics of the slave trade had long determined that traders fill their ships as tightly as efficiency and safe management allowed, the *Zong* was more crowded than most slave ships of the period. A typical British slave ship of that size and at that time would only have carried around 193 Africans. Of 223 British slavers which departed from Africa with more than 440 Africans on board, only eight were of 110 tons or less.[1]

The image of a vessel teeming with humanity is perhaps *the* most durable, popular idea of a slave ship. It is an image which derives largely from the many thousands of pictures of another Liverpool ship, the *Brookes*, used to such great propagandist effect by the abolition campaign after 1789. The *Brookes* carried 609 Africans, but at 267 tons she was a much larger ship than the *Zong*.[2] More than these statistics, it is the drawing of the cross-section and plan of the ship that most impresses upon the modern mind (as much as it did upon contemporaneous abolitionists) the ruthless crowding of slave ships, with Africans squeezed, sardine-like, into every available inch of space. This remains the quintessential idea of a slave ship, reproduced time and again to portray the barbarity of the trade.

In the three centuries before 1860 something in the region of twelve and a half million Africans were loaded on to such ships on the African coast. Eleven million survivors landed in the Americas.[3] The largest proportion went to Brazil and the Caribbean, to work, initially at least, on sugar plantations. Those plantations had a voracious appetite for enslaved African labour, and as the West consumed ever more sugar in its food and especially its hot drinks, the Atlantic slave ships were called on to transport more and more Africans to bondage in the Americas.

Whatever moral or religious scruples Europeans may have had about the enslavement of Africans, the practical and economic evidence about slavery was hard to dispute. African slaves made possible the lucrative world of sugar cultivation in the tropical Americas, and much other production in British colonies to the north. A learned tract, written during the controversy over the Royal African Company's monopoly, affirmed that 'The Negroe Trade on the Coast of Africa is the chief and fundamental Support Of the British Colonies and Plantations in America'.[4] So too Malachi Postlethwayt, a prominent essayist and commentator on trade and commerce, recognised that Britain was 'indebted to those invaluable People, the Africans, for our Sugars, Tobacco, Rice, Rum and other Plantation produce'.[5] Indeed slavery brought complex economic change and benefits across Europe itself. Everyone agreed: the slave trade, and the trade to and from Africa, was vital. It was 'the main spring of the machine, which sets every wheel in motion ... The African trade is so very beneficial to Great Britain, so essentially necessary to the very being of her colonies, that without it neither could we flourish nor they long subsist.'[6] In his survey of trade, published in 1718, William Wood wrote that 'the Labour of Negroes is the principal Foundation of our Riches from the Plantations', and the trade to Africa 'is the greatest Value to this Kingdom, if we consider the Number of Ships annually employed in it, the great Export of our Manufactures, and other Goods to that Coast'.[7]

The only problem was how to provide sufficient numbers of Africans for the plantations. There were plenty of Africans on the Atlantic coast drawn to the lucrative business of exchanging other Africans for European goods. And in the words of John Hippisley, author of one of the earliest extant commentaries on the populousness of Africa, published in 1764, 'It appears at one glance, that Africa not only can continue supplying the West Indies in the quantities she has hitherto, but, if necessity required it, could spare thousands, nay, millions so, and go on doing the same to the end of time.'[8] But the *delivery* of that labour – the transportation of African captives – hinged on the myriad slave ships crossing the Atlantic: to Brazil and throughout the Caribbean sugar colonies, further north to the tobacco plantation of the Chesapeake, and, later, along the rice coast of South Carolina.[9]

As the slave ships delivered ever more Africans, many European colonies came to look less like European settlements and more like African outposts on the far side of the Atlantic. Across swathes of the Americas in the colonial period, it was the African who dominated the land, and who was often the key pioneer of settlement and development. By the 1820s, for example, of the 11 million people – Europeans and Africans – who had crossed the Atlantic to settle in the Americas, only two and a half million were European: the rest, more than eight million, were African.[10] And all of those Africans had crossed the Atlantic on the infamous slave ships.

This massive oceanic transportation of millions of Africans was not simply the result of *ad hoc*, unplanned circumstance. It derived from carefully devised political strategies and economic policies in government and commercial offices throughout Europe. It was a thoughtfully crafted process, designed to advance and promote personal and national self-interest (if possible, at the expense of rivals). These concerns reached the highest political levels. In the quarter-century after 1690, for example, parliament spent as much time and effort discussing how best to organise the slave trade as it was to spend debating its abolition a century later.[11]

The early phase of English slave trading was, in keeping with contemporary economic theory, dominated by monopoly. The arguments pro and con the slave-trading monopoly granted to the Royal African Company after 1672 were not about the *morality* of slave trading, but about the most effective means of organising it. When that monopoly was finally ended in 1712, the predictions of those who had argued for open trade rapidly came true. People from all corners of Britain sent ever-increasing numbers of ships, and tens of thousands of sailors, to the African coast. The commercial need to bolster the wellbeing of the plantation colonies joined with simple greed for the dazzling and irresistible riches suddenly available – notwithstanding its risks and dangers.

What made this remarkable boom in commerce even more striking was that it grew despite the frequency of warfare across the century. Four major periods of European – and therefore global – warfare (1688–97, 1702–13, 1744–7 and 1756–63) caused serious disruption to trade of all kinds. Yet the British emerged from their conflicts with the slave trade intact – indeed, in a healthy, booming condition. At the end of each war in the years 1688–1763, the British slave trade actually entered a new expansionist phase, as British victories and strategic gains were generally followed by the commercial exploitation of new possessions and openings.[12]

The colossal figures and massive geography of the British slave trade, sliced, divided and aggregated in any number of ways, can also serve to deceive. On the one hand they convey a good idea of the immense commercial machine, delivering goods – but above all people – around the littoral of the Atlantic with profitable efficiency. However, though the sheer volume of ships, sailors, cargoes and Africans suggests an effortless flow of people and commodities, each and every voyage was enormously complex and difficult for slaves – and for sailors.

The sophistication of the slave-trading system ought not to deceive us about its real nature. It was, from first to last, a business of organised brutality and inhuman regimentation of its African victims.

That regimentation began the moment a slave ship was first purchased, or from when its construction was first designed.[13] Every step was meticulously planned. Building and equipping a slave ship was more costly than for traditional merchant vessels. Merchants shopped around for the best deals – for ship-builders, and for equipment. Sometimes they sent equipment across the Atlantic to fit out a ship being constructed in America. A custom-made ship was more costly than a traditional merchant ship, and the men who master-minded the business from offices in Bristol, Liverpool, Bordeaux or Nantes knew precisely what was required, from the design and layout of a ship through to the daily seaborne management of its African captives.

The presence of the Africans determined key features of the ship itself. Though slave ships were constructed wherever was convenient and viable, rising European timber costs in the eighteenth century saw shipbuilders in North America (where timber was cheaper) emerge as major providers of British slave ships. When in 1745, for example, the Liverpool merchant Joseph Manesty ordered two slave ships from builders in Newport, Rhode Island, he specified the timber to be used and laid down precise physical details for the ships' length, depth and width, asking that they be built 'for the more commodious stowing [of] Negroes twixt Decks'. Raised decks for the security of the crew, special gratings, collapsible racks to create extra accommodation for captives, provision for the bulk and weight of the huge amount of metal goods (chains and shackles, as well as firearms) – all and more made a slave ship an expensive investment. Even then, the value of the cargo to be shipped far outweighed the cost of their transportation.

The slave trade became so attractive an investment that ships of all sorts and conditions, of all sizes and ages, were dispatched to the task of buying and shipping Africans. Something like three quarters of all slavers had been used for other purposes before being turned over to the Africa trade. Even vessels as tiny as eleven tons – little more than a pleasure craft by design – were used for the purpose, miniscule in comparison to the largest ship we know of, originating from Liverpool, of 566 tons.[14] Here was a Dunkirk in reverse: the whole spectrum of a nation's sailing vessels rallying to the lucrative task of transporting Africans across the Atlantic, with profit rather than rescue in mind.

The most straightforward part of any slave voyage was the first leg from Europe to West Africa – but, once on the African coast, new routines took over. With the dangers of disease, and the threat of the increasing numbers of Africans accumulating below decks, ships remained there just long enough to secure sufficient numbers of slaves for the Atlantic crossing. But it was always a protracted business.

African captives were bought piecemeal, in small batches, a few here, a few elsewhere. Often their enslavement had begun much earlier, deep in the African interior, most of them captured through acts of violence, warfare or kidnap, or for criminal activity, and they had already travelled great distances even *before* they caught their first sight of the ocean and the strange-looking vessels riding at anchor. Captains listened to advice and rumours from other slavers about where enslaved Africans might be had, and where prices might be better. They sent trusted crew members to local villages to negotiate, and they haggled with African traders who brought captives alongside by canoe. Sometimes they parleyed on beaches, attracted by telltale smoke signals indicating that slaves were available. They also bargained with established African slave traders in prolonged sessions which developed their own elaborate conventions and protocols. John Atkins told in 1735 how, in the trading he had seen on the coast, local African leaders asserted that 'a Bottle of Brandy, a Sabre, Knife, or any ordinary Apparel is acceptable; the Chief loves to distinguish himself by an Imitation of our Dress, and is often so preposterously set out with Hat, Wig and Breeches . . .'[15] So did the slavers' influence spread.

Often, time on the coast seemed interminable, and weeks turned into months. In 1750, John Newton, captain of the *Duke of Argyle*, spent seven months on the African coast.[16] A generation later Alexander Falconbridge, a surgeon on four slave voyages, wrote that 'From the time of arrival of the ships to their departure, which is usually near three months, scarce a day passes without some Negroes being purchased and carried on board.'[17] Sailors invariably fell victim to tropical illness, sometimes without any warning. One of Falconbridge's ships lost sixteen men on the coast: '11 deserted and 5 died.'[18] This story was repeated from one slave ship to another throughout the entire history of the Atlantic slave trade. And no sooner had African captives begun to arrive on board than they too began to die off. Their ailments often infected other Africans who shared their increasingly restricted and crowded quarters. Despite the crew's efforts, the squalid intimacy of the slave decks was a perfect breeding and transmission ground for certain diseases, especially dysentery (the 'bloody flux'), the main killer of Africans on the slave ships. Crewmen who had to deal with the aftermath of these ailments (sluicing out the decks and removing the corpses) were themselves inevitably contaminated, hence the higher rates of sickness and death among those men whose work brought them into close contact with the Africans below decks.

The spaces in the ships allocated for Africans would usually be modified further upon reaching the African coast. Carpenters rigged up extra platforms and shelving to create more room for Africans – although this of course meant *less* room for each individual.[19] Women and children were separated from the men, and generally granted more freedom in their own corner of the deck. There were usually more men than women on slave ships, and the men, manacled at the ankles and wrists, occupied the largest space below. Fresh air was fed to them by overhead gratings and via ventilators in the side of the vessel, designed to scoop up air and funnel it below as the ship sailed. Such strategies and designs, however, rarely managed to dispel the oppressive, stinking atmosphere of the slave decks, especially in bad weather, when all hatches and gratings were closed, or when the ship swung at anchor or was becalmed. The space below decks was often too low to allow adults to stand upright, too hot and unaired to be anything other than fetid and stifling.

Slave traders quickly learned that the most dangerous time of any voyage was there, moored off the African coast; the dangers of disease enfeebling and diminishing the crew's ranks, and the threat from accumulating Africans, were most acute, and often came together. Indeed the crew on every slave ship nurtured a real and deep-seated fear that they were handling people who could not be trusted and who could, in an instant, erupt and overwhelm them. Shipowners every-where recognised this danger and repeatedly warned their captains: 'be allways upon your Guard and defence against the Insurrection of your Negroes'.[20] From the early days of the Portuguese trade to the mid-nineteenth century – that is, for four centuries – merchants counselled their men to remain alert. Crews knew, before they had even set sail, that their control would be precarious and always at risk from poten-tially rebellious African captives. John Newton believed that the threat of insurrection was endemic, if only because 'the Men Slaves are not, easily, reconciled to their confinement, and treatment'.[21] He warned that 'One unguarded hour, or minute, is sufficient to give the Slaves the opportunity they are always waiting for. An attempt to rise upon the ship's company, brings an instantaneous and horrid war.'[22] A careless moment by a crew member, a simple lapse of attention, an incautious move, could provoke a violent African response. In 1721, Captain Francis Messervy ignored a warning not to walk among the African men while they ate, without a heavy armed guard. The Africans 'laid hold on him, and beat out his Brains with the little Tubs, out of which they eat the boiled Rice'. The ensuing revolt was only quelled when eighty Africans had been killed.[23] No crew, counselled John Newton, could relax entirely, even when the Africans were subdued; 'when most quiet they were always watching for opportunity.'[24] Such stories and guidance made sailors edgy, paranoid, and resolved to do whatever it took to stave off African attack.

They surrounded themselves and their ships with defensive metalware. Some ships had a raised 'after-deck', with mounted guns, to provide the crew with a vantage from which to muster a defence against possible slave revolt.[25] Other ships had a barrier, a *barricado*, behind which the crew could defend themselves against rebellious Africans: 'there are small holes in it, wherein blunderbusses are fixed, and sometimes a cannon . . . for quelling the insurrections that now and then happen.'[26] Swivel guns were also strategically placed for the same purpose, and the crew were always amply provided with small arms.

Most widespread, striking, and best-remembered of all the means of control was the necessary ironware of slavery – the fetters and manacles, the chains and restraints which enabled small numbers of sailors to keep some semblance of domination over overwhelming numbers of Africans. Slave ships also carried a *speculum oris*, a metal device designed by surgeons to deal with lock-jaw, but used on slave ships to force-feed resistant Africans. When Thomas Clarkson bought one in Liverpool, the shopkeeper told him 'the slaves were frequently so sulky, as to shut their mouths against any sustenance, and this with a determination to die; and that it was necessary their mouths should be forced open to throw in nutrition'.[27] Chains and metalware came to characterise the slave ships, and to this day the manacled African remains one of the most powerful visual images of the age of Atlantic slavery. Today this image is in great disfavour, because it appears to speak to African subjection and defeat. But there is another way of considering the chains of slavery. Chains represented both the fearful apprehension of the enslaver *and* the ubiquitous, resistant defiance of the enslaved. Without these metal goods – disgorged in great volumes by British metal industries – no slave ship could have survived for long. But while chains and shackles provided some security for the crew, they offered nothing but painful aggravation to millions of Africans. Chains were, at one and the same time, an emblem of African bondage and an inescapable physical torment which enraged the spirit as much as they chafed the flesh.

Slave traders were choosy about who they bought. Sometimes they had specific instructions about what kind of Africans they should procure. Most obviously, they sought young, healthy Africans, who were sure to survive the crossing and attract a profitable price in the Americas after a smooth passage – so traders avoided those groups with a reputation for causing trouble. Captains and surgeons, along with experienced crewmen, all made their own assessments of each African brought on board. They needed to know something about each captive, both for the commercial success of the voyage and even for its physical survival. Facial scars and 'tribal' background provided some clues, but the crew looked for other signs: which Africans looked threatening, which ones seemed depressed (and likely to harm themselves), which ones might be trusted?

Africans who proved more accommodating were often chosen as helpers. Men and women who seemed to have status in the eyes of other Africans, or had skills which might be turned to their captors' advantage, were employed for the better management of the enslaved Africans. Intermediaries and interpreters, for instance, were invaluable on board a slave ship. Sailors also looked for sexual partners for crewmen starved of female companions. Sometimes captains selected African women for their own gratification on the voyage, removing them from the slave decks to their own quarters. Though captains were generally keen to prevent predatory sexual attacks by crewmen, some allowed their men to have sex with captive women. John Newton, himself no sexual innocent in his early slave trading days, thought that the ship's captain set the tone for sexual behaviour on his ship:

> It depends much upon the disposition, and attention, of the Captain. When I was in the trade, I knew several commanders of African ships who were prudent, respectable men, and who maintained a proper discipline and regularity in their vessel; but there were too many of a different character. In some ships, perhaps in most, the license allowed, in this particular, was almost unlimited. Moral turpitude was seldom considered, but they who took care to do the ship's business, might, in other respects, do what they pleased.[28]

Long before the abolition campaign revealed to the reading public the levels of sexual abuse, the sailors' 'licentious liberties among the Women Slaves' were discussed in print.[29] In the last twenty years of the eighteenth century, however, the stories of sexual terror on the slave ships were openly publicised by Africans and by sailors alike. The ex-slave Ottobah Cugoano, living as a free servant in London in 1787, declared in disgust that 'it was common for the dirty filthy sailors to take the African women and lie upon their bodies'.[30]

All relations between black and white were complex on a slave ship. They turned more complex and fraught as the ranks of Africans increased. Africans and sailors were squeezed together in diseased and noisome conditions of gluey, dangerous intimacy. Each and every aspect of daily life seemed designed to irritate and anger the enslaved, and to alarm and frighten the crew: the pervasive stink, the human filth, disease and death, the grating of naked bodies on hard planks and the chafing of flesh against metal fetters. As if all this were not enough, there was the distress and terror of oceanic travel: the storms and howling winds, the pitching and rolling, the juddering and grinding of a small sailing ship driven by strong currents or struggling against hostile wind and water. Slave ships were uniquely horrible and terrifying, and conditions for the Africans were often unimaginable. If hell existed, it was not so much hell on earth, as hell at sea in a crowded slave ship.[31]

Each day in the early morning (weather and crew numbers permitting) small groups of Africans penned below would be brought on deck for spells of exercise, feeding, washing, and the inspecting of their chains. In good weather the Africans were fed on deck; in poor weather, they ate below, communally, from small tubs, in the foul and contaminated environment they lived in. Water – normally a half pint with each meal, so vital to people dehydrated by their sweltering living conditions – was also passed round, hand-to-hand.[32]

The Africans remained shackled at all times – upwards of fifty men, held on a chain strung along the deck. Sometimes they were prompted to 'dance' and sing in the hope that the exercise would be good for them. One surgeon told how 'onboard his ship they sometimes sung, but not for their amusement. The captain ordered them to sing, and they sang songs of sorrow. The subject of their songs were their wretched situation, and the idea of never returning home.'[33]

The loathsome task of unoccupied crew members was now to go below to clean out the 'necessary tubs' and scrub the foul decks. If possible, sick slaves – and there were soon plenty of them on all slave ships – were shifted to other parts of the ship, but when sickness affected large numbers of Africans this was impractical. The Africans were expected to relieve themselves in large buckets – tubs – located around the decks. But Falconbridge described how, in stumbling to reach them, especially when sick, they often 'tumble over their companions, in consequence of being shackled . . . In this distressed situation, unable to proceed, and prevented from getting to the tubs, they desist from the attempt: and, as the necessities of nature are not to be repelled, ease themselves as they lay.'[34] At sea, and especially when storm-tossed, the sick and the healthy, the dead and the dying, endured unspeakably wretched conditions, their shackled lurching and sliding on the pitching decks all lubricated by the human waste and the bilious discharges of seriously, often fatally, ill shipmates.

By late afternoon, the Africans were again led below decks for their night-time incarceration, with sailors posted as guards.

It was a terrifying and much-hated post. Armed with a whip, the man on guard supervised ranks of sullen slaves, who muttered and plotted, the night's silence punctuated by the metallic noise of their fetters. Every African was a suspect, and every sailor was distrustful and wary. Regular searches revealed hidden weapons and tools: knives, chisels, axes, pieces of metal or wood – anything a careless sailor might have left unattended for a moment. Even the children and women were suspect, because their greater freedom on the ship allowed them to acquire potential weapons and then pass them to the shackled men. In 1751, a young African on John Newton's ship, the *Duke of Argyle*, was left unfettered because of an ulcerated leg, and then for his good behaviour; he passed 'a large marlin spike down the gratings' and twenty men managed to break their shackles.[35] The crew, however, were able to subdue them.

Compounding the miseries of the enslaved Africans was their total ignorance about their situation. They had no idea where they were, where they were going, or what was going to happen to them. Africans and sailors alike recalled that, when Africans were first brought on board, many believed they were about to be eaten. The crew soon disabused them of this fear, but what the Africans could *not* have guessed was the duration of their shipboard torments, and the range of sufferings they were about to endure over the next few months. The Africans were invariably terrified of the world around them, of the ever-changing and threatening sea, and the strange noises of a sailing ship. For all that, it was the man-made horrors which dominated the enslaved Africans' seaborne lives: the interminable hours in appalling conditions, the pain and discomfort of being shackled, the miserable food and lack of exercise, the permanent irritant of sharing such close quarters with strangers, the indignity of communal existence on the slave decks – and the disease and death. For all they knew, their miseries would never end.

It is a safe guess that the very great majority of the Africans hauled on to the slave ships had never seen white people before the initial contact with their captors. From that first moment of encounter onwards, the Africans' experience of white people was characterised by brutality and humiliation, which for some infused with their angry resentment; they simmered, waiting for the opportunity to strike back. But many simply gave up hope. One witness told a parliamentary inquiry that all the Africans he had seen 'appear dejected when brought on board. Some are so for the whole voyage, others till they die'.[36] Some tried to kill themselves – hence the nets around slave ships – and some succeeded. The slave ship was the human crucible which poisoned relations between black and white throughout the history of Atlantic slavery – and long afterwards.

Despite the slave ships' desperate overcrowding and the crews' potent fears of African insurrection, there were good reasons not to treat Africans harshly on board. Captains and officers received commissions, incentives and bonuses for a successful voyage, and had good financial reasons to try to maintain the health and wellbeing of their African captives for sale in the Americas.[37] In the accountancy of the slave ship, where every African had a monetary value, violence and ill-treatment of Africans could easily be counterproductive: injured and sick slaves would not bring the expected price at sale in the colonies. Dead Africans represented a financial loss. No slave trader would consciously damage the prospects of a good sale, after such risk and efforts, and after so prolonged and dangerous a voyage, simply to ill-treat the Africans wilfully. And here lies the puzzle. Why *were* Africans treated so brutally on the slave ships?

Though the history of the slave ships could be written in terms of the violence meted out to the Africans, the real, fundamental cruelty of the slave ships was not so much *ad hoc* and personal, not so much the result of sadistic whim and capricious violence (though there was plenty of both), but rather *institutional* – the brutality was basic to the whole system. On board the slave ship, as on the African coast and on the American plantations, violence was deemed essential. Without the violence of shipboard management (the manacles, the guns, the daily regime) no slave ship could have hoped to survive. What this meant in practice was that on every slave ship there simmered a toxic human brew, an ethos and culture of violence, which infected every member of the crew, and which damaged or threatened every African on board. It was this culture of violence which forms the background to what happened on the *Zong*.

When John Newton finally decided to speak up for abolition in 1787, he spoke with a unique combination of moral authority, clerical eminence and personal experience as a slave trader. We also know from the journals he kept as a slave captain that, like others, he never hesitated to dole out brute violence to his African captors; he had liberally flogged Africans and crew members, and had even tortured Africans to extract information about a plot. He was understandably reluctant to reveal the details many years later, at the height of his abolitionist work, but – looking back on the deeds of his younger slaving days with mortification and contrition – he was forced to explain himself: 'I considered myself as a sort of gaoler or turnkey, and I was sometimes shocked with the employment that was perpetually conversant with chains, bolts and shackles. In this view, I had often petitioned, in my prayers, that the Lord, in his own time, would be pleased to fix me in a more humane calling.'[38]

Such a plea is likely to irritate a modern reader, not least because we know that Newton's high principles went hand-in-hand with low financial cunning. This 'disagreeable' work earned him a great deal of money and he only stopped slaving when illness prevented him taking command of another slave ship. In his later life, when he had evolved into a revered cleric and prominent abolitionist, Newton masked the brute reality of his work as a slaver. 'What I did, I did ignorantly; considering it as the line of life which Divine Providence had allotted me . . .'[39] His ship's log reveals a very different tale: of excruciatingly painful treatment doled out to Africans whenever he thought it necessary – 'Put the boys in irons and slightly in the thumbscrews to urge them to a full confession'.[40]

To modern eyes, such contradictions seem strange: godly men going about a godless task, and great cruelty displayed by sophisticated, educated and religious individuals. Yet John Newton was no different from hundreds of other slave captains. He knew that his post, indeed his very survival, demanded a severe, unbending management of everyone – black and white – under his control. The command of a slave ship was a unique position, which required the severity of gaol management with whatever violence was thought appropriate by military command. All this took place in an age when corporal and capital punishment were commonplace and largely unquestioned. But perceptive slave captains also recognised that violence was *cultivated* on the slave ships, and that crewmen quickly lost any sense of humanity and decency through the brute grimness of their daily working lives: 'It was a business with a tendency to efface the moral sense, to rob the heart of every gentle and humane disposition, and to harden it, like steel, against all impression of sensibility.'[41]

Few showed less 'humane disposition' than the rank-and-file sailor confronted by a ship packed with Africans.

It was often difficult to secure a full complement of crewmen for slave ships, and no wonder. Sailors hated the slave ships for all the obvious reasons: they stank (when filled with slaves they could be detected miles away, downwind at sea), they were disease-ridden and they were extremely dangerous. Their reputation inevitably went before them, and no man who signed on could have been under any illusion about the risks awaiting him, though none could have appreciated just *how* hellish the ships were until they were at sea.

After 1787, when the abolition campaign began seriously to undermine the credibility of the slave trade, supporters of the trade argued that the ships provided a bruising nursery for raising and training crew for the Royal Navy. The evidence, however, was quite different. One of the most potent discoveries (by Thomas Clarkson) about the slave trade was that the slave ships actually *devoured* their sailors. The slave trade, far from being 'a nursery for our seaman', actually destroyed 'more in one year, than all the other trades of Great Britain, when put together, destroy in two'. It could be proved that, of the 5,000 men who left Britain on slave ships in 1785, fewer than half – only 2,320 – returned home. The slave ships' muster rolls revealed that the death rate among their sailors was far higher than in any other form of seafaring, though much of that high crew mortality was in West Africa and resulted from the

European's lack of resistance to the ferocious regional disease environment. In the words of Thomas Clarkson, 'every vessel, that sails from the port of Liverpool in this trade loses more than seven of her crew, and [. . .] if we refer it to the number of seamen employed, more than a fifth perish.'[42]

These were, by any standards, horrifying death rates, and such attrition could clearly impair the ability of the crew to manage and control their enslaved Africans with any degree of confidence. The crew's numbers fluctuated throughout the voyage: 'While the number of Slaves increases, that of the people, who are to guard them, is diminished, by sickness, or death, or by being absent in the boats: so that, sometimes, not ten men can be mustered, to watch, night and day, over two hundred . . .'[43] These were precarious ratios, and it was clearly in the crew's best interests that the Africans remained ignorant of just how few men controlled them; at sea, dead sailors were thrown overboard out of sight of the slaves in the hope that they would not notice the thinning out of the crew's ranks.

The story of the slave ships is of course dominated by the inescapable misery of the Africans and, understandably, we tend to overlook the lives of their onboard tormentors. But the sailors' experience on the slave ships was overwhelmingly miserable. They were badly paid, obliged to undertake the most hideous of tasks, and their lives were permanently at risk. They lived with the stink of the slave decks in their nostrils and were always (even on the best-manned ships) greatly outnumbered by hostile Africans who were keen to harm them. It was a brutish, repulsive and often short-lived working life.

Though it may seem odd to discuss this alongside the suffering of the Africans, it is essential to any understanding of the social history of the slave ship. Oppressors and oppressed were inextricably linked in an infernal system. The violations and sufferings of the Africans were at the hands of men who found their work repellent and who openly admitted hating their work. Work on a slave ship was always close-quarter: eyeball-to-eyeball, intimate engagement between humans who shared only the squalor of the environment and a simmering hatred of one for the other.

These were not the usual jobs required of sailors. No other deep-water work required such minute and unflagging attention to the 'cargo'. When bad weather struck, the Africans endured the worst of times, neglected by a crew fully stretched by coping with a battered vessel until the storm blew itself out. But it was then, after Africans had endured the unimaginable, that sailors were confronted by conditions at their worst, and when the crew had to bring some sort of relief to slave decks which looked like a cross between a neglected stable and a slaughterhouse. Men obliged to clear up such filth took out their resentment on the Africans. One slave ship surgeon told how they 'grew angry with the slaves, and used to beat them inhumanly with their hands, or with a cat [whip]'.[44] The ships brutalised everyone on board.

These tasks and dangers of life on a slave ship were well known, and became the gossip of dockside life in the ships' home ports. It is no surprise then that merchants and captains were always on the look-out for crew, and used every means available to them to fill their ranks. In the long century before abolition in 1807, when British ships carried three and a half million Africans across the Atlantic, around one third of a million sailors went with them – white, black and mixed-race.[45] Some 210,000 of them were ordinary seamen,[46] persuaded perhaps by the offer of an advance on their wages – though many spent all their wages even *before* the ship left its home port. The wonder is that *anyone* volunteered to work on board a slave ship, though the explanation was simple. Most joined because they were poor and desperate and had no real alternative – though even among destitute sailors 'slave trading was regarded as an uncommonly abhorrent occupation'.[47] The personal stories of slave ship sailors repeat a depressing and familiar tale: of poverty, debt, drunkenness, violence – and utter confusion – driving them to work in the slave trade. There were some exceptions, but overwhelmingly they were poor men, recruited from the meanest of circumstances. Many were victims of a 'crimping' system – a form of press-ganging operated by publicans in collusion with crimps (recruiters) for the slave ships: 'to pay their debts, and to furnish themselves with a few clothes, and a little modicum of liquor, they are obliged to make a will and power of attorney, in favour of their rapacious landlady.' Men indebted to such publicans were then given a choice: a slave ship or gaol.[48]

Crew members were to be counted among the most exploited of workers, toiling away at the most oppressive and dangerous of jobs. Captains and senior officers at least had a financial stake in the business, were relatively well-paid, and could earn substantial bonuses on a successful voyage. At the end of one voyage to St Kitts, John Newton sent to his wife in England 'a piece of paper value £50 sterling money', supplemented, three days later, by 'a bill for £207.3.10 which with that formerly sent to you is the amount of my Guinea Commissions and privilege'.[49]

Such incentives lured senior men back to the slavers time and again. The captain was critical to the success (or failure) of any slave voyage. A good slave ship captain had to possess an unusual range of qualities. First and foremost, he had to be a good mariner, able to handle a valuable ship and its human cargo for months on end, in the turbulent waters and unpredictable weather systems of the Atlantic and Caribbean. He also needed to be tough and adept at handling a difficult and often brutal crew; their thieving, their violence (to each other and towards the Africans), drunkenness, disobedience, sexual attacks on slave women – all and more tested a captain's ability to handle the whole enterprise. In addition, he needed to be commercially alert and have skills and knowledge to haggle with African traders and their agents while observing the requisite conventions. Slave ship captains on the coast also needed each other, especially for security but also for information and advice about the prices asked at different parts of the coast. Throughout, the captains tried to stick to the owners' instructions, which were written out before they left their home port. In 1700, for example, the captain of an early Liverpool ship received specific instructions from the ship's owners to leave 'with the first fair Wind and Weather', first for Kinsale in Ireland where 'Mr Arthur Kreise Mercht' would provide provisions for the voyage, and then 'with the first fair wind and weather make the best of yr way to the Coast of Guinea'. There, he was instructed to 'dispose of what of the cargo is proper to purchase the slaves ye can'. If problems arise 'make what haste ye can down to Angola where the Doctor is well acquainted and who will inform you what goods most propper for that place'. From Africa, he was to 'to touch at Barbadoes where if you find the marketts reasonable good sell there if Dull go down Leeward to which Island you shall see convenient where dispose of your Negroes to our best Advantage and with the Produce load the ship with sugar cotton ginger if to be had'. At each place, the owners specified the best local contacts: men who knew the state of local trade and could be relied on.[50]

Such instructions might change, however, when new orders caught up with the ships, months after they had left home, via a vessel freshly arrived from Britain.[51] During their stay on the coast, masters also kept in touch with their owners back home 'from time to time with quick Intelligence'. The bigger merchants became very adept at this, because they could 'keep imployed a number of Ships, that like a Thread unites them in a knowledge of their Demands.'[52] A flow of letters from company offices to captains on the African coast changed or supplemented earlier instructions, and demanded information about the state of business on the African coast. Equally important, a well-trusted and dependable slave captain was authorised to change the focus of his mission if an unforeseen opportunity arose on the voyage.

The simple rule of thumb for slave captains was that they should make the most of whatever commercial prospects came their way. They were after all entrusted by the ship's owners in Britain with a costly venture, and were expected to use their experience and commercial instincts to enhance the profits of the voyage. They carried cash, bills of credit, and personal sureties allowing them to deal with unexpected opportunities. If a captain found more Africans than he could carry, for example, he looked for extra shipping capacity elsewhere. On the last day of 1753, John Newton struck a deal to buy an empty vessel, the *Racehorse* of 40–45 tons, lying idle at Sherbar, off Sierra Leone, for £130 sterling 'in a bill on Jill & Compy, with my own security for acceptance'. He appointed one of his own officers, Job Lewis, as captain of the *Greyhound* 'and sent him away to trade on the ship's account', though Lewis died shortly after of a fever.[53]

Slave captains had to be literate, numerate and commercially alert: unsurprisingly, most did *not* emerge from the ranks of the generally uneducated ordinary sailors on the slave ships.[54] Liverpool's ability to attract and train up masters for its slave ships proved an incalculable advantage in enhancing the city's dominance in the slave trade. There were, quite simply, many more experienced slaving sailors, of all ranks, in Liverpool than in any other port – and they were drawn there from all corners of Britain, and from North America. Whereas merchants in Bristol and London often struggled to put together a crew for a slave voyage, the task was much easier in Liverpool. This availability of captains in the city enabled Liverpool's merchants to hire experienced men quickly (and turn round their ships promptly). In return, Liverpool captains were well rewarded. Commissions on successful voyages, the right to ship a few slaves of their own for sale in the colonies, could amount to a considerable income on a successful voyage. Such rewards also recognised the enormous risks those men took – not least with their lives.

Captains also passed on their trading skills, training up junior officers, mates and surgeons in the peculiarities of successful slave trading. They introduced them to African traders (and local customs) on the coast, and helped to forge personal links – and trust – which lasted for decades, and all to Liverpool's great advantage. It was these men, the captains and senior officers, whose skills and tested experience, at sea and on the African coast, enabled Liverpool to outstrip its rivals in Bristol and London, and become the dominant port in the Atlantic slave trade in the second half of the eighteenth century.[55]

One notable career path for a man wishing to command a slaver was first to serve time as a slave ship's surgeon. The life of a ship's surgeon was rarely less than grim, but there was nothing to match the ghastliness of employment on a slave ship. Their prime duty sounded simple but was enormously difficult: to keep the crew and the Africans alive as they crossed the Atlantic.[56] Slave surgeons were men who saw African slavery at its most brutal and inhumane. From the moment the first African was hauled on board, to the moment the last one staggered off the ship in the Americas, the surgeon's regime was unpleasant, dangerous and unhealthy. Quite apart from any technical medical skills (rarely more than rudimentary), only a man with a strong stomach could tolerate the job. The surgeon physically inspected the Africans when they first came on board, visiting them regularly, weather permitting, below decks throughout the voyage. He handled and examined them intimately, in what was, for the Africans, a regular public humiliation, doling out the appropriate medicines, keeping a tally of their ailments – and recording their deaths. John Atkins, a surgeon in the Royal Navy in the 1730s, described how the Africans were 'examined by us in like manner, as our brother Trade do beasts in Smithfield; the Countenance, the Stature, a good Set of Teeth, Pliancy in their Limbs and Joints, and being free of Venereal Taint, are the things inspected and governs our choice in buying.'[57] What the surgeons dispensed was, of course, only the most basic of medical treatments, and their efforts were often overwhelmed by the crowded squalor and contagious filth of the slave decks. In 1792 the ship's surgeon on board the *Lord Stanley* on the African coast listed the suffering and deaths among the Africans in his care. Some improved and recovered from their complaints; many did not. In June, for example, he recorded how 'A girl, No. 4 yesterday complained of a pain in the head for which she had no medicine as she did not seem otherwise ill, this morning at 3am. She was seized with delirium, a few hours afterwards convulsions came on and at 8am. She died.'[58]

The surgeon got to know the Africans better than anyone else on board, and, however ineffective the surgeons' work might seem today, contemporaries thought their presence vital. When, in 1788, as a result of early abolitionist pressure to ameliorate slave conditions on slave ships, parliament passed Dolben's Act, it insisted that all British slave ships carry a surgeon.

There were times when the surgeon had to change roles, and take over the command of the vessel. Over the many months of a slave voyage, disease and violence thinned out the ranks of the crew. Men were drafted in from other ranks, sometimes from other ships, to fill the gaps. Captains too succumbed, especially to tropical ailments on the African coast. But captains, with their particular skills and qualities, were much harder to replace once the vessel had departed for Africa. Not surprisingly, experienced surgeons, who were among the best educated men on slave ships, and who had the necessary literate skills, were sometimes promoted to captain. In the twenty years before abolition in 1807, we know of at least thirty-six men who served both as surgeons and captains on slave ships.[59] The two positions – captain and surgeon – were pivotal in the success or failure of any slave voyage. The disaster on the *Zong* was to stem directly from the confusion created by a ship's doctor being elevated to the position of ship's captain.

The crew of slave ships were remarkably mixed, and constantly changing, with men coming and going at all points of the voyages, on shore and at sea. Sailors died in accidents, deserted when they reached port, or were impressed by hard-up warships (and some tough incorrigibles also found themselves handed over to the Royal Navy by exasperated slave captains). And ships required more men on the Atlantic crossing, simply to guard the crowded ranks of Africans, than were needed on the other legs of the voyage. The gaps left by the dead, the sick, the deserters and the transferred were filled by new men coming aboard wherever the ships docked: in the Atlantic islands, in West Africa or the Americas. But through this regular ebb and flow of men, it was the sheer attrition of manpower which stands out, as sailors succumbed to, or fled from, the sickness and violence of the slave ships. Those who knew the slave ships would not have been surprised to hear the evidence given by one witness to Thomas Clarkson: 'the seamen in general are treated very ill in the slave trade.'[60]

The story of the men who came to form the core of the crew on the *Zong* reflects the wider patterns of the slave ships. The Gregson syndicate dispatched its ship the *William*, captained by Richard Hanley, in October 1780, with a crew of thirty. Three men were to die on the voyage, twelve were transferred to form the crew for the *Zong*, four men joined the Royal Navy ship *Champion* in May, and another man was described as 'Runaway' in Jamaica. A further sixteen men joined the vessel for the last leg of its voyage back to Liverpool.[61]

When at last the slave ship finally turned away from the sight of the African coast, for the long haul westwards, the sailors felt some relief. Heading into the Atlantic meant putting the dangers of Africa behind them. For the Africans, however, it was a departure from everything they were familiar with. The ship was now alone and had to be self-sufficient. The crew and hundreds of Africans had to be sustained all the way to the Americas.

The last chore on all slave ships was to ensure that it had been loaded with sufficient provisions for the Atlantic crossing. Slave ships took on board African foods that would be familiar or palatable to the enslaved, to add to the dried fish, biscuits and other items carried from Europe. The standard food was horse beans, boiled into a pulp and mixed with yam and rice, sometimes with a little beef or pork, seasoned and mixed with oil and pepper, or with whatever ingredients the ship's cook had to hand. Ideally, Africans received water three times a day, though on many ships water was distributed twice a day, after the food. The rule of thumb was that a voyage of two months would require one barrel of water per slave: a ship with 600 slaves would carry 40 tons of water for the Africans. Equally important, the casks had to be kept in good condition.[62]

Crowded with apprehensive and traumatised Africans, and managed by overworked and edgy sailors – and provisioned with enough food and water for the crossing – the slave ship put the fading sight of Africa behind it, and nosed into the long weeks of an Atlantic crossing. Few such crossings were without their terrifying moments. For the Africans, the apprehensions of oceanic sailing were compounded by the stark human miseries unfolding around them. As the weeks at sea slipped by, their manacled shipmates succumbed to distressing ailments, and many of them died in the most abject of conditions. Mass suffering, sickness and death formed a distinctive, inescapable background noise – and smell – from the slave decks. But what was to happen on the *Zong* was altogether different.

CHAPTER 4

The making of the *Zong*

WHEN THE WILLIAM GREGSON SYNDICATE BOUGHT THE *Zong* in 1781, it was just the latest addition to what, by then, was William Gregson's remarkable slave-trading empire. By the time of his death in 1800, Gregson had become one of Liverpool's leading citizens and businessmen, a highly successful slave trader who had diversified into insurance and banking, with an associated political career culminating in election as Mayor of Liverpool in 1762. It was a rags-to-riches story, for, like so many of his fellow traders to Africa, William Gregson came from humble origins: his father had been a porter, and his own early working life had been in rope-making (itself vital for Liverpool's shipping industry). But William Gregson's early involvement in the slave trade would have daunted many men.

In 1744, along with four partners, he invested in the new, locally built 80-ton *Carolina*, one of only about thirty slave ships trading out of Liverpool at the time. The *Carolina* collected 332 Africans on a slow trawl along the coastline of the Bight of Biafra,[1] before heading for Kingston, Jamaica. Forty-eight Africans died *en route*, and the crew also suffered heavy losses. Furthermore, the ship itself never made it back to Liverpool, but was lost at sea soon after delivering the Africans. This disaster did not deter William Gregson, and two years later his next ship, the *Blackburn*, co-owned with three partners, sailed for Africa: it too was lost, though this time seized (along with the Africans on board) by the French.[2] Unbowed, Gregson pressed on, and over the next half-century he invested in ever more slave ships. Thanks to good management, better fortune than with his first two voyages (and presumably good insurance), William Gregson slowly rose to the top of Liverpool's mercantile and social tree.

In that half-century William Gregson became the sole or part owner of large numbers of slave ships. Year after year, his ships transported huge numbers of Africans to different plantation colonies in the Americas, but largely to Jamaica. In the 1750s, Gregson's vessels shipped more than 8,000 Africans across the Atlantic, and a further 7,000 followed in the 1760s. By the end of his life, the 152 slave voyages in which we know William Gregson had a stake had carried 58,201 Africans, 49,053 of whom survived to landfall in the Americas.[3] Even in the desolate world of slave statistics, these are astonishing figures for an individual slave merchant, and they speak not only to Gregson's commercial fortunes, but also to his entrepreneurial skills. Yet Gregson was just one personal example of the slave-trading success which transformed the city of Liverpool. His rise paralleled almost exactly Liverpool's transformation from being a poor rival to Bristol, to becoming Britain's pre-eminent slave port. In the decade Gregson entered the trade, Liverpool dispatched 43 per cent of all

Britain's slave ships; thereafter the graph was ever upwards. It was as if the stories of William Gregson and of his home port went hand-in-hand.

William Gregson's initial forays into the slave trade provide clues to his later success. Two aspects of his early career were crucial. It began in the 1740s, and it was shaped by using partnerships with other investors. The war of the Austrian Succession (1740–48) exposed all ships sailing from southern ports (like London and Bristol) into the Atlantic via the English Channel to French enemy warships. Ships from Liverpool bypassed this by going round northern Ireland. By avoiding the risks of conflict and capture in the traditional sea lanes into the Atlantic, Liverpool ships not only gained more and safer business but also secured cheaper insurance than their southern competitors – and hence Liverpool ships could undersell their rivals.[4] Thus, for most of the 1740s and 1750s, enterprising Liverpool merchants took advantage of wartime conditions to carve out a powerful position in the Atlantic slave trade. Equally important for Liverpool's story in those decades was the way the city's merchants and entrepreneurs coalesced (sometimes with associates from outside Liverpool) into partnerships of investors to finance and dispatch slave ships to West Africa and the Americas. Liverpool's powerful slaving community of the late eighteenth century evolved from a series of (often interrelated) commercial associations among men who knew each other (and who were often related to each other) who pooled the costs of investments, shared the enormous risks of slave trading, spread the burdens of the associated insurance, and who, with luck, acumen and good fortune, would share the profits. In William Gregson's case this pattern survived a full half-century, from the

Carolina in 1744 through to his last ventures in the early 1790s (when he effectively handed over to his sons).

In the pioneering 'take-off' period of the 1740s, Gregson invested in five slave ships: the *Carolina* (1744), the *Blackburn* (1747), the *Elizabeth* (1747), the *Clayton* (1749) and the *Nancy* (1749). Each ship was jointly owned by partnerships of between four and six men, some of whom came from humble stock, but who featured time and again in other partnerships throughout Gregson's career. Like Gregson himself, some of his partners went on to invest in dozens of later slave voyages. Matthew Strong, a 'rector' from Northern Ireland, was to have nineteen voyages to his name, James Gildart thirty-seven, and John Kennion twenty-five. Peter Holme, a Manchester grocer, was a partner in fifty slave voyages, John Bridge, a cooper by trade (like Gregson's rope-making, an invaluable skill in the shipping industry), forty-five, and Thomas Dunbar, a soldier, thirty-five. In Laurence Spence, a London merchant (who went on to to notch up thirty slave voyages), Gregson and friends had a personal link to the important world of London's business and finance.[5]

The pattern set by those early voyages of the 1740s laid the foundations for much of Gregson's remarkable career. His slaving investments were secured among men he knew – and clearly trusted. They came together, time and again, for new voyages and new ships, their vessels 'going north about', outflanking, outpacing (and therefore under-pricing) their rivals from the southern slave ports. In so dangerous a world as oceanic trade, in handling such volatile cargoes as enslaved Africans – and much of this during periods of intense global warfare – disasters were inevitable. Over the next fifty years, the commercial losses which followed such maritime disasters were, if not commonplace, then regular. Eleven of Gregson's ships were shipwrecked between 1745 and 1791, and four were seized by French or Portuguese enemy vessels in wartime. Perhaps even more revealing, three of his ships, the *Fanny* in 1765, the *John* in 1776 and the *Viper* in 1789, were overwhelmed by Africans. The first was 'Cut off by Africans from the shore' though later recaptured and the slaves sold in Kingston, Jamaica. The *Viper* and the *John* was also attacked and overwhelmed by Africans from the coast.[6]

Here in miniature – the simple outline story of one slave trader, William Gregson – lies the wider story of Liverpool's slave ships. Good fortune and disaster followed each other. But Gregson's accumulation of ever more slave ships, his year-on-year reinvestment in slaving voyages, his commercial, personal and civic rise to eminence in his booming home city, also reveal the prosperity yielded by African slavery. Although Gregson and friends suffered the occasional commercial catastrophe, every single one of his voyages entailed a tragedy of a very different order for the Africans packed below decks. The survivors from the almost 60,000 Africans loaded on to his ships found themselves cast ashore in slave colonies from Pernambuco to Demerara, from Tobago to Tortola, though the largest number – more than 25,000 – were set to work on the plantations in Jamaica.[7] The disasters which befell the Africans are perhaps beyond measure. But Gregson and his colleagues had a different kind of calculus at their disposal. They could offset the hazards and dangers to their business by prudent housekeeping. William Gregson learned, from his first two slave voyages, the commercial risks of slave trading. Slave traders knew that they must insure their ships against the disasters which lurked on all sides of the enslaved Atlantic.

Despite these obvious risks, William Gregson prospered more than most. Among 199 leading Liverpool slave merchants in the years 1750–99, only ten other men came close to Gregson's number of slave voyages (152). And only two other merchants, William Boats (157) and William Davenport (155), had more slave voyages to their names.[8] Such men, and the commercial empires they created on the back of enslaved African labour, made Liverpool what it was.

The ships of Gregson and his partners developed important links in specific locations in Africa and in the enslaved Americas. Their ships traded along a huge stretch of African coastline, from Sierra Leone to Loango, but overwhelmingly they secured their human cargoes in the Bight of Biafra – especially at Bonny and Calabar, where they acquired more than 28,000 Africans. The second most fruitful area for Gregson's slave ships was the Gold Coast, his ships acquiring 12,000 Africans at Anomabu, Cape Castle and other unspecified Gold Coast ports.[9]

A successful slaving voyage also had to know which slave market to head to in the Americas. Here Liverpool swept past its rivals after 1741, coming to dominate every slave market in the British Atlantic empire (except for the Chesapeake, which remained in the hands of Bristol slave merchants). Liverpool's slave traders were quick to spot a market for Africans wherever it opened up. A newly acquired British colony (Grenada and Tobago), the demand in a post-war, slave-starved island, or in a colony newly acquired by the British at the latest peace settlement, all were quickly noticed.[10] William Gregson was among those able to provide African slave labour to old and new colonies alike. His ships delivered Africans across a wide arc of Caribbean islands, and even dispatched some as far south as

British Guiana. Above all, however, Liverpool's ships – including Gregson's – headed for Jamaica. From mid-century, Jamaica had entered another expansive phase, as new sugar plantations were developed in previously untouched and remote areas of the island, notably along the west and north coasts. In the years between 1741 and the end of the British slave trade, 594,499 Africans were taken to Jamaica – and more than 65 per cent of them were transported in ships from Liverpool. Of the 57,413 Africans taken to the Caribbean in Gregson's ships, almost one half were sold in Jamaica, while 7,490 went to Grenada (acquired by the British in 1763), 6,902 to Barbados, and a further 6,156 to Dominica (also acquired in 1763, though the French took it back, briefly, in 1778).[11]

William Gregson's initial disasters with the *Carolina* and the *Blackburn* in 1744–7 soon receded and his dramatic commercial success ultimately encouraged a degree of family pride. One of his vessels even bore the family name, making fifteen slave voyages between 1769 and 1794 before it was seized by the French in the latest of the Anglo-French wars that dominated much of the eighteenth century. The *Gregson* alone loaded 6,501 Africans, of whom 5,638 survived to land-fall in the Caribbean. The great majority, 3,423, were sold in Jamaica, another 1,647 in Dominica and 568 in Tortola.[12]

Slave trading was, by definition, a risky business, but by the time William Gregson handed over his commercial dynasty to his sons in the 1790s, Liverpool's slaving community faced a new kind of threat – the fierce attack from British abolitionists. Yet the rewards for the founding father had clearly been great. William Gregson's personal estate at his death was calculated at £10,000, a sum exceeded by only twenty-one other Liverpool slave traders.[13] By the last years of his life, his name was to be seen not only on the prow of one of his ships but also on a bank in the centre of the city – 'Messers Gregsons, Sons, Parke and Clay' – with offices on Lord Street.[14] The bank, like the slave ship *Gregson*, and so many of his other slaving ventures, was a partnership.

This commercial success brought William Gregson an assortment of material and social rewards. His prosperity enabled him to be among the first of the city's major slave traders to move out of the city centre to the suburbs, when he settled in Everton, a village 'situated on an agreeable eminence about a mile north-east from the town of Liverpool', which has 'of late years become a very favourite residence, and several excellent houses are built along the western declivity of the hill.'[15] William Gregson had become a man to be reckoned with.

As befitted a man of his economic standing, Gregson became a force in the political life of Liverpool. By dint of being a 'free burgess' (a privilege he bought for himself and his three sons) he joined the Corporation, Liverpool's governing body. In 1762 he became mayor of the city (his son John was to follow him in 1784), serving on various Corporation committees which actively steered civic affairs with the city's commercial interests in mind. It was in these years that the Liverpool Corporation embarked on that string of civic and commercial improvements which sought to make Liverpool a more pleasant place to live while providing the port-city with an infrastructure better suited to the commercial life of the men who governed it. The massive expansion of Liverpool's docks and warehousing, undertaken at some financial risk to the Corporation, were all improvements which hugely helped the mercantile community. Under the watchful eye of its resident slave traders, Liverpool successfully blended 'civic power and mercantile self-interest'.[16]

The apparently irresistible rise of William Gregson's fortunes disguised a number of obstructions, most notably the regular havoc caused by warfare in the Atlantic and the Caribbean. Warfare inevitably did short-term damage to the Atlantic slave trade. The British trade suffered especially during the conflict with the American colonies between 1776 and 1783 when warfare, and the support of other European nations (notably the French and the Dutch) for the rebel Americans, both served to intimidate the slave merchants. In the five years before the American war the British had embarked 215,915 Africans on their slave ships. But in the first five years of that conflict the numbers fell to 85,408 – a drop of 60 per cent. Slave ships which persevered had to be on the look-out for enemy ships, as well as natural hazards – and the Africans. Slave traders, including William Gregson, clearly felt that to dispatch ships to Africa and the Caribbean was to invite disaster.

The last of William Gregson's ships to sail before the American war intervened was, appropriately, the *Gregson*, which left Liverpool on 17 July 1777, delivering 328 Africans to Jamaica before returning to its home port on 20 April 1778. Concerns about the dangers posed by the war meant that it was three years before another ship belonging to William Gregson and associates shipped Africans to the Americas.

When a Gregson ship next reappeared off the coast of Africa, it did so courtesy of William Gregson's sons. It was common for successful Liverpool slave merchants to incorporate male family members into their businesses when the moment seemed right. And in September 1780 three of

Gregson's sons, John, James and William junior (all of whom were to become seasoned slave traders over the next twenty years), joined four others, George Case, Edward Falkner, James Aspinall and Richard Wicksted, in a seven-man ownership of the *Swallow*. Case (who was married to William Gregson's daughter) and Aspinall were among the city's pre-eminent slave traders, and Wicksted (a 'gentleman' from Cheshire) had previously been part-owner of a slave ship. More relevant perhaps, two of them, Aspinall and Case, had previously owned slave ships along with William Gregson senior. Their new ship, the *Swallow*, sailed for the Gold Coast on 1 September 1780, acquiring 200 Africans before leaving the African coast on the last day of the year. It delivered 186 African survivors to Tortola. Soon afterwards, however, in an eerie repeat of their father's first venture in slave trading thirty-seven years before, the Gregson brothers' ship was lost in a shipwreck.[17] Like their father's before them, this was a disaster which did not deter the sons from further slave voyages. Nor did it deter their father from returning to his old business habits.

Even as his sons' ship traded on the African coast, William Gregson decided that the time was ripe for him to re-enter the trade. The destination was, again, the Gold Coast, thence to the Caribbean. But now, in October 1780, as he put together his new business partnership of five men for the voyage, William Gregson opted for what was essentially his first family-based venture. The new ship, the *William*, was to be owned by William Gregson along with his sons John and James, his son-in-law James Case, plus two familiar and experienced slaving partners, James Aspinall and Edward Wilson.

The 120-ton *William*, built in Liverpool in 1778, was to complete five voyages for the syndicate before being shipwrecked in 1787. They appointed as captain the well-trusted and experienced Richard Hanley, who had captained ships for William Gregson as early as 1762. In fact Hanley was to be master of five different vessels on twelve different voyages for various Gregson partnerships over a span of almost twenty years between 1762 and 1782. When he sailed on the *Gregson* on its five voyages between 1770 and 1775, Hanley was both master and part-owner. All but one of Hanley's previous voyages had been to the Bight of Biafra and to the Gulf of Guinea islands. Only once, as far back as 1765, had he traded for slaves on the Gold Coast. He had delivered his African captives to a string of slave colonies: Barbados, Grenada, Dominica, the French Caribbean and Jamaica.[18] Richard Hanley was clearly a very experienced slave ship captain, familiar both with the African coast and with various slave colonies scattered across the Caribbean. Time and again Gregson and his colleagues entrusted Hanley with their assets, even incorporating him as a partner on five of the voyages, before they appointed him captain of the *William* in 1780. If William Gregson had any concerns about re-entering the slave trade in 1780, he could have found no steadier pair of maritime hands than his trusted captain and sometime partner, Richard Hanley.

There was nothing exceptional about this new mission. True, it marked the beginning of a fully-fledged Gregson family slave-trading concern, with the head of the family now joined by sons and son-in-law, and it marked William Gregson's return to the business after an enforced absence of almost three years. The ship's owners clearly felt that the wartime risks had diminished if not totally vanished – and the capable and enterprising Handley was alert to the commercial opportunities that war also, on occasion, threw up. One such opportunity dropped into the lap of Richard Hanley when he arrived on the African coast early in 1781.

When the *William* dropped anchor at Cape Coast on 14 January 1781 the war with the North American rebel colonies seemed very far away indeed. But the ramifications of the conflict were just starting to be felt worldwide, especially in the Caribbean, and even along the slaving coast of West Africa. Britain's traditional European enemies saw the war in America as a tempting opportunity to settle old scores. France and Spain, for instance, were keen to assert their international power, and to increase their overseas possessions. They also hoped, in the process, to discomfort and hinder the British. The end result was that overseas colonies were gained and lost in a gigantic game of imperial and military chess, particularly in the Caribbean. That arc of islands, stretching 2,000 miles from the Bahamas to Trinidad, was more central to the North American conflict than might first seem likely. A great deal of the shipping heading to North America took a southerly arc, skirting the Caribbean and Bahamas. In addition, many of the European ships carrying supplies for the American rebels (notably arms and ammunition) often came via the French, Dutch and Danish West Indian islands.[19] Consequently, possession of the slave islands, and the trade routes to and between them, formed an irresistible enticement, both in themselves and as part of a grand Atlantic strategy. Once the French sided with the Americans, they became particularly aggressive, taking a number of Caribbean islands between 1778 and 1782. The British war effort in North America needed to end this French threat, and staunch the flow of maritime assistance to the Americans through the Caribbean. The British thus attempted to seize the ships of those nations which sided with the Americans, which traded with the Americans, or otherwise showed them political or commercial sympathy. But to do this, on both sides of the Atlantic, placed enormous strains on the British, and required more extensive naval power than even the Royal Navy could muster.

Extra help came via the Vice-Admiralty Courts. Though usually used to arbitrate on disputed legal matters of British maritime commerce, those courts now extended British military power by issuing 'Letters of Marque' to armed merchant vessels. Such letters were

> extraordinary commissions granted by the lords of the admiralty, or by the vice admirals of any distant province, to the commanders of merchant ships for reprisals, in order to make reparation of those damages they have sustained, or the goods they have been despoiled of by strangers at sea. Or to cruise against and make prize of an enemy's ships or vessels, either at sea or in their harbour.[20]

One such ship was a 100-ton former French slave ship, the *Alert*, now in the hands of Bristol merchants and commanded by Captain Llewellin.[21] Only six days after the British had made a declaration of reprisal against the Dutch for supplying the breakaway Americans, the *Alert* received Letters of Marque on 26 December 1780. Those reprisals against the Dutch fell short of a full declaration of war, but enabled an authorised British ship to impound Dutch vessels and their goods. The *Alert*, trading at Cape Coast, lost no time, and by late February 1781 had captured three Dutch vessels off the African coast: the *Aurora*, the *Eendracht* and the *Zorgue*. She escorted the captured ships to Cape Coast Castle, where they were joined by another British ship, the *Union*, which had itself captured three Dutch ships. Two of the captive Dutch ships, along with some of the Dutch crew members, were released – but the *Zorgue* was too valuable a prize to let go: it came already loaded with 244 Africans. Richard Hanley, captain of the *William* fresh in from Liverpool, stepped in, and on behalf of the Gregson syndicate in Liverpool, using bills of exchange drawn on Liverpool, he bought the *Zorgue* and its African captives. This change of ownership was followed by a change of name; henceforth the ship was known as the *Zong*.[22]

William Gregson had been unwilling to ship Africans across the Atlantic for three years, and here was an opportunity to double his trade at a stroke – and for a relatively small outlay. There was no need to fit out the ship for its first leg to Africa, to fill it with goods to trade on the African coast. The *Zorgue* was a ready-made commercial enterprise: a slaving ship partly filled with Africans and ready to sail. Hanley clearly thought it too good an opportunity to miss – but it was not without its predicaments.

Many of the *Zong*'s original crew had dispersed following the British seizure and the time subsequently anchored off Cape Coast. Recruiting a full complement of crew for a slave ship in Britain was hard enough, but acquiring an under-manned vessel on the African coast posed even greater difficulties. Captain Hanley was forced to piece together an effective crew from whoever was available. He managed to assemble a crew of twenty, by transferring twelve men from his own ship, the *William*, keeping three of the original Dutch crew, and acquiring the rest from among the transient, rootless men to be found at anchorages along the coast.[23] Hanley had no intention of commanding the new ship and was content to remain with the *William*, and to complete his commission ordered for the Gregson syndicate.

In that case, who was to command the newly named *Zong*? Though Hanley had cobbled together a crew of sorts, manpower alone was not enough for a successful slave voyage. Every ship clearly required a competent master. Fortunately, Hanley had sailed from Liverpool in the company of a man with extensive experience of Atlantic crossings – his surgeon Luke Collingwood, who, it was later said, had 'gone 9 or 10 or 11 voyages', though never as captain.[24] In March 1781 Luke Collingwood transferred from his post as doctor on the *William* and was handed the command of the *Zong*. Although twelve of his men had worked together on the *William* on the outbound leg from Liverpool, this makeshift crew was relatively new to each other. Neither did Collingwood or his men have any knowledge or experience of the 244 Africans who already crowded the *Zong*'s decks; they had not chosen or inspected them as they would usually do when buying slaves, and they certainly had not yet gained that intimate knowledge of the Africans' individual appearances, quirks and characters through the rough manhandling required on a voyage. As a slave cargo built up, over weeks on the coast, the crew normally developed some sense, however imprecise and uncertain, of the people they were handling. Collingwood and his men were confronted by ranks of hostile and unknown strangers. In addition, everyone on board the *Zong* was now under the command of a man who was a widely experienced slave surgeon and Atlantic mariner – but a totally inexperienced ship's master. It was, from its inception, a very unusual slave ship.

On 16 March Captain Hanley wrote to his Liverpool head-quarters informing them that he had bought the *Zong*.[25] The

Gregson syndicate promptly took out insurance, 'upon the whole of the Ship and on Goods . . . valuing Slaves at £30 Sterling per head' and covering everything for £8,000.[26] They placed the insurance with another local syndicate consisting of Liverpool businessmen (and one from Warrington). Captain Hanley instructed Collingwood to remain on the coast and trade for more Africans before departing for Jamaica, and, with the problem of the *Zong*'s crew and captain apparently resolved, turned the *William* into the Atlantic with 382 Africans on board, eventually delivering 350 survivors to the company's agents in Kingston, Jamaica, in late May 1781. Two weeks before the *William* arrived, however, Richard Hanley died (on what was his thirteenth slaving voyage), and command passed to William Daniel. The *William* eventually docked back in Liverpool 248 days after it had departed.[27]

Collingwood remained on the African coast for a further five months, trading between Cape Coast and Accra. Finally, on 18 August, heavily loaded with 442 Africans, the *Zong* left the African coast. She did not sail due west, however, but rather set a south-easterly course towards São Tomé, a tiny island nestling in the Bight of Biafra some 250 kilometres off the African coast (in Portuguese hands in 1781). This might look a strange, slightly roundabout way of embarking on an Atlantic crossing, yet São Tomé had long been the favoured last port of call for slavers heading to the Americas.[28] In fact William Gregson regularly sent his ships to the Guinea Gulf islands. Beginning with his very first ship – the ill-fated *Carolina* in 1744–5 – Gregson ordered no fewer than ninety-one of his voyages to stop there before heading into the Atlantic.[29]

Luke Collingwood was, then, just the latest master to sail one of Gregson's ships to São Tomé for a final provisioning stop. With so many people on board – 440 Africans, nineteen crew, and (unusually) one passenger, a Mr Robert Stubbs – the *Zong* would require large volumes of food and fresh water to sustain them during the next few months at sea. But by 1780 the procedures for victualling a slave ship had become a well-oiled routine. Slave captains knew exactly how much food and water was needed, per African and per crew member, for the expected duration of an Atlantic crossing. For the best part of a century, slave ships had often covered themselves for all eventualities by carrying *twice* the amount of food and water they would require for the crossing.[30] Even so, the best-laid plans might be jeopardised by the quirks of circumstance: food and water could spoil and become too foul to consume; termites and rodents could quickly eat their way through supplies, and even gnaw through water casks. Water might run short when voyages were prolonged by weather, navigational errors, warfare or accident. Even with extra provisions on board, there were times when a voyage went badly wrong, when food and water were in short supply, and everyone on board was reduced to minimal rations. Hunger and thirst were well known to experienced sailors on long-distance sailing ships. On the *Zong*, however, the problem was to take an utterly different and murderous twist.

The origins of the subsequent disaster which overwhelmed the Africans on the *Zong* can be traced to events in São Tomé. On 24–25 August 1781, the ship took on fifteen or sixteen butts of water (of 162 gallons each) for the crossing. The first mate, James Kelsall, was the man traditionally responsible for the process of loading and storing food and water, as well as for the subsequent checking of supplies as the voyage progressed. But when the water was being loaded at São

Tomé, Kelsall was on shore, at a local factory. More seriously, the ship's cooper had been taken ill, and in retrospect Kelsall could not vouch for the 'Management of the Black Coopers who trimmed the Casks as the Cooper belonging to the *Zong* was sick and unable to work at the time.' Yet when the *Zong* left São Tomé, there were no such concerns about competency or supplies, and no indication of any problems to come. The men in charge must have felt confident that they had enough water, for all on board, to last until arrival in Jamaica. For a predicted voyage of eight weeks, there was enough water to allow three quarters of a gallon per person, per day – a simple average which takes no account of different allowances for Africans and crew, nor for any subsequent loss of life which would leave fewer people to provide for. Nor does it allow for a longer than average transatlantic voyage, or for wastage by leakage or pollution. Still, at first glance, the water stored on board the *Zong* seemed more than adequate for the voyage – unless something went dramatically wrong.

Almost precisely three months later, on 21–22 November, by which time the *Zong* was well into the Caribbean, someone noticed 'That a large Quantity of Water had leaked from the lower Tier of Water Casks'.[31] Why had it taken so long to spot the problem? Had no one, as a matter of shipboard routine, regularly checked the ship's supplies? If James Kelsall had concerns about the coopers in São Tomé, why had he not checked the water supplies and the casks *before* departure, and during the voyage?

On 6 September the *Zong* left São Tomé for Black River, on the south-west coast of Jamaica, around 4,000 miles away. By that point, the Africans who had first joined the *Zorgue* had already endured an extraordinary experience, even by the standards of the slave trade. Two hundred and forty-four Africans were on board when the vessel had been seized by the British, though we have no idea how long they had been there. Another six months passed before the ship set out on its Atlantic leg under British command. So in addition to the initial trauma of enslavement and loading on to the *Zorgue*, the captive Africans had lived through the tumult when the vessel had been seized by the British, followed by long fetid months as the ship collected more Africans, first at Cape Coast, then at Accra, before the final stop at São Tomé. All this – month after month – took place *even before* the *Zong* nosed out into the open Atlantic. Some of the captives might well have already been imprisoned on the ship for a year.

When the *Zong* departed from São Tomé, she was just another slave ship: a crowded, stinking, dangerous and volatile floating prison, packed with frightened and utterly confused Africans who had no idea what would happen to them. They were kept in place by a makeshift gang of sailors, most of whom barely knew each other, and who, like slave sailors everywhere, seemed all too willing to dominate by intimidation and brutality. All the Africans could see, when brought on deck, was the heaving Atlantic in all its immensity. Worse – much worse – was to come.

In Liverpool, William Gregson, his sons and associates knew only that their latest ship was on its way to Jamaica. Here, after the past three lean years for Liverpool's slave traders, Gregson seemed to have acquired an unexpected bonus in the *Zong*. These men must have been pleased to feel they were getting back into their commercial stride. It was an auspicious start for William Gregson incorporating a new generation into his endeavours. Meanwhile, they began to prepare the

William for yet another voyage, this time under Captain Cumberbatch, to take Africans from Calabar to Jamaica.[32] It was just the latest venture in an apparently unstoppable flow of Gregson's ships shuttling in and out of Liverpool to Africa and thence to the slave colonies. Of course, like slave traders everywhere William Gregson was accustomed to receiving bad news about losses: the deaths of Africans and of crewmen on his ships, even the entire loss of a ship. But in 1782 the *Zong* was to confront him with an utterly new problem. How would the Gregson syndicate react to the news that the crew of the *Zong* had deliberately killed more than one third of the Africans on the ship as it closed on Jamaica?

CHAPTER 5

All at sea

Before the Zong left the African coast she had been joined by a man who was to play a critical, though somewhat murky, role in subsequent events on the ship. At some point during the months the ship was anchored there, a Mr Robert Stubbs clambered aboard, joining the Zong as the sole voluntary passenger returning to Britain.

Though it was unusual, it was not unknown for a slave ship to carry passengers. There were, however, patently obvious reasons why passengers would want to *avoid* a slave ship at all costs. Not only was the journey, via the Americas, extremely protracted, but it was unavoidably dangerous and never less than unpleasant. Anyone who visited a slave ship on the African coast would have known, immediately, of their hazards and foulness. Moreover Robert Stubbs could have been under no illusion about the kind of experience facing him on the Zong, because he had done it all before. Almost thirty years earlier he had himself captained a slave ship.

Robert Stubbs had been master of the *Black Joke*, one of the most ironically named of all slave vessels (and surely no accident). Seized from the French, this 100-ton ship had sailed from London to the Gambia in 1757 under Stubbs' command and had taken on board 230 Africans. But the *Black Joke* was again seized, repossessed by the French. The surviving Africans were delivered not to a British colony, but to the French island of Martinique.[1] Despite this failure, Stubbs maintained his interest in the slave trade, subsequently becoming part-owner of another slave ship and finding employment throughout the 1770s as a ship's broker in London. In that time, he developed good relations with the Company of Merchants Trading into Africa (formerly the Royal African Company), and in 1780 he was appointed Governor of Anomabu, one of their smaller trading forts on the Gold Coast. It was to prove a disastrous appointment.

The Royal African Company had once been the face of British slave trading on the coast, but by the time Stubbs took up his post, the company was a shadow of its former self. Its initial monopoly, to provide enslaved Africans, was ended partially in 1698, and fully in 1712. Thereafter, the opening of the slave trade led to a massive growth in the British trade – 'to four times more since its being open, than it was under an Exclusive Company', in the words of an official study of slave imports in those years.[2]

Fierce economic and political argument had raged throughout the early history of the company, but through the confusions of the debate about monopoly or free trade,[3] little thought was spared for the Africans. All sides shared a broadly based consensus that the African was a commodity, an item of trade, something to be bought, sold, haggled over and used. It was this core belief which was to be a central but particularly lethal issue on the *Zong* in 1781. No one doubted the indispensability of the African, and most sides were united in the view that without African labour the American plantations could not function. Without the plantations, and all that flowed into and out of them, British economic wellbeing, at home and abroad, would falter.

Despite losing its monopoly in the supply of African slaves, the Royal African Company maintained its London offices and conducted its business in Africa from a string of forts along the Gold Coast and Senegambia, maintaining a regional HQ in the massive castle at Cape Coast.[4] The company remained an important presence on the coast, a commanding economic and military power based around its fortified trading posts. But its commercial activity had always been burdened by the heavy overheads of maintaining its costly forts. By 1750 its power had waned hugely, and the reorganised company was henceforth charged largely with maintaining the forts and trading posts.[5]

The British controlled more than thirty of these buildings heavily concentrated along the 'Gold Coast', and, though the forts offered an apparent strategic advantage, they also proved a financial headache. Their specific location is the clue to their real purpose. In common with other European slave-trading nations, British forts and castles were constructed along a relatively tight stretch of coastline. From Beyin in the west to Keta in the east (a coastal stretch roughly corresponding to the coastline of modern Ghana), a string of forts were built and maintained by (and sometimes rotating between) the Dutch, Portuguese, British, French, Danes and even the Brandenburgers. Though the forts handled regular flows of captive Africans from African traders, through the holding cells and dungeons, thence on to the slave ships, they also guarded supplies of gold from the fabled Ashanti region to the north. Buying and accumulating coffles of Africans did *not* require the protection of such massive fortifications, and most traders successfully traded far away from the forts in villages, on beaches, or on board their ships.

Even so, the forts also offered good trade for a number of British merchants. William Gregson and his Liverpool associates were one such group which frequently dispatched ships to the Gold Coast to buy Africans. They had the experience and commercial know-how to choose the best locations to find superior qualities and quantities of slaves. Before 1780, Gregson's favourite trading site on the Gold Coast was at Anomabu: his ships took away almost 3,000 slaves from that fort in the twenty-five years to 1775. Until 1781, however, they seem to have bought no Africans at the major British fort, Cape Coast Castle. But *after* 1780, Cape Coast rivalled Anomabu for the attention of Gregson's slave ships, providing 2,193 slaves. A further 4,379 Africans joined Gregson's ships from unspecified locations on the Gold Coast. Inevitably, then, when Gregson felt confident enough to send vessels back to Africa in 1780, they returned to their favourite spot – Anomabu.[6] They arrived at the same time as the new Governor, Robert Stubbs.

Like all west African forts, Anomabu readily crumbled in the tropical conditions, and through the intermittent warfare between Europeans in their vicinity. In addition to stout defences, the forts also needed efficient and competent officials, ideally men with experience of the Africa trade, and who knew something about the protocols (and dangers) of slave trading. They also needed men who could exert some authority and control over the motley bunch of inhabitants in and around the forts, and in the nearby African communities: soldiers, clerks, even clerics in places, passing sailors, local Africans (enslaved and free), and the offspring born of local women by this shifting male presence. In 1780 the latest recruit to the task at Anomabu was Robert Stubbs. His was to be a very short-lived, disastrous and almost inexplicable appointment.

Anomabu lies only a few miles east of the major fort at Cape Coast, so close that its officers travelled for the weekly meetings at Cape Coast by canoe. It had been established, along with a string of other small establishments, in the last quarter of the seventeenth century, and from the first, Anomabu had a reputation as a miserable, isolated location for white men; there might only be twelve of them there at a time compared to the hundred resident at Cape Coast.[7] West African posts were unforgiving positions at the best of times, and white men at Anomabu died easily and unexpectedly, or took to the bottle to keep Africa's miseries at arm's length. By the time Stubbs took up his post in 1780, the physical fabric of Anomabu, like many of the other British forts, had suffered major decline. Some of the fortifications had been reduced to heaps of rubble, walled defences had corroded, guns were few and many did not work, and the morale of the residents had declined in similar measure. In 1771 a Mr Tweed (reportedly the pseudonym of an ex-governor who had lived in Africa for more than fifteen years) had described the forts of the Gold Coast as 'A disgrace to the nation ... a nest for filth and vermin – without influence, degraded and stigmatised, as mere burlesques on fortifications; laughing stocks for Europeans and the derision of the natives.'[8] Six years later, conditions at Anomabu were, if anything, even worse. The captain of a

British warship reported in 1777 that holes had appeared in the side of the fort, 'most of the gun carriages are rotten, and falling to pieces . . . the castle gate is rotten and the frame separated, which renders our situation very unsafe . . . Almost every room in the fort is in a rotten, ruinous condition.' At the time the fort housed five soldiers, fifteen men, three women, one child, and a group of castle slaves.[9]

In early 1781, this small band was placed under the command of Robert Stubbs. His dealings with them – the way he behaved and conducted himself, in his new position of responsibility in Africa – provides clues about what may have happened, months later, on the *Zong* itself. Indeed the shadow of Robert Stubbs was not only to haunt the events on board the *Zong*, it also came to shape the way in which historians have recalled and understood those events.

The African Committee appointed Robert Stubbs to be Governor of Anomabu early in 1780 (a post which also made him vice-president of the Council of Cape Coast Castle). He sailed out from England in the company of the new governor of Cape Coast, John Roberts. The two men became instant enemies, and, in the words of Captain Llewellin, their master on the outward voyage, 'the whole passage out was nothing but one continued scene of Riot and quarrelling'. They continued in much the same vein on the African coast: 'the language that passed between the two principles on all Occasions was very unbecoming', the tactful captain explained.[10] It was clear enough, long before they reached Africa, that both men were utterly unsuited for their jobs. One witness stated, 'I am convinced they are the two most unfit Men in the Kingdom for the posts they were appointed to.' Within weeks, both men had managed to alienate their staff in their respective forts. 'Mr Stubbs is as fit to be Chief of Annomaboe as I am to be the pope of Rome' was the dismissive comment of one of his staff.[11] John Roberts, the senior of the two, lost no time in denouncing Stubbs to anyone who would listen ('a Scoundrel, Rascal, Highwayman, Livery Servants etc etc . . .') when not slandering his employers, the London committee, as 'blockheads' and 'a parcel of Fools and Old Women'. Roberts also openly denounced the very basis on which the African Committee functioned, talking incessantly of the time when the African trade would be handed over to a joint-stock company.

Yet, for all their personal animosities, the two men were much alike: 'entirely given up to Drunkeness and every Species of Riot and Debauchery'. One witness to their lives on the coast described how they were drunk 'every Day for a week together, and that as often before Dinner as after it'. As if that were not bad enough, one man who worked with Stubbs accused him of 'being of such low Education that he can neither read nor write'.[12] To make up for his shortcomings in literacy, Stubbs appointed as his personal secretary a sailor who had been discharged by Captain Llewellin for repeated misbehaviour. (Roberts went one better, appointing to his staff the 'Mulatto Son' of a local. The man promptly took to the bottle and developed the habit of dancing naked among the Africans.[13])

The hatred between the two men festered on the coast. Roberts refused to allow Stubbs to dine at the communal table at Cape Coast Castle – and similarly banned anyone who consorted with him.[14] Not surprisingly, the activities of these two leading officials had a disastrous impact on relations within their forts, among the whites, and between black and white.

Their behaviour 'rendered them so contemptible to the Natives that the Black Servants hooted them even in the Castle'.[15]

Predictably, the very reason for their presence – to run the business of trading from the forts – collapsed around them. Roberts and Stubbs were 'inadequate to the Task of conducting the Service: either with credit to their country or themselves.' They simply could not manage affairs properly 'either to their own credit or the satisfaction of the Committee'.[16] They were 'mere Cyphers, daily seeing the Trade pass their Gates to the Dutch and Danes'.[17]

At Anomabu, Robert Stubbs neglected the fort and its supplies, and cheated his local staff and local traders of provisions, clothing and money: one called him 'a bankrupt Scoundrel'. Africans – the vital link to trade in captives and gold – simply refused to deal with him. His inexperience, and his refusal to listen to more experienced men who could have helped him, were evident in his dealings with Africans. Stubbs blustered before them, hoping to illustrate the strength of his command at the fort by a parade and a display of his men and 'A Shew of exercising his great Guns'. To do this, he closed the main gates on Sunday morning, 'when the Natives regularly go to the Fort for their Weekly Allowance'. Far from being impressed, the Africans realised his 'Weaknesses, his poverty; his Inability to exert himself; and therefore demanded so many ankers of Liquor for shutting them out'. Local Africans knew he had 'so wretched a Garrison, and no provisions',[18] and the end result was a display of African disaffection and tumult directed at the fort. It also strengthened the resentment among Anomabu's military and clerical staff, who were already seething against their governor. The days of Robert Stubbs as governor of Anomabu were numbered – and that only months after arriving.

The London committee, alarmed at what they heard –
many weeks after the events, of course – recalled the two men
on 22 December 1780, 'to give an Account of their proceedings'.[19] Stubbs was withdrawn 'from his litigious Disposition,
neglect of Duty and contempt of their Authority'.[20] But
before that order arrived on the African coast, both men were
suspended by the Council at Cape Coast on 23 January 1781.

Stubbs' fate went far beyond dismissal, for three days later, at
breakfast time, he was physically seized by a group of men, led
by a Council member from Cape Coast Castle. They bound his
hands, dragged him down the stairs, and dumped him on the
beach next to Anomabu fort: 'On his Back, [and] pulled his
shirt and breeches almost off and exposed him in a cruell and
shameful manner there in that posture amongst a vast number
of Blacks, both men and women'. He was alleged to have abused
his position by slave trading in his own interest and was
suspended from the company's council.[21] The accusation may
have been true – but it was clearly a cover for a much deeper
resentment at his scandalous behaviour ever since his arrival.

The only escape from Robert Stubbs' extreme embarrass-
ment at Anomabu in January 1781 was for him to join one of
the cluster of British ships anchored and trading close to the
fort. Stubbs thus found floating sanctuary aboard Richard
Hanley's slave ship, the *William*, owned by the Liverpool
Gregson syndicate. Later, when Hanley had cobbled together
a crew for the *Zong*, Stubbs simply transferred from the
William to the *Zong*. There was another ship preparing to sail
back to Britain, but its master, Captain William Llewellin,
had had more than enough of Stubbs on the inbound voyage.
Indeed, he had been so incensed by Stubbs' disruptive, menda-
cious behaviour (which had begun even before they left

England) that he wrote a letter of complaint to London denouncing him as a 'wicked and Treacherous Character'.[22] Not surprisingly, Stubbs did not take a berth on Llewellin's return voyage. Another option would have been to leave Africa on Hanley's ship, the *William*, ready to sail via Jamaica. But opting for the *Zong* may not have been accidental.

The *Zong's* makeshift crew was commanded by its new master, Luke Collingwood, lately doctor on the *William*, with James Kelsall as first mate and Joseph Wood as second mate. When Hanley welcomed Stubbs on to the *William*, he may have thought that Stubbs' experience would be a valuable addition to the meagre ranks of senior men currently being assembled for the *Zong*. Hanley, an experienced slave captain, was clearly aware that the *Zong* was short of practiced senior men. Robert Stubbs – despite his recent failings at Anomabu – had captained a slave ship (albeit thirty years earlier) and was experienced at dealing (though not altogether successfully) with Africans on the slave coast. In any case, Richard Hanley was in no position to be choosy, and Stubbs may have seemed an unexpected bonus. However serious his flaws and personal shortcomings at Anomabu, which Hanley must have known about, Stubbs brought important knowledge to the ranks of the men on the *Zong*. It is tempting to imagine that both Hanley and Collingwood would have welcomed the addition of Stubbs. Even so, he joined the *Zong*, and remained throughout the voyage, *as a passenger*. The ship's muster roll confirms that he was never entered as a serving sailor during his time on the ship.[23] Two years later, in an English court, he was anxious to underline that point: he had been simply a passenger, an innocent bystander as the murderous events unfolded on the *Zong*. But why should we believe a word he said?

Stubbs had, obviously, been greatly despised by colleagues, acquaintances – and Africans – at Anomabu. The feeling was widely shared by men both on shore and on the ship which had carried him from England. The world of slave captains and African-based traders was not known for its refined etiquette, and Stubbs shared the company of men whose world was coarsened by the brutishness of slave trading, and by the miseries of white life in the tropics. Yet even in such calloused company, Stubbs had caused great offence – to black and white alike.

It is important then to be wary of Robert Stubbs, and to be cautious about everything he said or claimed. After all, he shuffled on to the *William* and the *Zong* with opprobrium and condemnation ringing in his ears. Even his account of joining the *Zong* raises suspicions. Stubbs claimed that he joined the *Zong* in 1781 along with four personal African slaves who had 'lived with me many Years'.[24] Yet Stubbs' career at Anomabu had lasted only nine months, from March 1780 to January 1781; and how likely is it that he had brought four Africans with him from London to a slave trading post in Africa? The most probable explanation is that Stubbs joined the *Zong* in the company of four Africans he planned to sell in Jamaica for personal profit. This was, after all, a common bonus for officers on slave ships, and if the accusations were true, Stubbs already had a sideline in informal, personal slave trading. Of course, Stubbs' claim may also have been a complete fabrication.

How *truthful* was Robert Stubbs? How much confidence should we place in this testimony? The irony is that while we have very good reason to doubt him, Stubbs' version of events on the *Zong* has become the accepted, factual version of what happened on that ship. His word has been critical to the entire

Zong story. This 'wicked and treacherous character' was the *only* witness to give evidence in court in London about the *Zong*. And the record of those proceedings form the basis for most of what we know about what happened. English courts in 1783, and every commentator on events subsequently, have relied on that evidence for an understanding of how and why the *Zong* killings took place.

In 1781, Stubbs became part of the *Zong's* complement of men when it left Africa for Jamaica. However distant his slaving experience, it was soon to be put to the test. Stubbs, who had not commanded a ship for thirty years, and whose recent position of responsibility at Anomabu had been such a lamentable failure, was soon to be thrust into command – at sea.

At some point Captain Luke Collingwood fell ill, and was unable to command the vessel. In such circumstances, the normal procedure was that the first mate, in this case James Kelsall, would assume command. Instead, Collingwood took the highly unusual step of turning not to Kelsall, but to the ship's sole passenger, Robert Stubbs. James Kelsall, clearly aggrieved at being passed over, disputed the issue with Collingwood, and on 14 November, eight weeks after leaving São Tomé, he was suspended from his position as first mate.

We do not know precisely what was wrong with Collingwood, who, after a protracted illness, died soon after landing in Jamaica;[25] but it is reasonable to ask whether his illness had impaired his judgement as well as his physical powers. Whatever the answer, it seems clear enough that the captain's illness, and the decisions taken during his fatal illness, played a role in the disaster which unfolded on the *Zong* in the last weeks of 1781.

We have numerous distressing accounts of sailors dying on slave ships after bouts of delirium; stories of tropical sickness attacking both body and mind, and sometimes incubating over a long period, before a sudden, uncontrollable final crisis and death. Grievously sick crewmen ended their days on slave ships in bouts of horrible pain and wild behaviour. In the last generation of British slave trading, up to 1807, something like 20,000 crew members died on British slave ships.[26] The logbook of the French slaver *Diligent* recorded shipboard deaths in a very unusual and graphic manner. Crew fatalities were marked by a Christian crucifix in the margin of the log: African deaths were remembered by the image of a skull.[27] The death of a ship's captain was by no means uncommon: towards the end of the British slave trade, one captain in seven died on the voyage. Indeed shipowners often specified exactly to whom a ship's command should pass in the event of the master's death.[28] The danger of course was that because of a master's sickness or death, a ship might fall to the command of men who were less qualified, less skilled, or less experienced mariners. Few slave ships could boast of having on board a passenger who was a former slave captain. The *Zong*, however, had the dubious advantage of the presence of Robert Stubbs.

Stubbs took temporary command of a ship that was making slower headway than normal. Almost ten weeks had passed between the *Zong* leaving São Tomé and making landfall at Tobago between 18–19 November, whence it was to continue north through the Caribbean to Jamaica. There were many faster crossings than the *Zong*'s, though much depended on the point of African departure. When, for example, the *African* had left Sherbar in Sierra Leone on 7 April 1754, bound for St Kitts, she took seven weeks to cross the Atlantic; dawn on

20 May revealed Antigua dead ahead.[29] But like other ships departing the Senegambia region, the *African* had caught the north-east trade winds which pushed it towards the Caribbean.[30] The *Zong*, trading much further south, made slower headway, and it was to be 100 days before she finally reached Jamaica, compared to an average of sixty-one days for ships heading for Jamaica in the years 1770–1808.[31]

The longer a slave ship was at sea, the more complex and difficult the human problems on board. Sickness and death multiplied, and frictions between Africans and crew worsened, especially when crew numbers also decreased. On the *Zong*, four of the crew died on the Atlantic crossing. The second mate, Joseph Wood, died in a fall from the rigging in the Caribbean. The original makeshift crew was now becoming thinly stretched and the surviving crewmen more and more pressured, and likely more impatient and edgy. It was at such times that the crew found it harder to care properly for the Africans, or to keep them under control effectively. By the end of November 1781, sixty-two of the original 442 Africans had died.[32]

There was, on all Atlantic crossings, a worry about the ship's provisions. But concerns during the long weeks in the empty Atlantic were eased at first landfall. With Tobago in sight, the men on the *Zong* knew that provisions could be replenished, though even then, caution was needed. If Captain Collingwood (or whoever was in effective charge) had any concerns about the ship's supplies, the sight of land in the Caribbean should have been the time to seek a friendly port to stock up. But who exactly was checking supplies on the *Zong*? The mate, whose job it was, had been suspended. Replenishing supplies could, in any case, have been more dangerous than usual. No one could be sure which islands were friendly. A string of British islands had fallen to the French in the course of the current conflict, and no British ship wanted to sail close to enemy territory – and risk seizure by the enemy.

The *Zong* now entered the Caribbean, heading north on the last leg of the voyage, through the Caribbean to Jamaica. It was a journey which normally took ten days.[33] Then, on 21 November, three days after first sighting Tobago, a more thorough review of the ship's water supplies revealed a major problem. An earlier cursory examination had failed to spot that many of the water casks were not full. It was now clear that the demands of a long Atlantic crossing had made much deeper inroads into the water supplies than was initially appreciated.[34] But the *Zong* was now well into the Caribbean, some distance from friendly ports, and at risk of seizure if it ran too close to enemy territory. Who was at fault for the ship's predicament – for failing to spot the water shortage? Had it been a rushed job, a consequence of the crew being short-handed or overstretched, or was it a sign of a poor and divided leadership on the *Zong*?

The fundamental problem may have stemmed from the ship's structure of command. By mid-November 1781, it was not clear who reported what, and to whom. It was the first mate's job to check provisions, but five days before sighting Tobago, James Kelsall had been suspended from that position. So who *was* undertaking the tasks normally carried out by the first mate: who was ordering or handling the vital checks? Presumably not the sacked and aggrieved Kelsall. Captain Collingwood was clearly incapable. Was it Robert Stubbs? Who was taking critical decisions about the ship, about the Africans, indeed even about the sailing and navigation of the ship itself?

The checks on the water supplies revealed that the *Zong* now had only enough water for everyone on board for between ten and thirteen days, on full ration. Under typical circumstances this would have been sufficient to last the ship's crew and Africans to Jamaica, which by then was about eight days' sailing time away. Even so, prudence might have suggested a more cautious regime; the obvious strategy at this stage would have been to reduce *everyone's* ration until safety, an appropriate landing place, or the final destination, was in sight. But that decision was not taken – again, a hint of confused or poor leadership on the ship.

Water was especially important on a slave ship, more so perhaps than on most other vessels, largely because of the peculiar conditions on board, and because of the location of the voyage. Slave ships, packed with hundreds of people in a crowded, dehydrating and suffocating environment, plied their trade in the sapping heat of the tropics. The Africans needed regular water simply to remain hydrated, particularly when they were cramped below. The crew too needed ample supplies of liquid. Theirs was strenuous, back-breaking daily labour, compounded by the difficulties Europeans faced of debilitating toil in the tropics.

In the early days of the slave trade, Europeans were divided about how much water to give to Africans on the slave ships. Some ships' doctors had been reluctant to give Africans more than a few regular spoonfuls of water, from the belief that too much water caused diarrhoea, the great scourge of the slave ships. This early approach changed as medical men observed what was, and what was not, best for the Africans' wellbeing. Practice, however, varied between countries. The Danes, for example, allocated less water to the Africans than other slave traders. The French calculated they needed sixty gallons of water per African for an Atlantic crossing of two months. Portuguese law, on the other hand, specified that slave ships must provide three pints per person each day. This was about three-quarters of the amount allocated to Africans on Liverpool ships. By the late eighteenth century, the rule of thumb on slave ships out of Liverpool was that everyone needed two quarts (four pints) of water per day.[35] One man who knew the crossing as a sailor wrote that 'During the first part of the passage, our allowance of water was three pints per day: for the last month I was reduced to one quart, wine measure. A quart of water in the torrid zone . . .'.[36] But how much worse was it, in the 'torrid zone', for those penned below decks for months on end? Of course not all water taken on board was for drinking: much of it had to be used for cooking. Simple averages (gallons loaded, divided by the numbers of people on board) can give a misleading and even inflated impression of how much drinking water was available for the Africans. Then, ten days after entering the Caribbean Sea, with the *Zong* now only days from its destination, but with water running perilously low, someone on the vessel made a serious navigational error.

On 27–28 November the *Zong* sighted Jamaica, but believed it to be Cape Tiburon on the south-west point of St Domingue, the major French Caribbean possession, then at the height of its sugar boom. In 1781 it was, of course, enemy territory. The *Zong* moved away, sailing on to the west, unknowingly speeding further and further away from its destination.[37]

Such errors at sea were easier to make, and more common, even among the ablest of sailors, than we might imagine, largely because of inherent weaknesses in contemporary maritime navigation. There were plenty of published manuals providing instruction and guidance.

> The great End and Business of NAVIGATION is to instruct the Mariner how to conduct a Ship through the wide and pathless Ocean, to the remotest Parts of the World, the safest and shortest Ways, in Passages navigable.

Notwithstanding such readily available advice, 'several Accidents . . . may attend a Ship in one Day's Run'.[38] The greatest danger was the persistent difficulty of finding a ship's longitude.

Latitudinal coordinates could usually be located by reference to the position of the sun at noon, but sailors everywhere continued to have difficulty finding longitude. The Royal Navy used mathematics, quadrants and sextants to measure longitude via lunar distance, but even that posed problems, because the system could be used only for twenty days in a lunar month – and only then if there was a clear sky. Just five years before the *Zong* episode, Admiral Howe (later to be First Lord of the Admiralty) had used lunar calculations when crossing the Atlantic in 1776, but misjudged his position by 300 miles, arriving off Nantucket when he thought he was off Long Island.[39] Such errors led to periodic disasters, most spectacularly the loss of Admiral Shovell's fleet, which had sailed on to the rocks off the Scillies in October 1707 with the loss of 1,400 men, their reckoning not helped by naval charts that located the Scillies incorrectly. The disaster prompted the foundation of the Board of Longitude in 1714, with the apparently simple aim of encouraging the invention of a device which could accurately locate a ship's longitude: 'The

Discovery of the Longitude is of such Consequence to Great Britain for the safety of the Navy and Merchant Ships as well as for the improvement of Trade that for want thereof many Ships have been retarded in their voyages, and many lost.' Similar investigations were also launched in France, Spain and Holland. In fact the problem of calculating longitude attracted some of the finest scientific and mathematical minds of the seventeenth and eighteenth centuries, and the story of the search for a system, an instrument, to enable sailors to locate their precise position at sea became a well-known international saga.[40] Although effective chronometers had been devised and introduced by the time the *Zong* lost its way in 1781, they were costly and rare: even the Royal Navy began to use them in numbers only from the 1790s, and then only on ships bound for distant waters.[41]

A ship's navigational regime was in the hands of its officers, but in November 1781 who precisely was in charge of the *Zong's* navigation? Someone on the ship was clearly calculating the ship's position by dead reckoning, by using the last visual sightings. And therein lay the basic error. Their last visual sighting had been *not* the south-west tip of St Domingue, but the easterly point of Jamaica. Instead of moving closer to their destination, they pulled (and were driven) further and further away.

The shipboard custom for visual sightings was that they should be recorded by the captain or the first mate on the ship's logboard: 'The Captain or Mate generally takes the Bearing and Distance of that Land (according to his Judgement) and sets it down on the Logboard or in the Logbook'.[42] But on the *Zong*, the captain was sick, and the mate had been suspended. Who took the sightings and made the error about Jamaica/St Domingue? Was it the sick captain, the suspended Kelsall – or Robert Stubbs? Whoever it was, it proved a disastrous decision.

The *Zong*, her water supplies diminishing, rapidly sailed past Jamaica, driven ever further westward by prevailing winds and strong currents. Unexpected currents – like sudden storms or contrary winds – were recognised as part and parcel of the dangers of seafaring: 'The Error in the Ship's Reckoning is frequently attributed to unknown Current, for by various Causes yet undetermined', stated a manual of the time.[43] In the *Zong*'s case, by the time the navigational error was realised the vessel was 'about 30 Leagues to Leeward to Jamaica' – that is, about 120 miles. The precariousness of the ship's position was now recognised, and it was finally accepted that the vessel needed the experienced James Kelsall back as first mate. On 29 November he was reinstated, two weeks after his removal. But in that two-week period, a normal slaving voyage had slid to the edge of disaster.

It was calculated that the ship now had enough water for only four days, but that it would take between ten and fourteen days to sail back to Jamaica. Like so much of the *Zong* story, the details are confused: the exact amount of water left, and the precise number of days predicted to reach Jamaica remain unclear. By the time the story became public, in London in 1783, witnesses to the events (Robert Stubbs and James Kelsall) had good reason to offer a guarded interpretation of what had happened. Both men needed to distance themselves from the *Zong* murders, and place the responsibility (and blame) else-where. They had every good reason to inflate distances and sailing times, and to minimise available water supplies – all to make their case look better. One synopsis of the subsequent legal hearing recorded that the ship now had enough water for only one more day 'reckoning at 2 Quarts a Day per Man'. It was also claimed that it might take another (though scarcely credible) three to four weeks to reach Jamaica.[44] Moreover the *Zong* could not sail to a closer refuge: all the nearest islands (notably Cuba) were enemy territory.

In truth, it is impossible to be confident about what *was* happening on board the *Zong* in the last days of November 1781. Most crucially, it remains unclear *who* was in command of the ship. Luke Collingwood was formally captain, and it seems appropriate to identify him as cause and occasion of what unfolded on the *Zong*. But pointing the finger of blame at Collingwood also suited the survivors, the ship's owners – and Robert Stubbs – when the case came to court in 1783. Holding Collingwood responsible for what happened on the *Zong* contains obvious problems and confusions. The captain was so ill that he had been unable to function, and had been obliged to relinquish command. Survivors described how at times Collingwood was delirious. We do not know how long his illness lasted, but he was sick during the ship's voyage through the Caribbean. And he was clearly sick, though how acutely sick we cannot tell, when the water crisis was discovered, and when the navigational error was made. Was Collingwood in any condition to make rational decisions? Would not his enfeebled condition reduce his authority over the crew? Or was he, as seems likely by the end of November 1781, simply a titular figurehead, master in name only, with *effective* command passing to others on the *Zong*? And where in all this was the man to whom Collingwood had handed command, the shadowy Robert Stubbs? In the words of one legal report, Stubbs 'took the Command towards the end of the Voyage when the Captn was disabled and exhausted'.[45] Was Stubbs' advice and influence the critical ingredient in the unfolding difficulties on the ship?

Whoever *was* in effective charge on 29 November faced a very serious crisis. The obvious step was to impose strict water rationing for everyone on the ship. There were now an estimated 380 Africans on board, many of whom were sick. It was at this point on any slave voyage, only days from landing, that the ship's doctor and crew were usually busy preparing Africans for sale: washing and cleaning the captives, oiling their skin to give it a less sickly pallor. The most wretched, afflicted with dysentery, were bunged up with oakum and cotton. The Africans had to be scrubbed and smartened, and the blemishes of sickness and trauma disguised, to make them as attractive (and valuable) as possible to would-be purchasers. These last days on the *Zong*, however, took a very different direction.

On 29 November, with the *Zong* still far to the west of Jamaica, the crew (now numbering only eleven men) were assembled and asked what they thought of the suggestion that, faced with the water crisis, 'Part of the Slaves should be destroyed to save the rest and the remainder of the slaves and the crew put to short allowance.'[46] James Kelsall later claimed that he was shocked, and objected when he first heard the proposal. If that is true, his objections quickly subsided. The crew agreed to the proposal unanimously. No one on board objected to the suggestion that they kill some of the slaves. And they set about the murderous work immediately. At 8 p.m. that same evening fifty-four women and children were pushed overboard, as Kelsall later described, 'singly through the Cabin windows'. The timing was important: darkness was falling and the change in the ship's watch allowed all hands to be available for the killings. Two days later, on 1 December, a group of forty-two men were thrown overboard from the quarterdeck. A third batch of thirty-eight Africans were killed some time later: ten Africans, realising what was about to happen, jumped overboard to their deaths. Somehow, one of the Africans managed to clamber back on board.

As with much of this story, there is some confusion about the precise numbers killed. One report suggested a total of 150 Africans had been drowned. James Kelsall thought that 142 Africans had perished, but the legal hearings in London later accepted a figure of 122 murdered, in addition to the ten who had jumped to their deaths.[47] Whatever the exact number, no one disputed that a mass killing – a mass murder – had taken place on the *Zong*. The killings took place in small, manageable batches. The men were thrown overboard 'handcuffed and in Irons',[48] according to Kelsall, to make the process less dangerous for the vigilant crew. It was obvious to the other Africans, penned below deck, what was happening. They must have *heard* the killings. It was no easy matter to heave a human being overboard – even when they were shackled. Robert Stubbs (innocently marginal to those events in his evidence) later told the court 'I heard some of the Shrieks of some of them'.[49] People tend not to go to a violent death without a noisy struggle, and though the evidence about the last brutal moments of the murdered Africans is sparse, we know enough (and can easily imagine more) about the screaming terror unleashed in the waters around the *Zong* on those early evenings, only days short of Jamaica. This terrible scene, repeated over three days, killed one third of the Africans on board.

The murder of the last group of Africans in early December did not end this catalogue of African deaths on the

Zong. As the ship struggled on, with the diminished water supplies (though now with fewer African thirsts to quench), it was claimed that a further thirty-six Africans died before reaching Jamaica.[50] Stubbs said that the *Zong* arrived at Black River with '30 of the Negroes laying dead upon the deck . . . from famine.'[51] Perhaps Stubbs hoped his claim that Africans died *after* the murders would strengthen the argument that conditions on board were *so* desperate that only the deliberate killings of some could save the rest. There is no doubt, however, that by the time the *Zong* docked, the surviving Africans were in a wretched condition. A Jamaican newspaper reported that it arrived 'in great distress'.[52]

In little over three weeks, between the first killings on 29 November and the *Zong*'s arrival at Black River on 22 December, there had been a catastrophic loss of life among the Africans on that ship. The *Zong* arrived at Black River with 208 Africans on board. On 9 January 1782 a Jamaican newspaper ran an advertisement offering for sale 200 Africans from the *Zong*. These were the survivors of 442 Africans, squeezed into the *Zong*, when she had left São Tomé the previous August.[53]

Such a massive loss of life on any slave ship would have proved a commercial disaster for the owners, but when the Gregson syndicate heard about the deaths, they had other ideas. They intended to turn the loss of life into a profitable trade by claiming on the ship's insurance for the Africans murdered at sea.

The idea of claiming on the ship's insurance seems to have been raised initially in the crew discussion on the *Zong*, immediately prior to the killings on 29 November. But who among the men on a slave ship was likely to know *anything* of the ship's insurance cover? In the event, of course, any insurance claim could only be pursued back in Liverpool by the ship's owners. While the decision to kill the Africans had been taken at sea, and carried out by the men on the *Zong*, their actions were later fully supported by a group of businessmen in Liverpool. The response of the ship's owners is no less startling than the behaviour of the crew. Working on a slave ship clearly hardened the hearts of the crew, but the slave trade seems also to have dulled the sensibilities (and even the social alertness) of those involved in the trade in Britain itself. Upright God-fearing and law-abiding citizens of Liverpool, prominent and respected men in that city's community and politics – pillars of the community – felt no moral qualms about going to court (with all the attendant publicity) to claim compensation for Africans murdered on one of their ships. It is not merely that the ship's owners thus became *complicit* in the killings; by strenuously fighting the case in court, the owners were also responsible for publicising the murders. They brought the entire *Zong* story to public attention. Had they not pursued their insurance claim, who would have known about the killings? The Gregson syndicate was thus responsible for shifting the killings from a ship in the Caribbean into an English courtroom. Thereafter, however, an outraged genie was out of the bottle. But until the legal proceedings began, Gregson and friends seemed unaware of – and even untroubled by – the profound social and political shock waves that might follow. Those Liverpool slave traders were single-minded about the killings on their ship: they wanted their money from the insurers.

Through the welter of detail about the *Zong*, and through the subsequent blur of claims and counterclaims, one critical fact remained undisputed by everyone concerned. Late in

1781, a massacre had taken place on a Liverpool ship as it approached Jamaica. Subsequent arguments, played out in English courtrooms, were about *why* those killings took place, and whether the killing of the Africans could legally be compensated by the ship's insurance cover. Today, that legal discussion seems to capture a perverse historical moment: the Lord Chief Justice, called upon to sit in judgment, not of the killers, but of whether mass murder was covered by an insurance policy. As if the initial killings were not bad enough, English law now seemed intent on dishonouring the dead by assessing them as items of trade. African deaths were mere numerical and financial details in a commercial transaction, the demise of the Africans simply a fine point of commercial law.

The killings on the *Zong* were premeditated and discussed beforehand, by the men who carried out the killings: they were agreed to as a practical and commercial decision. It was a grim and, today, a barely credible decision. Yet anyone familiar with the Atlantic slave ships knew that killing Africans was *not* unusual – and at times it seemed to come as naturally to the men who sailed the slave ships as steering the Africans across the Atlantic.

CHAPTER 6

An open secret

L ATE-EIGHTEENTH-CENTURY ENGLISH NEWSPAPERS carried
brief factual statements announcing the departure and arrival of
slave ships at various locations around the Atlantic. These small
notices from the world of business formed a mundane feature
of the social and economic fabric of British life. The arrival of
slave ships in the Americas, loaded with Africans, raised no
moral issues for publishers or readers, ruffled few political
feathers, and attracted little comment save for the simplest of
factual notices. On 13 March 1782, for example, almost three
months after the *Zong* had arrived at Black River, a London
newspaper reported the bald facts: 'The following ships from
Africa are arrived at Jamaica viz *Zong*, Collingwood, with 208
ditto [slaves].'[1] Exactly one year later, the full story of what had
happened on that ship reached the British public, with the
extraordinary news that those 208 Africans were the survivors
of a mass killing.

At first glance, the story seemed a rather mundane legal
matter. On 6 March 1783 a group of Liverpool merchants

brought a case in London's Guildhall against the underwriters of one of their ships, who had refused to pay for the partial loss of a cargo at sea. But twelve days later, the real story behind the dispute emerged when the *Morning Chronicle and London Advertiser* published an anonymous letter outlining the details. The lost 'cargo' that was being contested by insurers and shipowners consisted of 132 dead Africans.

The anonymous letter described the reactions of people in court to what they heard on 6 March. The ship's mate, James Kelsall, admitted that he had helped throw the Africans over-board, 'by the Captain's order, which he thought was to him a sufficient warrant for doing any possible thing, without considering whether it was criminal or not'. He did this despite the fact that Captain Collingwood 'was in a delirium, or fit of lunacy, when he gave the orders'. These words in an English courtroom *'seemed to make every one present shudder'*. The anonymous letter-writer continued:

> That there should be bad men to do bad things in all large communities, must be expected; but a community makes the crime general, and provokes divine wrath, when it suffers any member to commit flagrant acts of villainy with impunity.

The author thought that the implications of the case were profound.

> It is hardly possible for a state to thrive, where the perpetrator of such complicated guilt, as the present, is not only suffered to go unpunished, but is allowed to glory in the infamy, and carries off the reward of it.[2]

The case was heard before a jury, which decided that the insurers were indeed obliged, under the terms of the insurance policy, to pay compensation for the murdered Africans. But the matter did not rest there. The newspaper report detailing the case was to have profound and unexpected consequences. Its immediate impact was to expose two related but distinct issues. Firstly, a mass murder had taken place on a British ship. Secondly, the men who committed the killings, and the shipowners who employed them, had not only got away with the killings, but had even profited from them by successfully claiming against their insurers.

News of what had happened on the *Zong* was greeted with horrified disbelief. Even to contemporaries familiar with the slave ships, and even in an era when African sufferings on slave ships was unexceptional, and killings on slave ships were commonplace, what happened on the *Zong* was horrifying. But why was that so? Was it the *numbers* of people killed that horrified people? Or was it the Liverpool merchants' heartless pursuit of compensation – as if they were dealing with an inanimate ship's cargo? Or was the shocked reaction to the *Zong* story a sign of a deeper, less obvious shift in contemporary sensibility? Whatever the cause, it is now clear that the affronted reactions to the *Zong* amounted to the beginning of a marked change in British attitudes to the slave ships and everything they stood for.

The man who brought the grim tidings of the *Zong* to Granville Sharp – a seemingly humble clerk in the Ordnance Office, but also a dogged defender and long-time friend of the black community – was Olaudah Equiano (Gustavus Vassa), a formidable, literate and well-connected African, and himself an ex-slave. Equiano had already led a remarkable life, both enslaved and free, at sea and on both sides of the Atlantic. His years as a sailor had taken him from the eastern Mediterranean, throughout the Caribbean and North and Central America. Equiano had forged friendships and networks in ports up and down the North American seaboard; he had been a pioneer settler on the Mosquito Coast of Central America; and had survived naval combat, shipwreck, and a hazardous expedition to the frozen wastes of the Arctic. When he learned about the *Zong* he was leading a less exciting life in London, but he knew instinctively to head to Granville Sharp. He called on him on 19 March.[3]

It was Sharp's blur of activity in the days following that helped to spread the awareness of events on the *Zong*. It may also have alerted the ship's surviving crewmen that they could face serious charges. Sharp made no secret of his plans to have the men responsible prosecuted for murder. Later, when James Kelsall and Robert Stubbs gave evidence about what had happened on the ship, they must have been aware of the need to tread cautiously, and not to incriminate themselves. To those who were outraged by what they heard of the *Zong*, Granville Sharp began to take on heroic status. In the words of the *Gentleman's Magazine* for that year, he was a 'true patriot, a true christian, [who] has nobly stepped forth, and at his own expense, instituted a criminal process against those workers of wickedness'.[4]

Thus, in the spring of 1783, these two very different men, Equiano – who today is the best-known eighteenth-century black Briton and whose image even appeared on a British postage stamp in 2007[5] – and the remarkable Granville Sharp, came to form an unusual but potent partnership. The one a freed African who had known the bitterness and violence of slavery at first hand; the other an eccentric Englishman who had, by sheer persistence, become a thorn in the side of Britain's slave lobby. He was resolved to bring down Britain's slave empire, though it seemed a hopeless task: what could one Englishman, however determined, hope to achieve in the teeth of such massive economic and political power? In fact, Granville Sharp's work was to prove the catalyst for major political change.

When news of the *Zong* became public in 1783, the myriad backers of slavery and the slave trade – huge vested interests across the face of Britain – must have felt secure enough behind the hundreds of slave ships juggling for space at various British quaysides. William Gregson and his colleagues knew that their strength lay in the massive economic and commercial benefits which the Atlantic slave system clearly brought to themselves and to Britain. The slave trade looked impregnable, and the *Zong*'s owners in Liverpool clearly felt no alarm when they pressed ahead with their legal claim against the insurers. Meantime, other Gregson ships were already plying their trade in Africa and the Caribbean. But their world was about to change – and very quickly.

What stunned people about the *Zong* in March 1783 was not simply the murderous brutality of events on that ship, but the incredible legal saga played out in London – *and* the implications of that legal debate. An English jury, sitting under the watchful gaze of the Lord Chief Justice, Lord Mansfield, 'rendered a verdict wholly favourable to the owners of the *Zong* for the loss of 130-plus slaves at £30 each'.[6] It was hardly surprising that the African Ottobah Cugoano thought the Gregson syndicate 'inhuman connivers of robbery, slavery,

murder and fraud'.[7] Initial outrage at the murders was quickly
followed by an added revulsion when the jury ordered that
compensation be paid for the murdered Africans. It was as if
English law was adding legalistic insult to the injuries
inflicted by the slave traders.

There was, however, a perverse logic to the jury's decision.
The entire slave trade hinged on the transportation of
Africans *as cargo*, and prudent shipowners took the precaution
of insuring their cargoes. As the *Zong* affair went through the
courts in 1783, two important issues quickly surfaced. First,
insuring the lives of Africans on slave ships was routine.
Second, killing Africans on slave ships was *not* uncommon,
and *under certain circumstances* the death of Africans could
be compensated. Moreover there was no secret about all of
this: the violence which characterised life on the slave ships
and which reached such extreme levels on the *Zong* had
frequently been discussed, in print, throughout the eighteenth
century. There was plenty of publicly available evidence
about the violence and killings on British slave ships, but no
one had seen it cast in such a sensational and shocking light
before.

Confronted by details of the *Zong* case in 1783, many more
people now became aware of some startling facts about the
slave trade: of Africans dying in large numbers on British
ships, of untold numbers of Africans trying to destroy themselves, and of Africans shackled for months on end to prevent
revolt. Despite its bleak extremes, and notwithstanding its
peculiarities, the story of the *Zong* exposed some essential
features about the Atlantic slave ships. Every slave ship
expected to face dangers from their African captives. What
happened to the *Zong* was a lesson in just how badly wrong a

voyage could go if simple errors were made by the men in charge. The wrong man, making the wrong decisions, could destroy an entire voyage. But, as far as we know, no one took the kind of decisions which were taken on the *Zong*, and no other merchant resolved to recover their losses in the way chosen by the Gregson syndicate.

Everyone involved in the slave trade – from the grandest merchant to the roughest of deck hands – knew that there were times when the crew might have to kill the very people they had been sent to trade for, and for whom they paid such high sums. Though no one would admit it openly, a crude human calculus had evolved at the heart of the slave trade and was accepted by all involved: to survive, it was sometimes necessary to kill, most commonly when faced by shipboard insurrection. Of course not all Africans boarded the slave ship in a rebellious mood; some were utterly crushed by the traumas of enslavement and dislocation (sometimes for months past), others were humbled by sickness, and still others rapidly slid into mental turmoil and could see no solution to their miseries but by ending their lives. Yet for all that, after the initial shocks, there emerged a persistent, rebellious instinct: an urge to escape, to resist the alien regime, to answer back by whatever means seemed possible. But Africans also learned that recalcitrance and revolt provoked violent reprisals from a vengeful crew. The crew took no chances when confronted by dangerous Africans: they shot at them, fired guns through the hatches into the slave decks, dropped lighted gunpowder through the gratings on to the Africans, doused them with boiling water and, more desperately, found themselves locked in hand-to-hand fighting with insurgent Africans. Sometimes a slave ship was reduced to a confused battleground. The *Ruby*, sailing to the Gold Coast in 1731, 'had the Misfortune to be cut off by the Natives down the Coast. Colwell [the captain] and most of the sailors were killed'. Two years later, the Africans on board another British ship trading on the coast 'Mutiny'd, rose, and killed a great Part of the Ship's Crew; the Captain himself had his Fingers cut by them in a miserable Manner, and it was with great Difficulty he escaped being killed, which he did by swimming ashore'.[8]

African revolts took place on slave ships of all nationalities.[9] In the 1720s we know of revolts on at least seventeen French slave ships. On one of them, the *Excellent*, seventy-four Africans died in the fighting or by committing suicide in the ocean when the revolt had been crushed. The crews also knew that African rebelliousness simmered and was hard to eradicate. On the *Dauphin*, Africans rose up three times, despite the leading plotter having been hung from the yard-arm and shot.[10] Sometimes the fighting became so chaotic it engulfed the entire ship and destroyed it. In 1786, the Revd Philip Quaque, an African trained in London now living at Cape Castle as a cleric, described 'a melancholy and unhappy circumstance' offshore. The Africans on a Dutch slaver were so badly treated that 'they rose upon the ship's crew' and seized the ship. When a group of English sailors fought to regain control of the ship, everyone was 'indiscriminately blown up upwards of three or four hundred souls'. Nor was this a solitary example.[11]

Incidents of such extreme violence obviously could not be kept secret. In the case of British ships, they were reported in Lloyd's annual shipping lists. In 1749, for example, Lloyds reported that 'The Scipio, Stewart, of Leverpool [sic], from Africa for America, was blown up on the Coast, occasion'd by an insurrection of the Negroes'.[12] Nor were formal maritime reports the sole source of such information. After 1787 abolitionist literature placed great emphasis on the commonplace brutalities of slave trading, but there had been plenty of published accounts, telling much the same story, earlier in the century. Naval officers, slave captains, explorers and geographers, all and more had published graphic accounts of the upheavals on board slave ships, of the desperate fighting and exemplary gory repression.[13] Readers learned that the bodies of rebel Africans were commonly dismembered and defiled. William Snelgrave, himself an advocate of better treatment of enslaved Africans on board the slave ships, was as fierce as the next captain when faced with captured rebels. In 1721, one of his men had been killed in a revolt on his ship riding at anchor near Anomabu. Snelgrave asked the captains of eight neighbouring slave ships to bring all their African captives on deck to witness the consequent punishment. They all watched the leading rebel being hauled to the yard-arm. As he dangled there, ten sailors shot him dead. 'The Body being let down upon the Deck, the Head was Cut off, and thrown overboard. This last part was Done, to let our Negroes see, that all who offended thus should be served in the same manner.'[14]

All this was not simply a matter of revenge and intimidation. Dismembered bodies were evidence of the power of the white men,[15] and desecrating the African's body was also a conscious effort to violate whatever beliefs Africans might hold dear about the body, and how it passed over into the afterlife – or even how the African might escape back to Africa: '. . . many of the Blacks believe, that if they are put to death and not dismembered, they shall return again to their own Country, after they are thrown overboard'.[16] Though slave traders had only the vaguest idea of African religious beliefs, mutilating the dead Africans was an attempt to dishonour the body and its prospects of an afterlife. Such stories had been paraded before the British reading public long before the *Zong* case gave the issue a new and totally unexpected twist.

Africans who survived such shipboard battles had no guarantee of safety. Those left with scars and wounds posed a problem for the slave captains. Obvious disfigurements would inevitably reduce the value of Africans when offered for sale in the Americas. One merchant complained that many recently arrived Africans had been injured in an insurrection on the crossing: 'many of those who lived to be brought to Market had wounds in this bodies which gave an unfavourable impression.'

Captains sometimes decided to solve this problem by simply disposing of wounded Africans. They killed them. When the Rhode Island slaver the *Sally* suffered a major insurrection, 110 Africans died in the fighting – but another eighty were forced overboard by the crew. A Bristol captain, faced with injured Africans on his own ship, drove them over the side, fearing their damaged bodies would 'have sold for nothing'. In 1788 – that is, *after* the *Zong* killings – a Pennsylvania newspaper reported how a slave revolt on the ship *Nassau* had resulted in much loss of life, with many survivors suffering gunshot wounds. After the ship's doctor had examined the wounded, the crew heaved overboard those Africans most injured, and therefore deemed worthless.[17] It was perfectly clear to all, long before and after the *Zong*, that Africans were sometimes deliberately drowned by slave traders. Pitching wounded Africans overboard was a simple and convenient way of cutting a slave ship's losses. And that raised the issue of insurance.

Jettisoning cargo was commonplace – to save the ship, or to save part of the cargo – and maritime insurance had developed legal conventions which accepted this as an essential feature of a ship's insurance cover.[18] When the Gregson group insured their African captives on the *Zong* for £30 per head in 1781, they were merely doing what hundreds of prudent slave merchants had done for years past: covering their investment against possible loss. William Gregson had traded in Africans for thirty years, and must have known that the cost of Africans killed in the suppression of a revolt, or who later died from their wounds, was recoverable on a ship's insurance.[19] John Wesket's authoritative study of insurance law, *A Complete Digest of the Theory Laws and Practice of Insurance* (published, coincidentally, in the year of the *Zong* case), stated:

> The insurer takes upon himself the risk of the loss, capture, and death of slaves, or any other unavoidable accident to them: but natural death is always understood to be excepted: – by natural death is meant, not only when it happens by disease or sickness, but also when the captive destroys himself though despair, which often happens: but when slaves are killed, or *thrown into the sea in order to quell an insurrection on their part*, then the insurers must answer.[20]

Africans who simply died, or killed themselves, on the slave ships were not covered. Indeed, sometimes the underwriters specifically excluded insurrections from their insurance cover. Owners of the *Fly*, for example, took out cover which specified that 'The insurers [were] free from any Loss or damage that may happen from the Insurrection of the Negroes.'[21]

This was an unusual stipulation, though, and one that we can imagine few clients would have been happy with, considering the very prevalent fear of African attack *en route*.

But what was the legal position if the crew deliberately killed Africans for reasons other than suppressing their uprising? It seems the question had never been asked before. But someone on board the *Zong* clearly knew that, under certain conditions, Africans killed on the voyage were covered by insurance. Was it Captain Collingwood (delirious and sick)? James Kelsall, who professed to be shocked when the killings were first proposed? Or was it Robert Stubbs – a man with years of experience in different branches of the Africa trade and a man of remarkable deviousness?

Whoever it was, understanding ship insurance at this time was no easy matter. The standard policy used for the cover of ships and their cargoes was itself a bewildering document. First issued in printed form in 1680–81, the format of the insurance policy did not change for the next hundred years, bar a 'Memorandum' (listing the particular details of a specific ship) attached at the end.[22] The policy's antique presentation became ever more outmoded and unfamiliar with the passage of time, exacerbated by the confusing language employed, which puzzled even the judges who scrutinised it.[23] Such was the standard policy used by slave traders to cover their ships and human cargoes. The section describing the risks covered by underwriters reads as follows:

Touching the Adventures and Perils which we the Assurers are contented to bear and do take upon us in this Voyage, they are of the Seas, men-of-War, Fire, Enemies, Pirates, Rovers, Thieves, *Jettison*, Letters of Mart and Counter-Mart,

Surprisals, Takings at Sea, Arrests, Restraints and detain-
ments of all Kings, Princes and People, of what Nation,
Condition or Quality soever, Barratry of the Master and
Mariners, and *of all other Perils, Losses and Misfortunes* [my
italics] that have or shall come to the Hurt, Detriment, or
Damage of the said Goods and Merchandises and Ship, etc,
or any Part thereof.

It was a policy which seemed to allow the shippers some
latitude in making a claim for losses. First, they could claim
under 'Jettison' – the enforced ditching overboard of cargo,
often necessary when a ship was in danger, running before a
storm or otherwise needing to lighten its load. There was, in
addition, the catch-all phrase of 'all . . . Perils, Losses, and
Misfortunes that have or shall come to the Hurt, Detriment,
or Damage . . . thereof'.[24] Lloyd's standard insurance policy
did *not* cover losses caused by 'common mortality', or by the
loss of perishable cargo.[25] Would the deliberate 'jettisoning' of
sick Africans fall under such a general cover?

Stories from the slave ships, of killings and violent rebellions,
periodically broke cover in the eighteenth century, and they
run like a refrain through the printed accounts of the slave
trade. At one level, it seems perplexing that people who went
to so much effort and expense to buy Africans sometimes felt
obliged to kill them, and sometimes to mutilate the African
corpse. But slave merchants and their captains everywhere
knew that the crew lived in a extremely dangerous environment. In the squalid intimacy of the slave ship, control over
the enslaved was uncertain, sometimes precarious and always
under threat from the Africans themselves. Killing Africans

was sometimes the crew's only ultimate guarantee of their own survival.

Brutal killings were normally not capricious; they were calculated, and had become an established cost in the wider business of slave trading, long before the *Zong* killings. Moreover such killings were not hidden away, part of a grubby maritime secret, known only to those most closely involved with the ships. They were openly discussed, in print, by men who commanded and owned the slave ships. Men who had worked on the African coast and on the Atlantic slave routes wrote about their lives and adventures, describing African sufferings in very great detail. Equally, shipping records periodically documented the extreme violence of African insurrections and their suppression. The men most directly involved, from the shipowners in British ports right down to the humblest of sailors, knew precisely what happened to insurgent, wounded or dangerous Africans. After all, they were the men who ordered or implemented the punitive steps taken against the Africans. There was, quite simply, no secret about the killing of Africans on the Atlantic slave ships.

In that hazardous and precarious business, shipowners and masters alike took appropriate steps to minimise or avert its inherent risks. Their immediate security lay in the physical control exercised over the Africans via the shackles, chains and guns, and the intimidation of the shipboard regime. But as with other forms of shipping, they also took out insurance policies to cover both the vessel and the cargoes. Legal disputes inevitably arose about claims on those policies. But the *Zong* case offered a totally new approach to the entire business of maritime insurance. Did an insurance policy cover the deliberate killings of Africans? The *Zong* legal hearings in

1783 revealed the links between the staid world of insurance and the violent world of the slave ships – and, in the process, the matter was transformed. The insistence of William Gregson and colleagues that they receive compensation for murdered Africans shifted the entire debate from a technical decision about the law of insurance into a public discussion about the very nature of slavery itself. Before 1783, arcane matters of maritime insurance had been the preserve of specialist legal debate. Now they were thrown into full public and political view.

1 A view of Liverpool from the Mersey conveying a sense of the city's shipping, shipbuilding and associated industries in the eighteenth and nineteenth centuries. In the background are the King's Dock, the King's Tobacco Warehouse and the Herculaneum Pottery.

2 The links between Liverpool and Africa were literally set in stone in the 1750s – in the elaborate friezes depicting African heads on the city's Exchange, now the Town Hall.

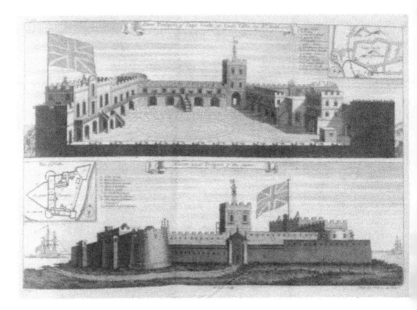

3 Cape Coast Castle, headquarters of the Royal African Company, and a formidable fortress that dominated the Gold Coast. Its vast underground vaults, constructed as prisons in the 1680s, could hold up to a thousand slaves awaiting shipment. It was here that the *Zong* was purchased in 1781.

4 African canoes transporting slaves from the coast to awaiting slave ships, off Elmina.

5 A Liverpool slaver, around 1780, at the height of the city's slaving activity. The four ventilation ports in the lower hull are a giveaway for the ship's main business, as are the small boats being rowed by Africans towards the vessel, and the predominantly wooden buildings on the coastline – almost certainly intended to represent West Africa.

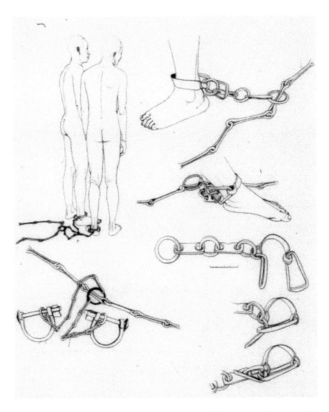

6 The ultimate security of the slave ships: Africans in fetters and manacles.

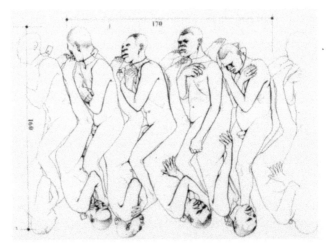

7 Crowding on board made the voyage a living hell for the Africans below deck, enraging some and driving others to despair.

8 The fear of all slave traders: an African revolt on board a slave ship. The crew have retreated behind the barricado and fire upon the rebelling slaves.

9 Sailors routinely cleaned Africans on arrival in the Americas so that they fetched the best selling price. They would be scrubbed, oiled and buffed; scars and other evidence of trauma and sickness would be disguised.

10 Olaudah Equiano, a key spokesman for Africans in the abolition campaign, in a frontispiece to his best-selling self-published autobiography of 1789.

11 Granville Sharp, the pioneering and steadfast friend of Africans and their claims to human rights in the late eighteenth century.

12 Lord Mansfield, the judge at the centre of legal debates about slavery in England – and, more particularly, about the *Zong* in 1783.

13 Thomas Clarkson, surrounded by his collection of African artefacts and, on the mantelpiece, busts of Wilberforce and Sharp. Clarkson was the resolute foot-soldier of the British abolition campaign after 1787.

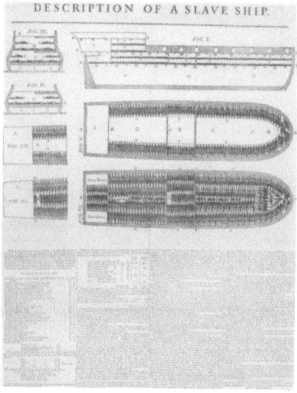

DESCRIPTION OF A SLAVE SHIP.

14 The graphic images of the *Brookes* slave ship, here reproduced on an abolition pamphlet printed by the Quaker James Phillips, captured public imagination and helped turn opinion against the slave trade.

15 The assertion of human rights, 'Am I not a Man and a Brother?', became an immensely successful icon in the campaign against the slave trade, here represented by a Wedgwood cameo.

16 As part of the bicentenary of the abolition of the slave trade act in 2007, a replica of the *Zong* sailed along the Thames.

CHAPTER 7

In the eyes of the law

Two men, Granville Sharp and Lord Chief Justice Mansfield, were to play key roles in the legal (and social) discussions when the *Zong* case came to court in 1783. Sharp campaigned against the crew and the owners of the ship both inside and outside the courts, and tried to bring murder charges against the men involved. Lord Mansfield made comments and a decision (taken down by a secretary employed by Sharp) which not only entered legal history, but – more critically, perhaps – soon passed into popular currency and demonology. What we know about the case was determined to an extraordinary degree by these two very different men: what they did, what they said, and, no less important, how those actions and words have been construed in the intervening years. Yet before we consider their roles in 1783, we need to take a longer view, for they were men whose paths had frequently crossed over the previous eighteen years. Theirs was a complex, confusing and always distant relation-ship, forged in the intimacy of the courtroom, but with profound consequences for society at large. Long before the *Zong* affair, Sharp and Mansfield had become the most unlikely of protagonists in that story's eventual climax.

Lord Mansfield, the nation's highest-ranking judge and father of English commercial law, had presided over two slave cases in which Granville Sharp, a vigorous defender of black rights, had involved himself. Throughout, Mansfield remained resolute that any legal pronouncements he might make should do nothing to harm Britain's commercial prosperity – even when it was anchored in the slave trade – and he took no formal notice of the openly critical Sharp who frequented his court-room whenever slavery was discussed. (In time Sharp realised that his presence in Mansfield's courtroom might, by irritating the Lord Chief Justice, actually be counterproductive, and he chose to stay away.) Mansfield's concern was simply to adjudicate and pronounce on specific matters of law, as he saw them unfold in the case before him. Sharp's role was different: to be a legal and political agitator for black freedom, and to act as an iconoclast within a legal system which gave sustenance to slavery, often unconsciously, by supporting England's thriving commercial system. Sharp was among the first to spot and to exploit the discrepancy in the English law, between its attachment to individual liberty on the one hand and, on the other, its commitment to a thriving commercial system – much of which was rooted in slavery.

Since the seventeenth-century revolution, English law had prided itself on the extension and maintenance of liberties at home. Yet the parallel rise of the Atlantic slave empire was based on the denial of liberty to millions of Africans. These two contradictory legal systems sometimes overlapped, and inevitably clashed, most simply when a single African slave moved from the Americas to English shores: was a slave brought from Jamaica, for example, freed by merely arriving in England?[1] Once drawn to the conundrum, Granville Sharp set himself the task of verifying that English liberties were enjoyed equally by black and white, and was to emerge as a hero in that story. Yet there was nothing in his early life to suggest the direction his life would take.

Born in 1735 in Durham, Sharp was one of fourteen children, the son of an Anglican cleric; his grandfather was Archbishop of York, his father Archdeacon of Northumberland, and two of his brothers were Anglican clerics. Theirs was a close-knit family, well known for their music-making and philanthropy. But Granville was the youngest son, and by the time he reached school age there was little money left for his education. Instead, he was placed in various apprenticeships. A ferociously industrious student, Sharp had an intellectual curiosity which drew him towards a range of disparate interests, from ancient languages to theology. (He taught himself Greek and then Hebrew in order to dispute theology with biblical scholars.) A natural and assiduous researcher, Sharp was able to turn his hand to any number of scholarly challenges, but was modestly employed, from 1758, as a civil servant in the Ordnance Department.[2]

His brother William practised medicine in Mincing Lane, London, and it was there, in 1765, that Granville Sharp had a chance encounter which transformed his life. Leaving his brother's house one morning, Sharp noticed a young black man, aged perhaps sixteen or seventeen, queuing with the other patients. The youth was in a wretched state: he had been viciously beaten, could scarcely walk, his face so badly bruised he could hardly see. As Dr Sharp dealt with his injuries, the two Sharp brothers talked to the youth, Jonathan Strong. What they heard shocked them. Strong had been brought from Barbados as a slave by David Lisle, a lawyer-planter. In a moment of anger, Lisle had beaten Strong senseless with a pistol, and then abandoned him on the street. The story is best told by Strong himself.

... I could hardly walk, or see my way, where I was going. When I came to him, and he saw me in that condition, the gentleman take charity of me, and gave me some stoof to wash my eyes with, and some money to get myself a little neccessaries till next day. The day after, I come to the gentleman, and he sent me to hospital: and I was there four months and a half. All the while I was in the hospital the gentleman find me clothes, shoes, and stockings, and when I come out, he paid for my lodgings, and a money to find myself some necessaries: till he gets me into a place.[3]

Restored to full health, Strong worked for the next two years as an errand boy for an apothecary in Fenchurch Street, before being spotted in the street by his former master, Lisle, who wanted to seize him and sell him. Lisle employed officers from the Lord Mayor's office to manhandle Strong into a London gaol to await transport and sale back in the Caribbean. When Granville Sharp was alerted, he hurried to the Lord Mayor's office, successfully demanding Strong's release. After much confusion, and in a welter of personal and legal threats, Granville Sharp prevailed and Strong was set free. Lisle attempted to prosecute the Sharp brothers for having prised Strong away; the loss of the case infuriated him to the extent that he challenged Sharp to a duel.[4]

Jonathan Strong's miserable story confronted Sharp with a number of related alarming realities: that there were slaves in England, that slaveholders assumed that English courts would confirm their right to own (and remove) those slaves, and that enslaved Africans could be shipped in and out of the country despite their wishes. Sharp was outraged, as was a small band of sympathisers who found this evidence about slavery in England deeply disturbing.

Quite apart from the basic human issue of Strong's maltreatment, Sharp's intellectual curiosity was now aroused. What was the *legal* basis for tolerating slavery in England? Sharp sought legal advice on the matter and was amazed at what he learned. In 1729, a group of West Indian traders and planters had asked the Attorney and Solicitor Generals for their legal opinion about slavery in England. Their judgment (the Yorke-Talbot opinion) affirmed that slaves were *not* freed simply by coming to England, *nor* were they freed by baptism (as was widely believed – Strong, for example, had been baptised). Sharp's legal advisors thought that a master could, legally, oblige his slave to return from England to the slave colonies.[5] Sharp also learned that Lord Mansfield agreed with that opinion. Yet this question was not new even when raised in 1729. Discussion about the legality of slavery in England long pre-dated the Yorke-Talbot opinion, in a string of slave-related cases heard in English courts going back at least to 1569.[6]

The planters were understandably pleased with the 1729 opinion, which seemed to guarantee their control over slaves brought to England. Forty years later Granville Sharp was astonished to learn that the opinion was thought to be definitive – and still binding. Sharp decided he would have none of it. Initially anxious to ensure that Africans were not removed from England and returned to the slave colonies against their wishes, Sharp's ambition grew. Although he confessed to having 'never opened a law book', Granville Sharp now resolved to study and master the law, and *prove* that slavery was indeed illegal in England. This highly personal decision, fired by his anger with the law which seemed 'so injurious to natural Rights', was to consume two years of his life, and it was to have a profound effect on the history of British slavery.[7]

Despite the 1729 opinion, English judges remained uncertain about the legality of slavery in England. What particularly angered Sharp was not this lack of clarity, but the harsh treatment periodically meted out to individual Africans whose rights were trampled underfoot by an English legal system which ought to protect them. He was also frustrated because a number of those slave cases came before Lord Mansfield, who appeared reluctant to make a clear legal decision in favour of black freedom. Thus, from 1765 onwards, the two men found themselves regularly involved in legal disputes about black freedom in England. Time and again, Lord Mansfield appeared more sympathetic to commercial interests, and was accused by Sharp of preferring 'pecuniary or sordid property, as that of a Master in a horse or dog, to inestimable liberty'.[8]

Although Granville Sharp had no *formal* role in any of the slave cases in Mansfield's court – cases that pitched Africans demanding their freedom in England against efforts to remove them to a slave colony – he emerged as the key figure behind the scenes, co-ordinating and advancing the legal argument promoting black rights. Sharp's aim was apparently straightforward: he wanted Mansfield to declare slavery illegal in England. For his part, Mansfield must surely have wanted

Sharp to disappear. Theirs was a courtroom relationship which was to reach its extraordinary culmination in the *Zong* case in 1783.

Sharp faced a formidable legal adversary. Lord Mansfield (1705–93) is widely recognised as a towering figure in eighteenth-century English law, his judgments and courtroom principles establishing a legal protocol and code of practice which proved deeply influential both at the time and through the years hence.[9] Born William Murray, into the Scottish nobility, Mansfield displayed great intellectual gifts from his early years, and was soon moved south to be educated, first at Westminster School then at Christ Church, Oxford. He excelled at everything he did: as a schoolboy, as a student, at the Bar, and, after 1742, in parliament and in government. By 1755 he was Lord Chief Justice (as Baron Mansfield) and now embarked on an important and long-overdue string of reforms to modernise a legal system still trapped in its mediaeval forms and procedures. But Mansfield's real interest – and the area in which he had abiding influence – was in the world of commercial law, especially insurance. He was, by experience and interest, an ideal judge to consider the issues lurking behind the *Zong* case.

Few men had such a remarkable range of judicial and political experience as Mansfield. He had been leader both of the Commons and of the Lords, and a government minister, and was greatly admired for his formidable legal talents. Throughout, he aimed to see that good faith and common sense prevailed in his courtroom, stating in one commercial case (regarding an issue of copyright) that the whole matter 'must finally resolve in this question, whether it is agreeable to moral justice and fitness'. Mansfield thought that mercantile disputes should hinge 'upon natural justice and not upon the niceties of the law'.[10] These were fine principles, yet later, when Mansfield heard the arguments about the *Zong*, they were found somewhat lacking. The judge was to show precious little 'natural justice' to the African victims on that ship.

Throughout his judicial career, Lord Mansfield was periodically confronted by the legal problems spawned by slavery. Though he 'doubted the validity of theoretical justifications of slavery' and attempted 'to reduce instances of individual cruelty to slaves', above all he fully accepted the commercial importance of the slave trade to Britain. He also realised that to declare slavery in England illegal would have untold economic ramifications for Britain's slave-based commerce.[11]

The massive expansion of Britain's global trade in the eighteenth century and the parallel growth in maritime insurance (by the late eighteenth century, British underwriters were annually insuring some £100 million-worth of goods at sea) generated a glut of complex legal questions. Time and again, English courts were called on to adjudicate on matters of commercial legality, and on the byzantine complexities of maritime insurance. Mansfield's legal career paralleled this massive expansion of British commerce and related insurance, and he made it one of his guiding principles as Chief Justice (a position he held from 1755 to 1788) to provide clarification of the law.[12]

It is no easy matter to grapple with eighteenth-century law, and even the best of students can be baffled by its impenetrable mysteries. It is a subject which seems designed to confuse, with its own specialist vernacular, and references back and forth to precedent, common law and legislation, the use of Latin terms to describe issues and events more comprehensible in English, all creating a fog of obfuscation. Mansfield was more aware than anyone of those difficulties, and throughout his legal career he was keen to make the law clear: 'The great object in every branch of the law', said Mansfield, 'is certainty, and that the grounds of decision should be precisely known.'[13]

Lord Mansfield imposed sense and shape on the earlier complex confusions of marine insurance law, across a series of cases establishing the basis for determining who was liable – shipowners or insurers – following accidents and misfortunes in maritime trade. One of his guiding principles was that insurers could only be liable 'for losses directly resulting from what they had insured against; they could not be expected to pay up for indirect losses'. Mansfield's work in this field was widely lauded by the legal fraternity. When, in 1786, the barrister James Allan Park published his definitive study of marine insurance, the book, dedicated to Lord Mansfield, was prefaced with praise for 'the many admirable improvements which you have made in that branch of law which relates to Insurances ... Your labours in this respect, were there no other cause, would be sufficient to render your Lordship immortal in a country, whose grandeur is founded on commerce'.[14]

Granville Sharp was aware of Mansfield's commitment to the overriding importance of commerce, and knew of his work as arbiter and architect of the law of maritime insurance. But Sharp in his turn was adamant that commercial interests should not triumph over English liberties. In effect the two men approached slavery from opposite (and conflicting) positions: Sharp anxious to defend individual rights, Mansfield keen to see no damage done to the nation's commercial prosperity.

Above all Sharp was keen to have Lord Mansfield persuaded, in court, that slavery was both illegal *and* contrary to natural justice. To achieve this he needed a case that could convert Mansfield to the idea that slavery stood condemned both as inhuman *and* as a violation of English law. But Mansfield, steeped in commercial law, was equally conscious that to threaten the slave system was to endanger British prosperity, and he remained deeply reluctant to offer legal succour to any man (in this case Granville Sharp) likely to disrupt or undermine that system.

There was much in Mansfield's make-up, particularly his strong ties to the government, to suggest he was no enemy to slavery. Yet throughout his judicial career he displayed a persistent attachment to the idea of fairness and personal justice. Above all, however, Mansfield was very much his own man, and was reluctant to be bound by the legal precedents established by his predecessors. In fact, his was a legal philosophy which angered a number of powerful opponents (ranging from the fiery polemicist *Junius* to the Virginian Thomas Jefferson) who wanted to see the law derive *solely* from precedents. Granville Sharp came to appreciate that here lay his best hope of breaking with the slaving past. Despite all the evidence to the contrary, Sharp hoped that Lord Mansfield could be persuaded, by legal arguments which Sharp would orchestrate, to reject the precedents and take a stand against slavery in England.

From 1767 to 1769, Granville Sharp set about mastering English law with the same tenacious application and industry he had earlier applied to Greek and Hebrew. Late at night, after work, he pored over legislation and earlier legal judgments about slavery. He was soon persuaded that the 1729 Yorke-Talbot opinion was wrong in law, and that slavery was indeed illegal in England. But how could a mere clerk from the Ordnance Office, however erudite or persuasive, hope to challenge, still less dislodge, a ruling from such eminent and high-ranking legal authorities as Yorke and Talbot, both of whom became Lord Chancellor later in their careers? Granville Sharp was not a man to be daunted by such realities.

Sharp first drafted a formal outline of his argument based on the recent case of Jonathan Strong, and circulated twenty manuscript copies among lawyers in the Inns of Court. Sharp's argument was greeted with widespread approval and agreement. He then published it as a tract entitled *A Representation of the Injustice and Dangerous Tendency of Tolerating Slavery; or of Admitting the Least Claim of private Property in the Persons of men, in England* in 1769. It offered a survey of legal evidence to show that, contrary to widespread belief, slavery had *never* been approved in English law. More immediately, in what was to prove a significant breakthrough, Sharp also claimed that all previous arguments justifying the removal of enslaved people from England contravened the Habeas Corpus Act of 1679.[15]

The long-winded title of Sharp's tract should not deceive us. This was no abstract treatise but rather a potent (and incontrovertible) attack which was ultimately to undermine the legality of shipping enslaved Africans back and forth from England against their wishes. More than that, Sharp's tract was effectively the beginning of a broader legal and political debate about the slave trade, and even about slavery itself.

The slaveholders' grip on enslaved Africans in England began to weaken, though not merely from Sharp's aggressive legal scrutiny. Above all, slave-ownership in England was being steadily eroded by the Africans themselves, many of whom simply refused to accept their enslaved status. Black slaves could be found in all corners of economic and social life in the slave colonies, but, despite the continuing popularity of employing black servants in fashionable society in England, slavery fulfilled no real function there. Enslaved domestics lived and worked among free working people, and freedom proved contagious. Slaves simply took matters into their own hands. They demanded baptism, asked for wages or, more dramatically, they ran away.[16] Granville Sharp kept a record of such occurrences, including advertisements seeking the return of the runaway:

> Ran away from his Master, a Negro Boy, under 5 feet high, about 16 years old, named Charles, he is very ill-made, being remarkably bow legged, hollow Backed and Pot-bellied; he had when he Went away a coarse dark brown Linen Frock, a Thickset Waistcoat, very dirty Leather Breeches, and on his head an Old Velvet Jockey Cap.[17]

In all this, those seeking freedom found encouragement and support among black friends who were already free and who were conscious of the social and legal possibilities for freedom in England.[18]

Apprehensive slaveholders, conscious of the risks of losing their slaves there, were especially keen to take them back to the colonies. The most effective way of doing this was brutally simple: to have the unfortunate African spirited out of the public gaze, and manhandled on to a vessel bound for the Americas. But those who tried this in London now faced the considerable obstacle of Granville Sharp himself. Following Strong's case in 1765 Sharp had established a reputation as *the* defender of Africans threatened in this way. Desperate African victims knew that their best, often their last, hope lay with him – if only they could get word to him in time. News of the latest kidnapping of an African sent Sharp scurrying to the courts, often in a breathless effort to secure the African's freedom.[19] Not all rescue attempts succeeded.

Sharp's reputation among British black people went far beyond such fraught, last-minute struggles, and he became a major source of advice and help in times of trouble. Time and again, distressed Africans found their way to Sharp's door. He briefed Africans about their legal rights, secured damages for them in court, attended their cases, and drafted reports on what had transpired in court.[20] Sharp's biographer, Prince Hoare, noted that 'His mind was now fully awakened to the magnitude of the abuses which existed with respect to African slaves in this country.'[21] Throughout the 1760s and 1770s, Sharp pestered and lobbied the good and the great about the issue of slavery, firing off letters and publications, and hoping all the while to raise the awareness of those around him about what he viewed as a national disgrace. Above all, Sharp was a devout man and was convinced that the disgrace of slavery was bound to provoke the wrath of the Almighty.

Granville Sharp wanted to secure much more than the freedom of each African he helped: he sought a declaration of a general principle, a legal denunciation by the Lord Chief Justice of the whole system of slavery in England. Lord Mansfield on the other hand was equally determined *not* to be drawn into so far-reaching and contentious a judgment. Both men – the meticulous and ever-cautious Lord Mansfield and the impassioned, fractious and irritated Sharp – regularly locked horns on this question of fundamental legal and social importance.

Sharp had been involved in a succession of nine such kidnapping cases before the ideal case came his way in 1772. A petition arrived at Mansfield's chambers requesting a writ of *habeas corpus* on behalf of James Somerset, a former slave now threatened with forcible repatriation to Jamaica. It was a familiar story.

James Somerset had been enslaved in Africa and shipped to Virginia in 1749. There he was bought by a local planter, Charles Stewart, and worked for him for twenty years. Master and slave had lived for four years in Massachusetts before sailing to England in 1769. Stewart had intended to return to Virginia later with his slave, but in October 1771, like so many others, Somerset simply quit Stewart's service and refused to go back. The master promptly had Somerset seized and handed over to Captain John Knowles, master of the ship *Ann and Mary*, anchored in the Thames and preparing for a voyage to Jamaica. There, Somerset, 'the slave and property of the said Charles Steuart' (according to the court documents), would be sold.[22] It was now James Somerset's turn, in the New Year of 1772, to ask Sharp for help.

It was clear to all concerned that here was a case of great significance. It was an apparently clear-cut matter: an African demanding his freedom and a planter insisting upon his right to ship his property where he pleased. Mansfield postponed the hearing, deciding that 'from the nature of the question, he should certainly take the opinion of all the Judges upon it'. Sharp, though again keen to help, was also anxious not to irritate or alienate Lord Mansfield, resolving 'Thence-forward to avoid the appearance of regular attendance in the Court'.[23] Once again Sharp worked closely with the threatened African on the case, even employing Somerset as a messenger to carry letters and publications between various interested parties. Three months later, the *London Evening Post* reported that efforts to have the two sides settle out of court had failed. It was now up to the judges:

> judgement should be giv'n according to the *strict letter of the law*, of which they (the Judges) only sat as expounders, without having it in their power to attend to the idea of compassion on the one side, or the danger of precedent on the other . . .[24]

The issue which Lord Mansfield was now expected to resolve was, in the words of Serjeant William Davy, leader of Somerset's legal team, 'as great a question and perhaps a question of as much consequence as can come before this or any court of justice.'[25]

Throughout the Somerset case, Granville Sharp buzzed behind the scenes, dispatching his publications and associated letters to a range of influential men in politics and the law, hoping in the process to widen the debate about to unfold in court. He felt that James Somerset offered the perfect opportunity to establish the general principle of black liberty in England. Sharp's point was asserted in May, in Counsel's blunt opening assertion: 'no man at this day *is*, or *can be*, a Slave in England.'[26] The case attracted keen public interest, with crowds turning up at court to follow the hearings, and late arrivals simply not able to get in. But Granville Sharp kept away, preferring instead to work behind the scenes for Somerset's legal team, and peppering them with verbal and written advice.

Somerset's team needed all the help they could get, for they faced a formidable opponent, not so much in the person of Mr Stewart the planter, but the entire West India lobby. The powerful fraternity of slave trading and plantation interests, which exercised such political and economic influence in London, had decided to support Stewart's case: 'to have the point solemnly determined; since, if the laws of England do not confirm the colony laws with respect to property in slaves, no man of common sense will, for the future, lay out his money in so precarious a commodity.'[27]

The case dragged on intermittently for six months, and as it progressed the legal tide clearly ran in favour of Somerset.[28] There was, in addition, much popular support; even in the courtroom, spokesmen for Somerset found their arguments for the African's freedom occasionally interrupted by outbursts of public approval.[29] Stewart's team on the other hand became increasingly desperate and resorted to scare-mongering, arguing that, should Somerset win, England would be rapidly overrun by Africans seeking their freedom, slavery itself would be undermined, and the nation would suffer a huge economic loss.

When both sides concluded their submissions at the end of May 1772, Mansfield declined to make an immediate judgment: 'The matter will require some deliberation before we can venture an opinion on it.' For his part, Stewart held out little hope of winning. In a letter written on 16 June 1772, he noted: 'Upon the whole, everybody seems to think it will go in favour of the Negro ... I am sorry for the load of abuse thrown on L . . . d M—d for hesitating to pronounce judgment in favour of freedom.'[30]

As the judges deliberated, letters in the press maintained public interest, continuing the debate both about the issues at stake and about the progress of the case itself. Finally, at around 10 a.m. on 22 June 1772, Lord Mansfield made his judgment. Sharp again stayed away from the court. Mansfield seems not to have read out a formal written judgment but, as he often did, spoke from notes. The three judges were unanimous, and their judgment brief, though the subsequent reporting of the case was confusing and has thus left many doubts about what precisely was said and decided. Perhaps the most accurate court report recorded Mansfield having stated the following:

> The state of slavery is of such a nature that it is incapable
> of being introduced on any reasons, moral or political, but
> only positive law, which preserves its force long after the
> reasons, occasion, and time itself from which it was created,
> is erased from memory. It is so odious that nothing can be
> suffered to support it but positive law. Whatever inconveniences, therefore, may follow from a decision, I cannot say
> his case is allowed or approved by the law of England, and
> therefore the black must be discharged.[31]

Years later, Mansfield said that his 1772 decision went no further than preventing a master from compelling an alleged slave to leave England.[32] Although he frequently insisted that his judgment had *not* outlawed slavery in England,[33] London's black community saw the decision as such a victory. The press reported that 'Several Negroes were in court . . . and after the

judgment of the court was known, bowed with profound
respect to the Judges, and shaking each other by the hand,
congratulated themselves upon their recovery of the rights of
human nature, and their happy lot that permitted them to
breathe the free air of England.'[34]

A few days after the case, a large crowd of black people
gathered 'At a public house in Westminster to celebrate the
triumph which their brother Somerset had obtained over his
master. Lord Mansfield's health was echoed round the room,
and the evening was concluded with a ball. The tickets to this
black assembly were 5s.'[35]

James Somerset, the African at the centre of the case, had no
doubt about the judgment. One of his relatives, named Dublin,
who was a slave to John Riddell in Bristol, absconded after 'he
had rec'd a letter from his Uncle Somerset acquainting him
that Lord Mansfield had given them their freedom.'[36] The
West India lobby also thought that the decision had been
broader than Mansfield suggested, denouncing it as a threat to
British (and West Indian) wellbeing. A hostile debate broke
out between those who approved of Mansfield's judgment
and those who disliked it, and who sought to limit its
ramifications.[37]

The Somerset case had an immediate impact in Scotland,
where another slave, Joseph Knight, had fled his master, John
Wedderburn, and, like James Somerset, demanded his right to
freedom. The Scottish judges followed their English counter-
parts and decided against the master. After years of further legal
wrangling, the Court of Sessions confirmed this judgment in
1778 – to the enthusiastic approval of the Scottish press.[38]

News of the Somerset case soon spread to North America.
Gossip, and overheard conversations between slave-owners,

ensured that Mansfield's judgment quickly percolated throughout the slave communities, and the belief that he had abolished slavery in England spread. On 30 September 1773, John Finnie, the owner of two runaways in Botetourt County, Virginia, had 'some Reason to believe they will endeavour to get out of the Colony, particularly to *Britain*, where they imagine they will be free (a Notion now too prevalent among the Negroes, greatly to the Vexation and Prejudice of their Masters)'. The owner of a runaway in Georgia thought that the man would 'probably endeavour to pass for a Freeman by the Name of *John Christian*, and attempt to get on Board some vessel bound for *Great Britain*, from the Knowledge he has of the late Determination of *Somerset's* Case.'[39]

Some colonial slave-owners even feared that Mansfield's judgment might be applicable to North America. In the event this did not happen, though the Somerset case established itself as an important landmark in legal debates in North America, and was widely cited in subsequent US court cases and legal judgments well into the nineteenth century.[40]

Whatever the confusions about the Somerset case, black slavery in England was dealt a severe blow by the 1772 decision. After that point, advertisements for slave sales and notices of runaway slaves in English newspapers effectively dried up. Africans active in the early abolition campaign believed that this was a landmark victory, and that Granville Sharp had been largely responsible for its success.[41] Even twenty years later, Sharp's work was remembered by Africans living in Philadelphia, who wrote to him: 'You were our Advocate when we had but few Friends on either side of the Water'.[42]

The Somerset case had focused public attention on the broader issue of slavery. The decision had gone the way Sharp had hoped, and was a major step towards his goal. But it was, nonetheless, a local, very *English* affair. The Atlantic trade continued to thrive and the slave ships continued to dispatch huge numbers of Africans to the Americas. And as long as the slave trade thrived, it was inevitable that, despite the Somerset decision, complex questions about slavery would continue to surface in English courts *after* 1772. Africans continued to be at risk of seizure and forcible transportation; in 1774, for example, Equiano unsuccessfully tried to save a shipmate, John Annis, from being sent back to St Kitts, where 'kind death released him out of the hands of his tyrants'.[43] Even the *sale* of Africans in England took place after Mansfield's judgment, albeit on a greatly reduced scale. A full seven years after the Somerset case, in October 1779, Granville Sharp received a cutting from a Liverpool newspaper: 'To be sold by auction, at George Dunbar's office, on Thursday next, the 21st inst. At one o'clock, *a Black Boy, about fourteen years old, and large Mountain Tiger Cat*'.[44]

Fully twenty years before the *Zong* case came to his court, Lord Mansfield had been obliged to wrestle with the peculiarities and confusions created by slavery. In the process, he had become very familiar with Granville Sharp and his work. Though the buying, selling and transporting of Africans across the Atlantic remained unaffected – indeed the slave trade boomed as never before – these English slave cases, and the Somerset case in particular, helped bring about an important transformation in social attitudes in England. Africans in England were emboldened to secure their rights, and a small band of English friends rallied to help them. If there was one person responsible for changing the public mood it was surely

Granville Sharp. Throughout the 1760s and 1770s, he and his legal friends had worked on a string of cases to secure black rights in the courts. What he had achieved was remarkable. But all the slave cases in which he had been involved, and which Lord Mansfield had judged, paled when Equiano called on Sharp in March 1781 with news of the *Zong* massacre. The events and political consequences simply dwarfed anything that Sharp had encountered before, and immediately raised compelling questions about what Mansfield would make of it. How would his reputed anger at acts of cruelty, and his famed efforts to redress injustice, sit with the cold-blooded killing of the slaves on the *Zong*? And how would the legal master of maritime insurance respond to a claim for 132 murdered Africans?

CHAPTER 8

A matter of necessity

Even in summer, Westminster Hall can be a cold, draughty place, its huge expanse of ancient flagstones draining the heat from anyone who stops to admire its mediaeval grandeur. But it rarely fails to impress. More perhaps than any other single building, Westminster Hall manages to convey a sense of the English past. Built by the Norman King William Rufus, it has been the location for an endless pageant of major English historical events – coronation banquets, royal entertainments, deceased monarchs lying in state, as well as the major state trials of Guy Fawkes and Charles I among others.

Westminster Hall was also the site of the nation's senior law courts from 1178 to the 1820s. After 1739, a screen was erected when the courts were in session to separate the courts from the rest of the Hall. The court sitting to the left of the screen was the Court of King's Bench,[1] and it was there, on 21–22 May 1783, that Lord Chief Justice Mansfield, flanked by Mr Justice Buller and Mr Justice Willes, reviewed the evidence and the legal arguments about the *Zong* case. What Mansfield and his colleagues listened to over those two days has never been considered as significant as some of the better-known legal proceedings conducted in Westminster Hall. Even so this hearing was to find its own special niche in the annals of English legal history.[2]

Mansfield, Buller and Willes had to decide if there was a case for a retrial of the initial case heard in the Guildhall in March, where the jury (under Mansfield's direction) had decided that the insurers were legally bound to pay compensation to the Gregson syndicate for the loss of the 132 Africans killed on the *Zong*. The insurers, still resistant, asked for a retrial.[3]

Mansfield opened the May hearing with a simple assertion: 'This is the case of a Policy of Insurance upon the ship the *Zong*.'[4] Yet he realised that the case revealed a troubling and morally perplexing story, and that no sort of determination to focus on the legal intricacies could shield him and his fellow judges from the ethical and political issues awaiting them. Indeed Mansfield only had to gaze at the courtroom to see those issues for himself: Granville Sharp, sitting in Westminster Hall alongside a shorthand writer hired to transcribe the proceedings. Sharp of course had his own ideas about what *ought* to take place in Mansfield's court, and, as with the earlier slave cases, his was to prove an impor-tant presence, both at the time and subsequently.[5] Sharp acted as advisor to the insurers' legal team of three lawyers (Mr Davenport, Mr Pigot and Mr Heywood). All four men were keen to expose the wider legal issues, and determined not to allow the hearing to concentrate uniquely on insurance matters – albeit for different reasons. On the other side, the

Zong's owners were represented, as they had been at the trial in March, by John Lee, the Solicitor General, and his assistant Mr Chambres.

In May 1783, both sides, for the insurers and the shipowners, were reviewing evidence which had been used in the trial two months earlier. There is, however, no full or formal record of what transpired in that initial jury trial in March. Lord Mansfield's trial notes for that law term are missing. Although there exists a lengthy, descriptive newspaper account, we have no *formal* record of what took place then. In fact, what we know about the initial trial has come to us via what was said about it at the second hearing, before Mansfield and his two colleagues in Westminster Hall.[6] To compound the difficulties, both the March and the May hearings took place without the benefit of the appropriate documentation. The obvious papers for the court to consider would have been the ship's log, but at some point in the *Zong*'s protracted journey, the ship's log disappeared.

A ship's log provides a formal, comprehensive account of a ship's existence. Kept by the master, it is a record – a daily, noon-to-noon account – of all the essential data about the vessel, from its crew and cargoes, to its movements, supplies and the weather.[7] The log was, in effect, the ship's collective memory, and remained on board to be handed on to the next in command when, for example, a captain died in post or left the ship. Under normal circumstances, the log would have recorded precisely what had happened on the *Zong*. But some time after the ship arrived in Jamaica in December 1781, the *Zong*'s logbook went missing, and all formal record of the killings on that ship – and what had preceded them – simply vanished. Try as they might, the insurers failed to secure any written evidence about the voyage from the ship's owners. They assumed that the papers had been 'altered obliterated defaced torn burnt or otherwise destroyed', and carried out, they alleged, 'with some unfair or fraudulent design' in mind.[8] All this was strenuously denied by the Gregson syndicate, who claimed that the ship's papers were left in Jamaica with Collingwood when he died – though of course they should never have left the ship at all.[9] If the lack of documentation seemed to point to some kind of fraud, it also made the insurer's arguments harder to prove. What sort of evidence could the insurers use to prove their case? Equally, how would the Gregson team conjure forth an argument that they should be paid compensation?

Suspicion about what had happened to the *Zong*'s logbook was compounded when it emerged that the first mate, James Kelsall, also 'Kept a journal untill on or about the 14th of November 1781 of the proceedings of the same Voyage.' He was ordered to cease his log-keeping by Captain Luke Collingwood,[10] on the day he was dismissed from his position as first mate, with the ship only days away from the Caribbean. Was Kelsall keeping a separate journal, or was he simply maintaining the formal ship's journal when Collingwood was sick? And where, in all this, was Robert Stubbs? His critics at Anomabu had alleged that Stubbs was virtually illiterate: did the *Zong*'s logbook fall victim to his educational shortcomings, when Collingwood handed over command to Stubbs? Or, more sinister, did Stubbs remove or destroy the logbook on arrival in Jamaica, realising the explosive nature of its contents? Whatever the answer, the end result is that the *formal* written record of daily events on the *Zong* either stopped or was subsequently lost or destroyed.

Any evidence about the events leading up to the murders, and about the murders themselves, would have to come from eye-witness accounts by those involved.

There were of course hundreds of eye-witnesses to the events on the *Zong*. The two hundred surviving Africans knew exactly what had happened. But by May 1783 those Africans had been scattered among their new owners 5,000 miles away in Jamaica. The other eye-witnesses were the few surviving crewmen. Their numbers, however, had been greatly reduced. Six of the original crew had died 'and more of them pressed in Jamaica into the king's service'. Two Dutchmen had returned to Holland from Jamaica, and three men had died at Black River.[11] But no surviving crew member was called to give evidence in court, even though their names and whereabouts were known, at least to Granville Sharp.[12] In any case, crew members had good reason *not* to want to appear in court. They had, after all, killed 132 people. But curiously, although Kelsall's written statement was analysed, no attempt seems to have been made to call James Kelsall from his home in Liverpool to testify in person.

Quite why the court failed to secure witnesses from among the *Zong*'s crewmen remains a mystery. But there was one man from the voyage who was living in London and who was readily available to give evidence in March 1783. The ship's sole passenger, Robert Stubbs, was called, and thus became the *only* witness at the March trial: in Lord Mansfield's words, Stubbs was the 'one Witness examined upon both sides'.[13] In the welter of detail, the confusion of arguments, and the complexity of legal issues which swirled around the *Zong* affair, the major evidence considered in court was that offered by Robert Stubbs. Indeed much of what we know about the

Zong derives from his testimony. Yet this is the same man who was denounced as a drunken liar and a cheat, by a host of men who knew him well – men of very different positions, ranks and persuasions: soldiers, sailors, administrators and even, in the wings, anonymous, jeering Africans.[14] Even as Mansfield and colleagues soberly weighed Stubbs' evidence, he was locked in a fractious dispute about money with his former employers, only a mile away from the court, in the City of London. It was a dispute which highlights the problem of Robert Stubbs as an honest witness: he said he was owed £444, but the accounts reveal the actual figure was £73.[15]

All this of course was unknown to the court. No one involved in the *Zong* case seems to have been aware that the sole witness was a deeply flawed character, whose word was regarded as worthless by men who knew him. Yet what Stubbs said about events on the *Zong* was central to the entire hearing. Both legal teams, naturally, subjected his evidence to close critical scrutiny, but no one thought fit to ask the simple question: why should anyone, still less a court of law, believe a word he said?

The legal teams for both insurers and shipowners dissected Robert Stubbs' words for evidence to support their respective cases. The insurers, angry at the initial verdict ordering them to pay, wanted their legal team to persuade the three judges to grant a retrial. Lawyers for the shipowners wished to confirm the original March decision in their favour, and to avoid a second trial. The central argument for the *Zong*'s owners was simple: with the ship's water running out, killing the Africans had become a matter of 'necessity'. The insurers countered that this claim constituted a fraudulent scheme devised to pass on an unprofitable voyage to the insurers. The ship's owners, they claimed, had hoped to achieve this by destroying all the relevant evidence – the paperwork – from the *Zong*.

Stubbs insisted that, although the idea of killing the Africans was Captain Collingwood's, 'according to his Judgement the Captn did what was right . . . they all apprehended they should die for want of Water if they had not thrown the Slaves overboard to preserve the rest'. There was, said Stubbs, 'an absolute Necessity for throwing over the Negroes'. The court soon became accustomed to the word 'necessity'. The decision to kill the Africans had been taken 'from the Necessity he was under to save the rest'. Stubbs had repeated the point time and again: the crew acted from 'Perilous Necessity'.[16] This 'necessity' was, in the words of Mr Davenport, made 'the ground of the Cause and of the Verdict' in March. But the insurers simply denied it.[17] The only legally acceptable basis for compensation paid on dead Africans would have been had they been killed during a shipboard revolt.[18] Yet there had not even been a *hint* of rebellion among the Africans. In the words of Mr Davenport, for the insurers, 'there was no insurrection not a Murmur amongst them'.[19]

The insurers' counter-argument was straightforward: the *Zong* found itself in dire straits because of human errors, notably the navigational error which sent the ship well beyond Jamaica. Then, faced with the prospect of a slow return leg to their destination, it had been decided to kill the Africans to reduce pressure on dwindling water supplies. It was 'a Blunder, and Mistake the Ignorance of those with whom the Ship was entrusted but it is not a Peril within the Policy.' These details hid, they claimed, the real intention: 'to saddle a bad Market upon the Underwriters instead of the owners.'[20] The insurers believed that Luke Collingwood was afraid that this, his first command, 'would make a bad voyage for the Owners'.[21] The insurers even claimed that, far from being 'distressed', the *Zong* arrived in Jamaica 'in perfect safety and with her Crew And the Rest of the Slaves in good health' – an assertion that seemed to be belied by the reports in the Jamaica press of the *Zong*'s state upon arrival. The insurers felt they were not liable 'either within the Words or meaning of the aforesaid policies of insurance'.[22] The entire business was a murderous fraud.

Despite Mansfield's opening assertion about insurance, a mass killing was the heart of the case. How could such killings be justified by an argument which hinged on matters of insurance? The insurers, naturally, wanted to move beyond the law of insurance, arguing that the crew had 'acted like men who had forgot the feelings of Men.' What they had done was 'a Crime of the Deepest and blackest Dye'.[23] On the other side, the Gregson lawyers had to *justify* those killings. That task fell primarily to John Lee, the Solicitor General, who fell back on well-established legal traditions in relation to slavery. But he did so with unseemly relish. There was no doubt, he argued, that English law made 'our fellow Creatures of the Negro Cast . . . the Subject of Property'. Further, the *Zong*'s insurance had *specified* that the Africans were 'goods and property and whether Right or Wrong we have Nothing to do with it'. The Africans were thrown overboard *as property* 'for the preservation of the Residue . . . That if a hundred did not die in this way 200 must in another.'[24] Robert Stubbs had made these same points at the trial in March. Now they were vigorously repeated, with approval, by the Solicitor General in front of the Lord Chief Justice.[25] John Lee went further, asserting that the killings had not even involved 'the least imputation of cruelty'. England's Solicitor General managed to reduce the whole murderous business to simple alternatives: 'the great evil was avoided by doing the less'.

Lee realised, despite his smooth interpretation of the killings, that he needed to anchor his reading within established provisions of maritime insurance; he did this by suggesting, contrary to all the evidence, that a slave revolt *must* have been brewing on the *Zong*. Had the killings not taken place, 'there must have been such an Insurrection All the blacks would have killed all the Whites'. He rounded off his argument by stating that the murdered Africans, being things, items of cargo, 'perished just as a Cargo of Goods perished'.[26] The killings constituted a sensible jettisoning of objects.[27] But John Lee was also asking the court to close its ears to the shrieks of drowning people, audible even to Robert Stubbs on the *Zong*.

It was clear enough, as the insurers' team argued, that events on the *Zong* had strayed far beyond the realms of insurance. No amount of forensic analysis of insurance policies could possibly justify such a mass killing. There could be, they argued, no 'such necessity as could justify such a very extraordinary Transaction.'[28] That a mass murder was committed because of a water shortage defied credibility – and outraged humanity.[29] It was a grotesque act which, at the very least, demanded a retrial. In advancing their case, the insurers' lawyers pushed their arguments beyond the particulars of maritime insurance. Indeed they developed an argument – which smacked of Granville Sharp's influence – which spoke to universal human rights. For example, when discussing so mundane a matter as the ship's water supplies, Mr Pigot asserted 'that as long as any water remained to be divided, these men [Africans] were as much entitled to their share as the captain, or any other man whatever'.[30] Beneath this simple assertion lay a startling theory: that everyone on board a slave ship should be treated equally. Such a theory was tantamount to turning the world of the slave ship upside down. If equality of treatment was to become the moral code of the slave ships, how could slavery survive? What possible circumstances, asked Pigot, could justify the killings? 'The life of one Man is like the life of another Man whatever the Complexion is, whatever the colour.' Mansfield's guidelines, though formally accepted by both legal teams at the outset, had been long forgotten: the Gilbert team anchored their case in outraged humanity.

The concept of 'humanity' – a counterpoint to the Gregson plea of 'necessity' – was at the heart of the insurers' submission. Mr Heywood, the third member of the insurers' legal team, argued that he and his colleagues 'appear as Council for millions of Mankind and the Cause of Humanity in general ... To say that wantonly or by Ignorance a Capn may throw 132 lives overboard is a Proposition that shocks Humanity.'[31] They openly claimed to represent not just the insurers, but armies of people who had no other legal spokesman. In Pigot's words, 'Were the compensation to stand it would be such an intent of Fraud and Oppression upon those Persons [the Africans] least capable of Protection.'[32]

The lawyers for the insurers took every opportunity to raise the question of murder – indeed that word was to be used nine times in the course of the proceedings. Pigot asked why some crew members had been allowed to leave the country: 'Is it strange that the parties concerned should be suffered to go out of the kingdom, when they ought to be tried for murder in another place?' Granville Sharp had tried to bring murder charges against the crew a mere three days after first being told of the *Zong* in March, and everyone in court knew of Sharp's involvement, and of his insistence that murder charges be brought. At one point John Lee, the shipowners' lawyer, glared angrily at Sharp in court, denouncing him as the man 'who intended to bring a criminal prosecution for murder against the parties concerned'.[33] Now, before the Lord Chief Justice, Gilbert's team demanded similar justice for Africans against the criminal behaviour of the crew.

The effect of all this was to widen the insurers' case from a technical challenge to the original decision, and a demand for a retrial, into a major defence of the Africans' human rights. This was precisely what Mansfield was at pains to avoid. On a different scale, it again exposed the tensions visible in those earlier slave cases (involving Granville Sharp) between the law of property (in the form of slaves) and that of equal rights before the law.

The insurers' lawyers raised questions in court which had far-reaching political implications. Indeed some of their arguments were more profound than almost any other contemporary discussions about the slave trade. Pigot's assertion about the universality of rights for both black and white – his declaration that all men should enjoy the same rights, irrespective of colour – was an astonishing claim to make in an English court in 1783. In essence, these were declarations of political and philosophical principles which might easily have been part of the famous debates swirling around the Revolution in North America. But as long ago as 1769, Granville Sharp had been advancing the case for equal human rights regardless of colour before the law. Now they found their most potent expression in the *Zong* hearing. Mansfield's court had become political in all the ways he had sought to avoid.

The insurers wanted a retrial. But that was unlikely to be achieved via grand social arguments. They had to make a very *specific* legal case before the judges. Yet the hearing soon revealed that even some of the basic facts about the key events on the *Zong* were unclear. It remained uncertain *who* had been in charge – and hence responsible. There were conflicting accounts about *how many* Africans had been killed. No one could convincingly explain *why* the ship's water shortage had remained undiscovered until so late in the voyage, nor why water rationing had not been introduced much earlier. Who, finally, had made the fatal navigational error? Though technically all these had been Collingwood's responsibility, it was far from clear that he was in charge.

On all these matters, both legal teams pored over the evidence supplied by Robert Stubbs, who, understandably, was keen to distance himself from the killings. With Granville Sharp threatening about murder charges, Stubbs presented himself to the court in March as a mere passenger and an honest outsider. Throughout, however, he was consistent on one major issue: key decisions, and responsibility for those decisions, lay with Luke Collingwood. But Stubbs' tendency to distort and deceive soon became apparent. He claimed, for example, that the *Zong*'s navigational error was *not* a result of Captain Collingwood's ignorance: 'This was an experienced and able Navigator that had gone 9 or 10 or 11 Voyages this Capn.' It is true that Collingwood was indeed an experienced sailor, but he had sailed the Atlantic, as Mr Pigot pointed out for the insurers, not as a master but 'As a Doctor'.[34] In distancing himself from the killings, Stubbs claimed he had been in his cabin when Africans were thrown into the ocean. But this raised the suspicions of the insurers' doubtful team: 'It makes an Impression upon my Mind,' said Mr Heywood, 'that the Man that could calmly and coolly commit such an Act as that and not remonstrate and endeavour to prevent it is not deserving much Credit here or any other Court of Justice.'[35] Equally, Stubbs asserted that he did not know who had thrown the Africans into the ocean. Was this conceivable, on so small a vessel, on *three* separate occasions? Only a short while before, when Stubbs had been in command of the *Zong*, he had needed to know *everything* about the ship and its crew. Now, when a large proportion of the Africans were being killed, Stubbs retreated to his cabin, on three separate occasions, shut off from the killings around him, and apparently unaware of who was involved.

Stubbs' credibility is most severely tested, however, by his apparently innocuous account of the fate of four individual Africans, those who he said had 'lived with me many Years'. He claimed that 'I never knew whether they were dead or living till we got to Jamaica',[36] and only then did he discover that they had been killed at sea along with the others. Stubbs' alleged ignorance about their fate seems odd, unless we remember that such a claim helped to absolve him of any involvement (and hence of any responsibility) in the killings. Is it plausible, however, that four people he claimed to have known for years would have been killed, without his knowledge or approval, on so small a vessel? Equally, had the Africans known Stubbs personally, would they not have turned to him in desperation, when their fate was sealed? In their last terrified moments, would they not have pleaded for the intervention of the one man on the *Zong* who might be able to save them?

If Stubbs did *not* own Africans on the *Zong*, why should he invent the story? Was it a fabrication designed to persuade the court that conditions on the *Zong* were *so* appalling that only a mass killing could save the voyage? That even a stakeholder in the bigger venture agreed with the killing, right down to the death of his own African slaves? Yet if those four Africans *did* indeed belong to Stubbs, and if he remained unaware of their impending fate, that would surely speak to a heartless detachment on Stubbs' part. He was a man who could, without challenge, allow the slaughter of people he knew. Perhaps Robert Stubbs did not mind if they were killed, providing their value could be recovered on the ship's insurance? Or perhaps – as likely as not – Stubbs was lying.

All these doubts about Robert Stubbs raise a really perplexing question. Why did Luke Collingwood entrust him with the command of the *Zong* in the first place? Once he was in command, problems multiplied for the vessel and for the people on board. It was during, or shortly after, Stubbs' command (and when Collingwood was in the throes of what proved to be a fatal illness) that three decisive incidents had happened: first, the slipshod monitoring of water supplies; second, the major navigational error; and finally, the decision to kill the Africans. Despite his pleas of personal detachment (and innocence) is it likely that Stubbs had *no* say, had played *no* role whatsoever, in the shipboard events which saw a commonplace slave voyage slide towards mass murder?

The devastating decision to kill the Africans in the hope of recouping the insurance cover was, according to both Stubbs and Kelsall, Captain Collingwood's idea. This allegation suited everyone, of course, because Collingwood was dead. But might the idea have been floated by someone else? Stubbs assured the court that 'He believed not a Man on Board knew that there was any such Thing as an Insurance.'[37] Did that

include Stubbs himself? Is it plausible that a man with experience of all branches of the Africa trade – at sea, in London
and in Africa – did *not* know about insurance policies on slave
ships and their human cargoes? If any man on the *Zong* was
likely to be familiar with maritime insurance it was surely
Stubbs.

Robert Stubbs was a man with many flaws. Even so, he
seemed an ideal witness for the ship's owners, and was
presented as such by their lawyers. He was 'unconnected
totally with all the contending parties no connection with the
Owners no connection with the underwriters he was the only
person onboard the Ship who had nothing to do with the
Ship who had nothing to do with the act . . . and therefore the
only person that could be said to be perfectly disinterested in
this question'.[38] This portrait of Stubbs as the ideal honest
broker, an outsider on the ship with no axe to grind, a man
who could be relied on to speak impartially to the case, was a
serious misrepresentation of the man and his role. Robert
Stubbs clearly *did* have an interest, and an involvement, in
what transpired on the *Zong*. And it was in his interest, along
with other surviving crewmen, to place responsibility, and
blame, on the dead Captain Collingwood. Robert Stubbs also
had good reason *not* to reveal the facts. Moreover we have
evidence, which was not available to the court, that Stubbs
often had trouble telling the truth.

As all this evidence was reviewed and scrutinised in those two
days in Westminster Hall, Lord Mansfield maintained his
famous diligent attention to the confusion of argument and
counter-argument, occasionally making a point or asking a
question.[39] Though he said very little, some of his interven-

tions have survived to become his best-remembered words. Indeed they have served to haunt (and to sully) his reputation. Mansfield pointed out that, in the trial in March, 'The matter left to the jury, was whether it was from necessity: for they had no doubt (though it shocks one very much) that *the case of slaves was the same as if horses had been thrown overboard.* It is a very shocking case'.[40]

In much the same vein, Mansfield intervened to comment on the practice of marine insurance. Since the initial trial, 'I was informed if they die a Natural Death they did not pay, but in an Engagt if they are attacked and the Slaves are kill'd they will be paid for them as much as for Damages done for goods and it is frequently done, just as if horses were kill'd they are paid for in the gross, just as well as for Horses killed but you don't pay for Horses that die a Natural Death.'[41] Mansfield intended to clarify a point of law, but the inhuman comparison of slaves with horses has gone down in history as his personal view.[42] The Lord Chief Justice was making the point that Africans were bought and sold as items of trade, and that their loss was therefore to be calculated like any other commercial transaction. But the comparison with jettisoned horses enraged critics, then and since. Despite his disavowals and qualifications, Mansfield appeared to adopt the language of the slave traders themselves. To many observers, the Lord Chief Justice appeared trapped by the very commercial system, with its intimate links to slavery, which his own legal career had helped to shape and refine.

In 1783, and today, the language and imagery used in Mansfield's court caused enormous offence. And the whole discussion was made worse by the air of unreality created by the insistence that murder was not an issue. The Solicitor

General exacerbated the irritation felt in court by his own blunt language and ham-fisted style. Granville Sharp was incensed by Lee's cavalier performance, describing him as 'A Yorkshire man, who spoke very broad in the provincial dialect of that country, which has seldom been so grossly profaned as by this lawyer.'[43] Later, when writing about Lee's support for the crew's right to kill their African captives, Granville Sharp could barely contain his anger, and his post-trial commentaries and letters were peppered with denunciations.[44] Sharp took particular offence at the language used in the courtroom, highlighting the ill-chosen words and phrases – *chattels, goods, property* – 'the Blacks were property'.[45] Sharp felt that the *Zong* case illustrated that English law, and Mansfield himself, simply accepted the vernacular, the idiom, even the cultural values, of the slave traders. Mansfield's court seemed to be playing the slave traders' game. There was a reluctance to say that the Africans had been 'slaughtered', 'massacred' or 'sacrificed', though Sharp angrily told the Admiralty in a later letter that '132 innocent human Persons were wilfully put to death'.[46] Mansfield desired a courtroom language which carefully skirted the brute realities by discussing 'jettisoning' or 'throwing overboard'. These were little more than euphemisms disguising an act of mass murder.

Lord Mansfield was, however, troubled by one simple point, raised in May for the first time, which cast new light on the whole case. The court was told that the last group of thirty-eight 'were thrown overboard a Day after the Rain'. This simple fact had not been revealed at the first trial. Mansfield remarked: 'it is new to me. I did not know any Thing of it.'[47] How could the shipowners' argument – that the last group had been killed from 'necessity' – be sustained when it had rained, and the ship's water supplies had presumably been amply replenished? That rain may have quenched the thirst of people on board, but it also washed away the credibility of the argument that the Africans were killed from 'necessity'.

Only a retrial could get to the bottom of all the confusion. Mansfield thus concluded that 'It is a very uncommon Case and I think very well deserves a re-examination.' It ought, he felt, to 'go to a new Trial'. Justices Willes and Buller agreed.[48]

There is no evidence that a second trial took place. Perhaps the Gregson syndicate realised the hopelessness of their case. Equally, they may have regretted the storm of protest which their claim and court case had provoked. Along with all other slave traders, Gregson and associates (by then back in their slave-trading stride) could do without threats of prosecution for murder hanging over the men on their ships. But, for more than a year after the Westminster Hall hearing, a different strand to the legal dispute continued, out of the public eye. In separate proceedings the insurers had initiated an action in the Court of Exchequer against Kelsall and the Gregson syndicate in the hope of securing an injunction which would stop the proceedings in Kings Bench. In the course of these proceedings, James Kelsall issued a signed statement, sworn on 26 July 1783 in a Liverpool solicitor's office, giving his own version of what had happened on the *Zong*. Solicitors at the hearing before Lord Mansfield clearly had a draft of a similar statement from Kelsall (John Lee made reference to it in court in May). Kelsall's affidavit in Exchequer differed critically from some of the key points made by Robert Stubbs.[49] Kelsall, like Stubbs, was no doubt aware of the need to be cautious about what he said. He may also have been settling old scores, mindful of his unhappy suspension at sea on the *Zong*. Whatever the motive, Kelsall's version of events contains some of the most extraordinary evidence about the *Zong*.

Kelsall's account rehearsed the broad outlines of events on the *Zong*, beginning in São Tomé. His suspension on 14 November, when Stubbs took command, was followed a week later by the discovery that 'a large Quantity of Water had leaked from the lower tier of water casks'. One week on, they realised their navigational error. Collingwood, said Kelsall, had been 'deceived in his Reckoning by the strong currents.' All this happened over a period of a mere sixteen days. When the crew were gathered to be told of the situation, the vessel had 380 Africans on board, 'all of them in good health and condition', according to Kelsall. It was decided on 29 November 'by the General Voice of the Crew that part of the Slaves should be destroyed.' The first batch – Kelsall thought between fifty and sixty Africans – 'all of whom were in good health and condition', were taken 'indiscriminately' from the 'women's and boys' room' and pushed to their deaths 'singly through the Cabin Windows of the said ship'. The second group, forty-two 'stout healthy Men slaves', were brought on deck 'singly in the Night and thrown overboard' from the quarterdeck 'handcuffed and in Irons'. Another batch of thirty-eight Africans were killed in a similar manner later. The surviving Africans, chained below, faced with the disappearance of so many of their shipmates, and hearing the screams coming from the waters around the ship, could have had no doubt about what was happening.

No one tried to pick out the weak to be killed. They were simply removed at random and drowned. At a stroke, Kelsall's evidence undermined the idea that the weak were sacrificed so that the stronger (and more marketable) might live. All of the murdered Africans, testified Kelsall, had been chosen 'without Respect to sick or healthy', and all were 'marketable slaves'.

Even so, Kelsall agreed with Robert Stubbs that the killings were 'necessary'. Had the killings *not* taken place, Kelsall argued, many of the Africans 'would have been seized with Madness for want of water.' As 'barbarous as it may seem', he thought that drowning was 'the shortest and least painful Mode of destroying them.'[50] There was, he said, no other solution 'but throwing the Slaves over'. Such killings were kinder, he claimed, 'than suffering them to expire by degrees'.[51]

James Kelsall's testimony is an important personal account of events on the *Zong*. But it has a significance far beyond the story of the *Zong* because of one brief section which offers a unique insight into the terrifying world of the ill-fated Africans. Kelsall recorded a brief, distressing exchange of words with one of the Africans about to be killed. No more than a mere snippet – only a few dozen words – it provides a haunting memorial to all those murdered on the *Zong*.

One of the Africans spoke some English, and told Kelsall that the people shackled below decks 'were murmuring on Account of the Fate of those who had been drowned'. Rumour had spread among the shackled Africans that they were being killed because the ship's supplies were running short: 'they begged they might be suffered to live and they would not ask for either Meat or Water but could live without either till they arrived at their determined port'.[52]

This unknown African was pleading for every surviving African on the *Zong*, all of whom knew that they were under a death sentence. All asked to be spared, despite the inevitably grim privations that would follow. They had seen shipmates marched on deck at dusk, had watched as their ranks below decks thinned out, and had heard the shrieks of the drowning. Anything – hunger and thirst – seemed preferable to the horrifying fate awaiting them in the dark waters west of Jamaica.

This despairing plea – little more than a throwaway line in a legal statement – is as haunting a fragment of evidence as any that has come down to us from the ranks of millions of Africans consigned to the bellies of the slave ships: a beseeching, desperate entreaty – a despairing plea from people staring at their own impending and brutal demise.

Did anyone else hear this haunting African plea for mercy? Was anyone on board likely to be swayed by the words of one doomed African? Why did the men on the *Zong* not accept his despairing plea? Why not let the Africans survive, hungry and thirsty, but still alive? Instead, the crew pressed on. Having embarked on their killing spree, it seems the crew could not turn back: in for a penny, in for a pound – courtesy, they hoped, of the ship's insurers.

Today, it seems strange that Gregson and his colleagues in Liverpool appeared to be perfectly content to have their names bandied around in court (and in public) as men seeking compensation for murdered Africans. In doing so, their actions revealed one simple truth for all to see: that some of Liverpool's most successful businessmen were demanding payment for Africans murdered by their employees, who, in turn, went unpunished for their crimes. But the *Zong* killings raised a string of new, perplexing questions: what made ordinary men – ordinary sailors – kill so easily at sea? And what inspired British businessmen to pursue a pitiless claim for compensation across the bodies of 132 Africans? Those questions take us well beyond the story of that ship, and expose the very heart (and heartlessness) of the contemporary culture of slavery. It was this culture which was reflected in the language used by John Lee and Lord Mansfield in court in 1783. Treating Africans as items of trade had a corrosive, demoralising influence on the way contemporaries spoke and wrote. The *Zong* killings, Sharp thought, offered 'proof of the extreme depravity which the Slave Trade introduces amongst those that become inured to it'.[53] And it was this cultural outlook which remained the prime target of Granville Sharp and his growing band of supporters.

In May 1784, the legal trail about the *Zong* went dead. But what happened on that ship was not forgotten, and was to prove a turning point in the way the British viewed their involvement with slavery – and with Africans. Granville Sharp had no intention of letting people forget the Africans who had died on the *Zong*. Nor would he let people forget the rights of African humanity at large.

CHAPTER 9

In the wake of the *Zong*

W<small>HEN THE</small> *Z<small>ONG</small>* <small>HEARING IN</small> W<small>ESTMINSTER</small> H<small>ALL</small>
concluded on 22 May 1783, the people most directly involved
returned to the routines of their everyday professional lives. But
for those who had been closest to the killings – the Africans
whose lives had been spared in the murderous cull fifteen
months before – life now consisted of a regime of arduous
labour in unknown Jamaican locations. A hearing in an English
court made little difference to their lamentable existences.

To the Gregson syndicate too the case made little difference:
it was business as usual. Yes, they had failed to secure compensation for the Africans murdered on their ship, and the decision that the dispute should be tried again in court – though
far from a clear condemnation – was effectively a rebuff to the
slave traders. But it did not prove to be commercially damaging
for the Gregsons, nor did it estrange them from the slave trade.
Even as the case went through its various legal stages in 1783,
the Liverpool men were busy organising new voyages destined
for the precise locations visited by the *Zong*. In fact the *Zong*

episode marked a *revival* in Gregson's slaving ventures, after the lull brought about by the uncertainties of the American war. Gregson's captains now showed a marked interest in Anomabu and the Gold Coast, though they also found good markets further west, at Bonny and Calabar. Between 1781 and 1790, for example, Gregson's ships transported 8,018 Africans from the Gold Coast; Anomabu alone yielded 2,427 enslaved Africans in the twenty years after 1780.[1]

William Gregson's ships scattered those Africans throughout the Caribbean islands, as the single-minded businessman exploited new slave markets wherever they emerged; newly acquired colonies, like Demerara in the 1790s, were always keen for new Africans to open up virgin lands. But Gregson's ships headed primarily to Kingston, Jamaica, to sell their human cargoes (although only another 200-plus Africans were to join the survivors of the *Zong* and disembark at Black River). Of the 34,931 Africans who survived the crossing on Gregson's ships, in the twenty years after 1780, 16,227 went ashore in Kingston, many destined to be shipped on again, most likely to Spanish America.

These were, again, extraordinary movements of people. But the numbers involved expose a broad contemporary paradox. The numbers of Africans transported in Gregson's ships after 1780 do not suggest that Gregson and his associates had been in any way intimidated by the *Zong* case. Nor do they even hint that here was a group of men who found the slave trade economically unattractive: in the 1780s and 1790s, the Gregsons' slaving interests – like Liverpool at large – boomed. Yet these were the very years when the abolition movement was generating enormous popular antipathy against the slave trade. The Gregson story after 1780 reveals a strange and confusing juxtaposition of forces: at the very moment when the British had begun to turn against the slave trade, Liverpool's slave merchants were busier than ever.

Closer examination of William Gregson's slaving business after the *Zong* case reveals that while his trade was indeed thriving, it was also changing. Before 1780, William Gregson's various slaving partnerships were forged overwhelmingly with business associates in and around Liverpool. Indeed some of those men became regular fixtures in his commercial life, joining with him year after year in owning a number of slave ships and financing slave voyages. But by the 1780s William Gregson was in his sixties and keen to involve his sons in his business affairs. It was clearly time to hand over. In the course of the 1790s, those sons effectively took over the business. Their father's last direct involvement in slave voyages was with three ships, the *Ariel*, the *George* and the *Will*, all in 1793. By then, William Gregson had been an active slave merchant for the best part of half a century, and henceforth the Gregson slaving empire was in the hands of his three sons and their associates.

Throughout this transfer to a new generation, there is no sense that a Liverpool slaving business was an unsuitable enterprise for a man's sons. All three Gregson sons (and a son-in-law) were introduced to the business by William Gregson. Indeed two of them, and a son-in-law, had been parties to the *Zong* court case seeking compensation for the murdered Africans. William Gregson, like many other Liverpool slave merchants, was happy to apprentice his sons to the brute realities of slave trading, and to bequeath his slaving heritage to his children when his time had come to step aside.

For Lord Mansfield, the *Zong* case in May 1783 had been just another legal conundrum: a mere two-day hearing, the latest of a myriad cases, appeals and trials which consumed his time. With the decision to allow a new trial behind him, Mansfield moved on to the next item in his crowded legal and political diary. In that same period overlapping with the *Zong* case, Mansfield acted as Speaker of the House of Lords under the Fox-North administration. By then, he had been Lord Chief Justice for almost twenty years, and though his health soon began to fail, he hesitated to retire because his protégé and choice as successor – Mr Justice Buller, who sat alongside him in the *Zong* hearing – did not have the King's support. For two years between 1786 and 1788, with Mansfield unable to sit in court, Buller acted in his stead: Mansfield finally retired in June 1788, without ever again speaking publicly about the *Zong*.[2]

For Granville Sharp, however, it had altogether different consequences.

For almost twenty years he had been busy forming friendships, contacts and correspondence with men at the top of all the major professions: in the church, politics and the law. Sharp's work on the slave cases, and his agitation about slavery and, more recently, about the American war, had created a series of overlapping networks and correspondents among London's influential elites. All now found themselves put to a new use in the wake of the *Zong*.[3] When he had no personal association with a well-placed man, Sharp had the tenacity simply to open up a direct correspondence with him. Although the formal *Zong* hearings were over, Granville Sharp was agitated into an angry blur of activity, and he renewed old contacts across all the major professions, seeking legal and political advice – and urging anyone who would listen to stir themselves against the slave trade.[4]

From first hearing about the *Zong* in March, Sharp had set the wheels in motion. He had hastened around London, telling all and sundry – if they did not already know – what had happened. He first called on Dr Bever, an Oxford legal expert, 'to consult about prosecuting the murderers of the Negroes'. A day later, Sharp was on home ground when he turned to the church, lobbying the Bishops of Chester and Peterborough about the *Zong*.

He then called on Dr Jebb, the Unitarian and reformer, before turning, a day later, to instruct solicitors 'to commence a prosecution in the Admiralty Court against all the persons concerned in throwing into the sea one hundred and thirty Negro slaves, as stated on a trial at Guildhall on the 6th of this month.'[5] Granville Sharp also took up the matter with General Ogglethorpe, founder of Georgia, politician, and friend of Dr Johnson with whom Sharp had corresponded for some years, mainly about the evils and illegalities of slavery (and of other forms of bondage – notably impressment for the navy).[6]

Ogglethorpe was just one of Sharp's many American friends and contacts. For years he had conducted a long correspondence with Americans, especially about the war and about slavery. Gradually, he had come to the view that Britain's involvement with African slavery was a national sin which invited divine punishment. The major outrages periodically thrown up by slavery provided evidence, he thought, that the nation could expect the Lord's retribution. And what outrage was more monstrous than the *Zong* murders? What terrible retribution might follow?

At the time of the *Zong* hearings, America loomed large in British life. Politics were overshadowed by the British disasters and defeat in North America. Yet despite the war, the

Americans had numerous friends in Britain, and Sharp found himself at the centre of a remarkable network of like-minded critics of the conflict: dissenters, Anglicans, MPs, writers and country gentlemen, all loosely bound together by pro-American sentiment. Sharp had become a familiar figure in London's radical circles, debating with others about how best to safeguard the defence of British liberties. Even in such circles, Sharp stood out as a resolute and vocal defender of liberties against a succession of British governments which seemed intent on trampling those liberties underfoot on both sides of the Atlantic. To Sharp and his friends, many of whom were later to rise to prominence in the radical societies of the 1780s,[7] it seemed obvious that slavery and the corrupt political system were linked. Stated crudely, an unreformed parliament could always be relied on to legislate in favour of the powerful slave lobby. (Their theory was to be confirmed, fifty years later. No sooner was parliament reformed in 1832 than colonial slavery was destroyed and the slaves emancipated.) Sharp viewed parliament's complicity in slavery as proof that it was not only morally corrupt, but also that it wilfully ignored the wishes of the British people.[8] Quite simply, Granville Sharp believed that the abolition of the slave trade and parliamentary reform went hand-in-hand.

Yet for all his zeal and his moral rectitude, there was something other-worldly about Granville Sharp. To his critics, he seemed not to understand political and economic realities. What were ethical or Christian objections from a few high-minded men of principle when set against the material benefits derived from slavery to the nation at large? Tackling so massive and entrenched an industry as the slave trade seemed both thankless and hopeless: economic prosperity had always seemed able to trump the ethical cards played by Granville Sharp and his friends. Yet what emerged from the *Zong* hearings confirmed everything he had repeatedly said about the business of the slave ships, and the time now seemed ripe to make use of the networks he had cultivated for years past.

Granville Sharp was easily provoked into a froth of religious indignation, but the *Zong* killings raised his anger to a higher plane. His handwritten letters and annotations to what others wrote and published all fairly rattle with outrage: angry words are slashed across the page, and the text is speckled with passionate interjections. He dispatched angry missives left and right – long, furious letters – to any individual or organisation he thought might help, or might need educating. Sharp 'employed every means in his power to give the utmost publicity to the circumstances that had happened, and the arguments that had been employed.' He contacted newspapers with 'a copy of the minutes (which he had procured in short hand) of the trial, and of the speeches of both sides.'[9] He sent copies to the Admiralty, to the chancellor of the exchequer and to the Duke of Portland, the prime minister. He urged Portland to consider the 'absolute necessity to abolish the Slave Trade and West-India slavery'.[10]

He had made a similar case to Lord North as long ago as 1772. But who, in 1772, would even listen? Now with the *Zong* killings public knowledge, the time seemed more conducive to expressing abolitionist sentiments. Even so, and even for those familiar with the enormities of the *Zong* case, abolishing the slave trade must have seemed a utopian ideal. As the Gregson family business illustrated, the slave trade was booming again. Who else was demanding an end to slavery itself?

Granville Sharp's immediate aim was to bring murder charges against the men who had committed the murders on the *Zong*. That could only be done through the Lords Commissioners of the Admiralty, who had jurisdiction for murders on British ships. He reminded the Admiralty that the *Zong* killings were an 'extreme wickedness', and any justification for the killings a 'damnable doctrine'. They were 'a flagrant Offence against God and against all mankind.'[11] He also asked them to investigate the killings and prosecute the men involved, citing Captain Luke Collingwood and the mate James Kelsall as the main suspects. It was obvious that other crewmen were also involved, and Sharp called on the Admiralty to scrutinise the facts he supplied, and then 'judge whether there is sufficient evidence for a criminal prosecution of the murderers.'[12] Nothing happened.

When Sharp sent a packet of documents about the *Zong* to the Admiralty on 2 July 1783, he must have known that his request for action confronted them with a major problem.[13] However outrageous the *Zong* case, and however uneasy the Admiralty may have felt about the killings, any scrutiny of killings on slave ships would likely open a Pandora's box of complications. How many Africans *were* killed on board British slave ships? Dozens? Hundreds? It would not be surprising in the tumult and terror of an African insurrection. Sharp's arguments may have been *legally* sound, but, if pursued, they could subvert the entire slave system (and Sharp knew it). Nor would the story of slave-ship killings have come as a surprise to senior officers in the Admiralty in 1783. The Royal Navy was familiar with the nature of life and death on the slave ships: naval ships had close dealings with slave ships on both sides of the Atlantic, and many men in the Royal Navy had served on slave ships. Indeed three of the men from the *Zong* had been impressed and transferred to Royal Navy ships in the course of the voyage.[14] Captains of slave ships who despaired of bringing to heel the more intractable of crewmen routinely transferred them into the custody of the Royal Navy. Even the most unyielding of hard men were normally broken by its disciplinary procedures. The Admiralty, then, needed no introduction to the brutalities of slaving.

It had clearly taken Sharp a great deal of time and effort to draft and assemble his packet of documents,[15] but his arrangement of those documents seemed haphazard, and not organised in any systematic or chronological sequence. They speak of the vehemence of his passion to make the *Zong* case known in the only way he knew how: bombarding influential figures and officers of state with long erudite letters and hard evidence of claim and counterclaim. But the oddities of the way he assembled and presented material about the *Zong* was of little importance compared to what he had achieved.[16] Granville Sharp's industry and persistence ensured that details about the *Zong* killings dropped on to the desk of the Prime Minister, the Chancellor of the Exchequer and the most powerful men in the Admiralty. They may already have learned of the case, and they might, of course, all choose to set aside Sharp's material, or simply ignore his request, but it was no longer possible for senior government officials to remain ignorant of the *Zong* murders. Sharp, the political and legal busybody, was determined to make the most powerful men in the nation aware of the *Zong*.

Inevitably, Sharp also turned his attention to the Church of England. His upbringing and intellectual schooling had been steeped in the theology and culture of the Anglican church.

As a result, he thought and wrote like an eighteenth-century divine, his reflections and publications spiced with religious analysis. Even when discussing legal issues, Sharp's scholarship remained rooted in theology and biblical exegesis. As he delved into slavery, he came to believe that it stood condemned on both biblical and legal grounds. For all his mastery of the law, and despite his familiarity with major figures of the legal world, Sharp was more at ease with clerics. For the same reason, Sharp also appreciated better than most the remarkable social and *political* power wielded by the Church of England: he knew that if he could win over prominent clerics to his side, he might be able to alert the slumbering Church of England to the outrages of slavery.

For years, he had lobbied the bishops, urging them to enhance the moral standing of the church by promoting the end of slavery. Bishops with seats in the Lords were showered with Sharp's tracts, hot from the press. To ensure that they got the message, he also approached them individually.[17] As early as 1779, when the slave trade was being discussed in parliament, he lobbied Anglican bishops *en masse*: 'I called on the Houses of all the Bishops that were in town to exhort them to oppose the Slave Trade in the House of Lords ... I had the honour of speaking with 22 Bishops out of the 26 a great majority of whom expressed a great Abhorrence of that Trade and a desire to suppress it.'[18] Not one of them disagreed 'with my sentiments on the subject'.[19] This early sweep through the ranks of senior Anglican clerics enabled Sharp to forge critical, personal links which he revitalised and used so effectively in the wake of the *Zong* killings in 1783.

Sharp had a number of clerical friends who had warmed to his earlier approaches, and who had, for a variety of reasons, already turned to the thorny moral and theological issues posed by Britain's slave empire. News about the *Zong* confirmed everything these abolition-leaning Anglicans already felt about the slave trade. Dr Beilby Porteus, Bishop of Chester from 1776, had been persuaded by Sharp's assertion that the American war was God's punishment for British wrong-doings.[20] As that war dragged on, Porteus had become increasingly worried about the very *purpose* of the British empire, and was especially concerned about the Church's neglect of Africans in the Caribbean slave colonies. Porteus's interest in America may have had family roots (his father was a Virginian), but it was more the widening literary and political debate about the colonies – and especially about the treatment and condition of Africans there – that nudged Porteus towards the abolitionist position for which he is best remembered.

In February 1783, a month before the *Zong* trial, Porteus preached the annual sermon for the Society for the Propagation of the Gospel in Foreign Parts. He took the opportunity to castigate the church for neglecting its own slaves on the Codrington plantation in Barbados. Sitting in the congregation were eleven bishops of the Church of England. Even when later issued as a tract,[21] Porteus's sermon seemed to fall on unresponsive Anglican ears. But Granville Sharp viewed Porteus as a major ally, and sent him the details of the *Zong* outrage. Porteus had already read about the case in the press, and had been alerted by a friend who had heard the court proceedings and shared Sharp's views on the *Zong*: 'Your observations are so just, and so full to the purpose, that I can add nothing to them but my entire approbation.'

Sharp also received support from John Hinchliffe, Bishop of Peterborough (and Master of Trinity College, Cambridge), who was already well known for his liberal speeches in the Lords. For some time past Sharp had worked closely with Hinchliffe, urging him to encourage discussion about slavery and freedom within the church. Hinchliffe's association with Cambridge enabled these early discussions about slavery to seep from the elite of the Anglican church into the university itself. But the process had been sparked by Granville Sharp.

Like Porteus, Hinchliffe was horrified by the *Zong* affair, 'one of the most inhuman barbarities that I ever read of . . . Were religion and humanity attended to, there can be no doubt that the horrid traffic would entirely cease; but they have too small a voice, to be heard among the clamours of avarice and ambition.'[22]

Men already primed by Granville Sharp to think about the slave trade were profoundly shocked by news about the *Zong*. People who had already given serious attention to the slave trade, and who knew about its inherent violence, were nonetheless taken aback by the case. Most revealing of all, even men who had *worked* on slave ships – Liverpool ships at that – looked back on the *Zong* killings with repugnance. John Newton, never too squeamish as a young slave trader to torture and brutalise his African captives, shuddered in his abolitionist old age when he considered the *Zong*: '. . . we have heard and read a melancholy story . . . of more than a hundred grown slaves, thrown into the sea, at one time, from on board a ship, when fresh water was scarce; to fix the loss upon the Underwriters, which otherwise, had they died on board, must have fallen upon the Owners of the vessel.' John Newton thought the *Zong* case was typical 'of the spirit produced, by the African Trade'.[23] Who better to judge than the old Liverpool slave captain, John Newton?

Newton was not the only man with Liverpool links to comment on the *Zong*. The Revd George Gregory, who in 1783 was the vicar of West Ham, had once been a clerk in the office of a Liverpool merchant, but came to prominence for his essays on contemporary and historical issues, first published in 1785. He too could barely believe what he learned about the *Zong* – 'The reader will scarcely be inclined to believe that the perpetrators of this horrid action escaped with impunity', he exhorted – and he clearly acquired much of his information from Granville Sharp.[24] Gregory asked a simple but obvious question: 'To those who think that the plea of wanting water was a sufficient justification for the above transaction, I will put one plain question – If those persons who suffered had been white men, and not slaves, would they have been thrown overboard?'[25]

What distinguished Gregory's account of the *Zong* was not so much his outrage – in fact, outside the courtroom no one spoke up publicly in support of the men on the *Zong* – but rather his comments about Captain Luke Collingwood. There was a very peculiar sting in Gregory's tail. Most commentators, then and since, have blamed Collingwood for the killings. But the captain found an unlikely defender in the person of the Revd Gregory, who felt that his memory had been 'injuriously treated, and by those from whom it was least deserved, the friends of slavery, who now affect to exclaim against him as a monster of inhumanity'. The reason for this vindication was that, when working as a clerk in Liverpool, Gregory had got to know Collingwood – a fact that he revealed in the second edition of his essays, published in 1788: '. . . I think it a duty to declare, that I knew Collingwood well – He had an education far superior to the generality of those engaged in the African trade – In his general conduct he appeared to me a liberal, benevolent, and well-intentioned man.' Such sympathetic support for a man who ordered a mass killing might seem odd and not very persuasive. Yet Gregory was an honest man, a robust critic of the slave trade, and an ardent abolitionist. He admitted that Collingwood was 'deeply infected with the same unjust prejudices that mark all who are connected with that iniquitous traffic, who consider the Negroes as an inferior race of beings, who we are entitled to treat as we please'.[26]

There was, of course, nothing exceptional in a slave-trade captain regarding Africans as inferior beings, but Gregory felt that Collingwood was different: '. . . I do, however, with the utmost sincerity, and with the utmost candour, believe, that he was rather of a milder and more humane disposition than most who are engaged in the slave trade . . .' It would be wrong to dismiss Gregory's opinion too quickly, not least because his view was based on a wide range of acquaintances among slave captains. In his time in Liverpool, Gregory had encountered a large number of men from the slave ships, and believed that most would have been willing to do what Collingwood had ordered: 'From repeated conversations with many of the Guinea captains and Guinea merchants, I can lay my hand on my heart, and solemnly give it as my opinion, that scarcely any of them would have scrupled to act the same part with Collingwood, if they were placed under the same temptation.'

Gregory's defence of Collingwood's actions seems very curious indeed. Here was an abolitionist cleric, able to find virtue and compassion in a man responsible for a mass murder. When Gregory published these remarks in 1788, he had little to gain from defending Captain Collingwood, and might possibly lose a great deal of face and sympathy from the ignominy and derision his remarks might provoke. Yet Gregory clearly felt the need to put his views on record, and did so in published essays designed to catch the attention of men of sensibility and compassion: the very men Gregory needed for support in his arguments against the slave trade. Assuming that Gregory's description was accurate, the problem of Collingwood and the murders becomes even *more* perplexing. How could an educated man, 'liberal, benevolent, and well-intentioned', order a massacre?

Why did Gregory wait three years, until 1788, before defending Collingwood? There had been universal condemnation of Collingwood for the killings, though supporters of the slave trade openly defended them – until they were silenced, as Gregory put it, by 'the clamour excited against it [which] rendered them somewhat more modest'.[27] It seems that Gregory felt honour-bound to defend the dead captain, knowing that he was no different than most other slave captains – and better than many. Blaming Collingwood let everyone else off the hook: the Gregson syndicate, the crew, even the law of insurance which lurked behind the entire episode. Gregory thought that most slave captains would have done the same. The fault lay not with Collingwood, but with the entire slave system.

News of the *Zong* killings horrified all sorts and conditions of people. But none were more troubled than the Africans living in England. They, after all, had direct personal experience of the slave ships, though most had found ways of raising themselves to the precarious status of free people. Today, the best-known of that group is Olaudah Equiano – the man who effectively broke the story by taking the news to Sharp on

19 March. Not surprisingly, perhaps, the most bitter denunciation of the *Zong* killings came from the pen of an African
friend of Equiano. In the 1780s, Equiano's friend and associate Ottobah Cugoano was working as a domestic servant in
fashionable London society, but, like many of his contemporaries, he had once been a slave. Born around 1757 on the
coast of what is now Ghana, he had been kidnapped at the age
of thirteen and transported to Grenada. He had worked in
slave gangs in various parts of the Caribbean before being
brought to England towards the end of 1772 by his owner. By
the mid-1780s Cugoano was a free man, working as a servant
for Richard and Maria Cosway, the painters of fashionable
London society (whose social pretensions of employing black
servants were lampooned by William Blake). Though
Cugoano was represented in a number of sketches and etch-
ings, today he is best known for his abolitionist publication,
Thoughts and Sentiments (1787).[28] Cugoano's words on the
Zong were harsh, and his conclusions bleak:

> The vast carnage and murders committed by the British
> instigators of slavery, is attended with a very shocking, pecu-
> liar, and almost unheard of conception, according to the
> notion of the perpetrators of it; they either consider them as
> their own property, that they may do with as they please, in
> life or death; or that the taking away of the life of a black man
> is no more account than taking away the life of a beast.

Cugoano recited the events, and the language used, in Lord
Mansfield's court, describing the Gregsons as 'inhuman
connivers of robbery, slavery, murder and fraud' and Captain
Collingwood as 'the inhuman monster', and concluding

grimly that 'our lives are accounted of no value, we are hunted after as prey in the desert, and doomed to destruction as the beasts that perish'.[29]

Once the *Zong* story became public in March 1783, the grisly details about the slave trade seeped from the courtroom into the wider public sphere. When scrutinised at close quarters – as it was in Mansfield's courtroom – the slave trade was revealed to be brutal, morally bankrupt and even murderous. Repeated and discussed in public and in print, the story of the *Zong* went from being an utterly exceptional story to becoming the very model for the slave trade itself. Here was the exception which became the rule. It shocked those people long inured to the realities of the slave ships – even those who had suffered on slave ships – and won over others who were unaware of the problem. Moreover, much of the impetus for the growing public awareness about these grim realities flowed directly from the efforts of Granville Sharp. It was, in John Newton's words, 'a melancholy story'.[30]

This 'melancholy story' seemed a perfect example of the slave trade itself, and of the heartless brutality that underpinned it. It provided ample ammunition for those who wished to attack the slave trade, and when the formal abolition campaign was launched in 1787, writers used the example of the *Zong* to press their arguments. One of the most notable essayists was the Revd James Ramsay. Formerly a surgeon in the Royal Navy in the 1750s, Ramsay had been called on to deal with a slave ship filled with Africans wracked by dysentery. It was a vile experience which persuaded him to change careers, and to preach to slaves in the Caribbean. Ramsay married into a prominent family in St Kitts, and he worked assiduously for the enslaved in the island. But his frustration at the deep-seated hostility of local planters edged him inexorably towards abolition, and he felt compelled to write about it.

The essay Ramsay subsequently wrote became an important abolitionist tract, but it had perhaps the longest gestation period of any abolition publication. He began his essay, on converting slaves to Christianity, in 1768, completed it in 1771, and finally submitted it to the Bishop of London in 1778. It was published in revised form in 1784, the year after the *Zong* hearing.[31] Few white men had experienced slavery at such close quarters as had Ramsay, both on the slave ships and on the plantations, but even he was astounded by the *Zong* case. He was especially shocked by the fact that the killers could speak so openly in 1783 about what they had done – and with no real fear that they might be charged with murder.[32] Ramsay was amazed at James Kelsall's role.

> Can humanity imagine that it was meant, in any possible circumstances, to submit the fate of such numbers of reasonable creatures to the reveries of a sick monster; or that his brutal instrument should dare to boast of his obedience, and even do it with impunity, in the highest criminal court of the best informed people of Europe?[33]

The story of the *Zong* killings was picked up and repeated by abolitionists across the country. In Manchester for example – *the* major centre of provincial abolition in 1787–88 – the story surfaced in a series of letters written by a local radical, Thomas Cooper, and published first in a local newspaper (*Wheeler's Manchester Chronicle*), and later in pamphlet form.[34] In Manchester as in all corners of the country, what gave the *Zong* story its significance was its *immediacy*. Although thousands of slave ships, and tens of thousands of sailors, left for Africa from British ports, slavery seemed distant, and hard to imagine. Despite the obvious ramifications of the slave trade for Britain itself (from British manufactures filling the outbound slave ships, through to the widespread consumption of slave-grown produce) the centre of gravity of the British slave system was far away, in West Africa and the Americas. People who had already grappled with slavery's philosophical and legal complexities had obviously been obliged to confront the brute realities of the slave trade; even so, the stark realities of what transpired on the slave ships generally remained elusive because so far away: the gory and stinking horrors of the slave ships remained hard to envisage because they were so distant. Notwithstanding the periodic slave cases in English courts, and the presence of England's own black community, slavery was essentially remote and indistinct – out of sight and generally out of mind. The *Zong* case helped to change all that by bringing the slave ships into closer focus. In essence, the *Zong* case, notwithstanding the deaths of 132 Africans, was a very British event. Mass murder had been committed on a British ship by British sailors. And British merchants had demanded blood money in court before the Lord Chief Justice. The ship, the men, the courts, the law officers, even the law itself, were all local, not exotic or foreign. The *Zong* case was an extreme and savage example of a very simple point: that slavery was not distant, foreign, out-of-sight. It was as British as a sweet cup of tea.

In the months and years immediately following the case, this growing awareness of the immediacy and of the realities of the slave trade filtered into British politics. Granville Sharp had struggled to ensure that such truths had been impressed on Britain's political, religious, military and legal elites. But for a similar message to reach a wider British audience – to reach the British people at large – required different tactics and a different type of politics. It also required a new and different kind of leadership.

The turning point in the entire history of the British slave trade was to emerge when animosity to the slave trade began to spill out from society's privileged elites (who had dominated the initial debates) and to spread through the country at large. Suddenly and quite unexpectedly, and a mere four years after the *Zong* hearing, abolition sentiment took on a popular dimension.

Within weeks of an abolition society being formed in 1787, abolition, like an uncontainable virus, spread with astonishing rapidity. As it did so it began to sap the previously unchallengeable strength and position of Britain's entire slave system. The corrosion had effectively begun in 1783 when the *Zong* case had demolished any moral standing affected by the slave lobby. The *Zong* killings were an event of such horror that it generated a deep-seated and widespread revulsion. And that was to lay the basis for a new form of frontal attack on the slave trade itself. After the *Zong*, proponents of the slave trade had to rethink their arguments. The debate about the slave trade would never be the same again.

It is possible to argue that the *Zong* case changed very little. The case did not stop slave merchants from shipping Africans across the Atlantic. Indeed, between 1780 and 1810 British ships carried an astonishing 947,163 Africans to the Americas.[35] The law still allowed slave merchants to insure their Africans as cargoes, and, under certain conditions, to claim for their loss on board slave ships. Moreover we now know that well into the nineteenth century Africans continued to fall victim to brutal killings on board slave ships, on the African coast, in mid-Atlantic and close to the Americas. Despite this litany of continuing brutalities and killings – and the continuing process of enslavement and enslaved transportation – something *had* changed, and changed profoundly. The British had changed. And they were to change even more rapidly and more profoundly in the years immediately after the *Zong* hearings. The *Zong* was instrumental in opening the eyes of the British to the realities of the slave ships. What they saw, they deplored. Growing numbers of them, of all sorts and conditions, resolved to put an end to it.

CHAPTER 10

Abolition and after

THE DEBATE ABOUT THE SLAVE TRADE, BOTH BEFORE and after the *Zong* case, had been conducted essentially among British people of education and substance – people like Granville Sharp and the men he had badgered for years. They were, by and large, people of sensibility from the small world of British educated elites. There was little hint of a popular dimension to that debate – with one notable and important exception: the presence of a tiny handful of remarkable Africans. Here were people who, though once enslaved, had acquired for themselves those prized individual qualities which brought esteem and respect in the eyes of others.[1] First and foremost, they were literate and devout, admired and respected by contemporaries for their learning, their writing and their Christian demeanour. Indeed we remember them precisely for those very qualities: the major figures – Ignatius Sancho, Ottobah Cugoano and Olaudah Equiano – became published authors, and their contemporary esteem and lasting renown stemmed largely from their literary achievements. But these men were utterly exceptional in a debate which was, over-whelmingly, the preserve of people born into the world of British privilege and education. There is no sense in the argu-ments before the *Zong* that there was a *popular* dimension to the debate; no hint that the discussion about slavery, *pro* or *con*, should involve anyone other than groups which already had a stake in political and educated life.[2] Ordinary people – the popular ranks of society, hard to define, but obvious enough in their numerous exclusion – remained on the outside of this, as they did in most other British political debates.

The recent upheavals in North America had, however, provided an indication of things to come: a far-off alert that seismic change might follow the involvement of the common folk in political life. Popular participation in the events leading to American independence in 1776 – including deci-sive crowd activity – had given the colonies a turbulence which the British and their agents found impossible to manage or control. North American political elites found their cause merging with popular discontents, and sometimes with disorders, to forge a new political formula. By the end of the war, ordinary urban and rural Americans had become a force in the land. It was an omen of things to come.[3]

In Europe, a similar upheaval is most commonly associated with the impact of the Revolution in France in 1789, and its ramifications in all corners of the Atlantic world (most notably in the slave islands of the Caribbean).[4] In fact, the emergence of a new form of popular politics – the expression of political views from men and women who had traditionally been kept *beyond* the political pale – can be seen in Britain, *before* 1789. It began with the growing outrage about the slave trade, and was harnessed and promoted by the campaign to bring it to an end. If it were to stand any chance of being more than a debate among the usual British political groups, abolition sentiment needed to break free of traditional politics. It was yet another great irony in this story that the means by which that breakthrough took place, and the location which became the launch pad for the rise of popular abolition, was the University of Cambridge.

In 1781 Dr Peter Peckard, a man who was greatly influenced by Granville Sharp's work against slavery, was appointed Master of Magdalene College, Cambridge. Peckard was the son of a Lincolnshire parson and an Oxford graduate who had put aside a riotous undergraduate and military past to become a prominent theologian and ardent proponent of liberty on a broad front. He had occupied a number of clerical posts, including Dean of Peterborough, before becoming Master of Magdalene. A Whig 'of the old school', Peckard became a fierce critic of the slave trade, moving towards abolition along a path familiar to a number of other low-church theologians and preachers. It was Peckard, in an anonymous tract, who was to coin the most famous phrase in the entire history of abolition: 'Am I not a man and a brother?' The phrase was to become the *leitmotif* for the abolition movement after 1787 and was to adorn Wedgwood's famous medallion of a kneeling, supplicant slave.

At Magdalene Peckard set out to reform and stiffen student education and discipline (along with the college's finances and physical fabric), and he quickly attracted a coterie of serious evangelical students. Like his friend Beilby Porteus, Peckard also used his Cambridge pulpit to speak out against the slave trade.[5] His first abolitionist sermon seems to have been given in 1781: 'Honour all men, love the brotherhood, fear God, honour the King.' Time and again, he returned to attack the slave trade, 'a Sin against the light of Nature, and the accumulated evidence of divine Revelation.' In his influential sermons Peckard denounced 'this most barbarous and cruel traffic', which was, he said, 'A crime, founded on a dreadful pre-eminence in wickedness; a crime, which being both of individuals and of the nation, must some time draw down upon us the heaviest judgment of Almighty God, who made of one blood all the sons of men, and who gave to all equally a natural right to liberty'.[6]

Peckard spoke to university congregations about 'the natural equality of the human race'. Sitting in one such congregation was a young undergraduate from St John's College, Thomas Clarkson, who was intent on a clerical career but whose life was to be transformed by his encounter with the theological and humane debate about the slave trade at Cambridge.

When, in 1784, Peckard was appointed vice chancellor of the university, one of his early initiatives was to attract the attention of 'the young and ardent minds of the undergraduates' by offering them an essay prize on the subject of slavery. The Latin title was *ANNE LICEAT INVITOS IN SERVITUTEM DARE?* ('Is it lawful to make slaves of others against their will?'). Thomas Clarkson, a brilliant student, already with a bachelor's degree in mathematics in 1783 and a prize for the best Latin essay in 1784, rose to the vice chancellor's challenge. Although the essay title was framed in very general terms, Clarkson, remembering what Peckard had said in a recent sermon, decided to concentrate on the African slave trade, though he felt under considerable intellectual and social pressure to perform well in the competition. To add to his anxiety, he knew nothing about the African slave trade:

'But alas! I was wholly ignorant of this subject; and, what was unfortunate, a few weeks only were allowed for the competition. I was determined, however, to make the best use of my time.' Clarkson needed to find as much evidence as possible, and quickly. Fortunately he 'got access to the manuscript papers of a deceased friend, who had been in the trade'. In addition, he collected information from 'several officers who had been in the West Indies'. His lucky break, however, came when he made a special trip to London to buy a copy of Anthony Benezet's *Historical Account of Guinea*, a pioneering abolitionist tract written by one of North America's most prominent Quakers, and published by London Quakers only months before. Clarkson found it a revelation: 'In this precious book I found almost all I wanted.'[7]

Benezet's book steered Clarkson towards earlier writers on the slave trade but, most important of all, it established Clarkson's habit of analysing the slave trade via men who had been personally involved: men who had been to Africa, and who had worked on the slave ships. By chance, Clarkson hit upon the means of discussing the slave trade via primary evidence: by finding and arranging hard data from the ships, and collecting verbatim accounts from men who had sailed them. He quickly learned how to acquire and process primary data from a first-hand source. In effect Thomas Clarkson had alighted upon a new methodology, which he was to perfect over the next few years. It was a method of research which yielded rich returns, providing statistical and first-hand data which was incontrovertible, and which became the shank of abolition activity thereafter – and well into the nineteenth century.

By following Benezet, and reading the older accounts of the slave trade, Clarkson realised that earlier authors were writing at a time when the slave trade was *not* a contentious issue: they had been able to write freely and openly about their experiences of the slave ships, without fear of incriminating themselves, or worrying about how their accounts might be interpreted. Theirs were open and honest accounts, unadorned by the sorts of qualifications and reservations that confuse Robert Stubbs' evidence about the *Zong*, for example. There was an authenticity to this voice which Clarkson wished to capture.

Thomas Clarkson's immediate task was daunting ('no person can tell the severe trial, which the writing of it proved to me'). He even kept a lighted candle at his bedside in case a night-time idea might strike, and he needed to jot it down.[8] Although he had looked forward to the intellectual exercise of writing the essay, he now found himself troubled by a frank reality he had not anticipated: not the discipline of research and writing, but the brutal horrors of the slave trade. 'It was but one gloomy subject from morning to night . . . I sometimes never closed my eye-lids for grief.' As he toiled with the task, Clarkson's essay was transformed, from 'a trial for academical reputation' into a work 'which might be useful to injured Africa'. Like Sharp before him, Clarkson was first shocked, then galvanised, by what he learned.

Clarkson's essay won the vice chancellor's prize. He then read the essay in the Cambridge Senate House, to approving applause. What followed has entered the folklore of the history of abolition. After delivering the lecture, and on his way back to London, lost in thought about the significance of the essay, Thomas Clarkson dismounted from his horse at Wades Mill in Hertfordshire. He realised that 'If the contents of the Essay were true, it was time some person should see these calamities to their end. Agitated in this manner I reached home.' That summer Clarkson lived in a state of some anxiety, plagued by the same recurring thought. 'Are these things true?' In his heart he knew that they were, but felt that he alone realised this.[9] He yearned to know of other people – politicians, clergymen – who might also take up the cause of the slave trade. Clarkson also felt powerless: what could an unknown twenty-five-year-old achieve on his own? Slowly, he came to appreciate that he *could* do something practical: he could translate his essay (from Latin), revise, extend and finally publish it – and hope for a public response. Thus, in mid-November 1785, Thomas Clarkson began the work, at home in Wisbech, that would transform his life and have an incalculable influence on the history of the British slave trade.

With the essay translated, in the New Year of 1786 Clarkson headed to London to find a publisher. An old Quaker family friend from Wisbech took him to meet James Phillips, the Quaker publisher and bookseller, who in his turn introduced Clarkson to a circle of prominent London Quakers.[10] As his network of London contacts expanded, Clarkson became aware of that coterie of Quakers and associates (and Granville Sharp) who had been active, for some years past, both for black legal rights in England and against the slave trade. This devout young man was now convinced that 'the finger of Providence was beginning to be discernible; that the day-star of African liberty was rising, and that I probably might be permitted to become a humble instrument in promoting it.'[11]

As Clarkson worked with James Phillips on the publication of his essay, his metropolitan friends reassured the young author through his periodic moments of doubt and uncertainty. Finally, in June 1786, one year after he had read his

Latin essay in Cambridge, Clarkson published his book under the title *Essay on the Slavery and Commerce of the Human Species, Particularly the African*. By then he had become part of a group of like-minded people, who were to form the core of the later 'Clapham Sect' and who met at Barham Court in Teston, Kent. Teston was to be the location and heart of the early evangelical attack on the slave trade, and the people around Clarkson at Teston were eminent and influential figures. Above all, they were busy people, preoccupied with their own political, personal or commercial interests. None was able to concentrate *solely* on the slave trade. Only the young Clarkson seemed in a position to devote himself uniquely to the cause of the campaigning against it.[12] Knowing that he would have to abandon his clerical ambitions (and thus disappoint his family) Thomas Clarkson nonetheless publicly pledged in 1786 'that I would devote myself to the cause of the oppressed Africans'.[13]

Clarkson had initially been astonished to learn that so many others were *already* arguing and writing about the slave trade. He had assumed that his was a lonely crusade, but by the summer of 1786 he was firmly embedded in a network of abolitionist sympathisers, and had become one of an expanding circle outraged by what they knew of the slave trade, and determined to end it. Even so, their numbers were small and they were confronted by a major, entrenched and prospering industry. Their opponents, the men behind the slave trade – merchants, financiers, shippers (the Gregsons, for example, who, in the years 1785–8, had ten ships at sea or preparing to transport Africans to the slave colonies[14]) – could never have imagined that this small coterie of critics, however articulate, influential and dedicated, would become such powerful political adversaries. Still less could they have dreamed that these critics would, within a generation, bring Britain's mighty slave trade to its knees.

The Society for Effecting the Abolition of the Slave Trade (SEAST) was founded in May 1787, setting itself the task of 'procuring such Information and Evidence, and for Distributing Clarkson's Essay and such other Publications, as may tend to the Abolition of the Slave Trade'. They also set out to raise money to make this possible.[15] The society was, in origin, primarily a Quaker organisation, as Granville Sharp told his brother John that July: 'A Society has lately been formed here for the purpose of opposing the Slave Trade: though the Members are chiefly Quakers, I thought it was my duty, when invited, to join them in so just a measure'.[16] This pioneering band of abolitionists realised that Thomas Clarkson's essay was too big, too densely argued, for popular consumption. They wanted a short, snappy tract for a more popular market, and therefore commissioned Clarkson to produce an eight-to-ten page *Summary View of the Slave Trade*. This was quickly followed by another sponsored tract, *An Essay on the Impolicy of the African Slave Trade*. Read to the Abolition Committee, and then suitably corrected, it too was printed, and 2,000 copies were published and distributed 'to various parts of the kingdom'. Here were the origins of the drive to win over the public by carefully crafted propaganda, all grounded in first-hand experience of the slave trade, and made available in accessible, cheap or free pamphlets. It was an appeal to the literate: to men and women who would heed published arguments if they were presented to them in an easily available and manageable format.[17]

In 1787, William Wilberforce had come into contact with Thomas Clarkson and a group of anti-slave-trade activists, including Granville Sharp, Hannah More and Charles Middleton. They persuaded Wilberforce to be spokesman for abolition in parliament. But the most remarkable and innovative aspect of the new campaign was the *public* agitation for abolition. That was led and organised by Thomas Clarkson in the country at large. Clarkson set out on a series of punishing national abolition lecture tours. By 1794 he had covered an astonishing 35,000 miles, speaking, organising new committees, and gathering new evidence about the slave ships from ports across Britain.[18] Demands for abolition of the slave trade, picked up by small local groups of like-minded people (often initiated by Quakers), swiftly gathered strength and voice across the country. In the process, the demand for abolition was quickly transmuted from a minority issue, the preserve of small handfuls of people, into a national clamour. By the end of 1787 the abolition campaign had become genuinely popular: nation-wide, it cut across boundaries of class and region – and gender. But how had that happened, and all in a matter of months?

Quite simply, abolitionist literature regaled the reading public with the truth from the ships: the brutal and sometimes unspeakable details about the fate of all Africans transported across the Atlantic. The slave ships were at the heart of the abolitionist message, and were portrayed in their full horror using images, data, and first-hand testimony. First of all those realities shocked, then angered, the British people. Angered by what they learned, they resolved to demand that parliament, so vital to the emergence and flowering (indeed to the very survival) of the British slave trade, should bring it to an end.[19]

The early abolitionist campaign, the *public* campaign which whipped up popular antipathy to the trade and lodged that feeling in parliament, was primarily a triumph for the barrage of information and argument generated by the early abolitionists. The speed with which antagonism to the slave trade sprang up across Britain surprised even the abolitionists, even though it came about because of their methods and tactics. After May 1787, the campaign against the slave trade generated an extraordinary volume of printed material. An increasingly literate British public found itself showered by an astonishing outpouring of cheap literature scattered around the country by abolition supporters. In the first year alone, Clarkson calculated that the Abolition Committee had issued, 'not at random, but judiciously and through respectable channels', 51,432 pamphlets and books, and 26,525 reports and papers. In addition scarcely a daily newspaper or monthly magazine failed to carry items about abolition.[20] All this was orchestrated by an abolitionist organisation which began in London but quickly sprouted local roots. Quakers (with their excellent facilities) were often the initial activists, but they quickly attracted a wide range of committed provincial followers. Within months, the pioneering abolitionists found that they had created a genuinely national organisation which, in its turn, spat out and distributed an ever-growing volume of publications, sponsored both by London and by local abolition committees.

To parallel the printed word, the abolitionist message reached huge crowds at lectures across the nation. Abolitionist speakers, led by the indefatigable Clarkson, were always guaranteed a full house and a good reception wherever they spoke. When Clarkson spoke in a Manchester church, he found it was 'so full that I could scarcely get to my place'.[21] The aim of all this effort was to generate public anger and direct it towards parliament, in the hope that it would recognise that the slave trade was wrong and would then abolish it. The most effective way of doing that in 1787 was to organise petitions against the slave trade. In that first wave of agitation, an estimated 103 abolition petitions, signed by tens of thousands of people, descended on parliament.[22] By the end of May 1788, only one year after the launch of the Abolition Society, parliament had been *inundated* by abolition petitions. The table of the House of Commons 'was loaded with petitions from every part of the kingdom.' In the words of the prime minister, William Pitt, no one doubted that the slave trade 'had engaged the public attention to a very considerable degree.'[23] The impact of abolition petitioning went far beyond the history of the slave trade, for it was to influence reforming politics for the next half-century, right down to the Chartist movement.[24]

Unparalleled numbers of ordinary people turned to the abolition cause, and scratched their names on to abolition petitions. By the summer of 1788, the slave lobby recognised 'The stream of popularity [which] runs against us.'[25] In the Lords, Lord Carlisle acknowledged that 'It was a matter of public notoriety, that the question of the Slave Trade had engrossed the attention of every part of the kingdom for above these twelve months'.[26] Both Lords and Commons recognised the national popularity of abolition and the nation's disapproval of the slave lobby, however much economic benefit flowed from its activities. The once unquestioned political sway of the West Indian lobby had been severely undermined. Spokesmen for the slave trade were roundly condemned and out-argued. Abolition had gained the political – and moral – high ground and was never again to relinquish it to the slave lobby.

These first abolition petitions were intended to coincide with a parliamentary scrutiny of the slave trade which had been initiated by the prime minister, William Pitt, who, in his turn, had been influenced by his old friend Wilberforce. Pitt also met with Clarkson, grilling him for two hours about the data he had assembled from the slave trade, and the prime minister thereafter initiated an inquiry by a committee of the Privy Council. For a year between 1787 and 1788, that committee listened to, and gathered information about, the slave trade. It was, once again, a reprise of Clarkson's method, of accumulating first-hand information from men with personal experience of the slave ships. Clarkson, once more, was central, choreographing key witnesses from the ranks of ex-slavers, clerical abolitionists and others well versed in the details of the trade. The abolitionist arguments presented to the Privy Council were, of course, fiercely contested by spokesmen from the slave lobby, but their main difficulty was that the bleakest of evidence about the slave trade paraded before parliamentarians was simply irrefutable. When abolitionists also lobbied MPs, they realised that they had strong support in the Commons (though the Lords was to remain resistant throughout). Although Burke scolded the House for not heeding the popular voice on the slave trade earlier,[27] by May 1788 it was clear that the question of abolishing the slave trade had taken root in parliament. Within a mere twelve months, the cause had secured a parliamentary foothold and had gathered national backing.

Thomas Clarkson's influence in all this was evident. Parliamentary investigations into the slave trade (within the Privy Council, and research by individual MPs) effectively copied the method he had devised for writing his Cambridge essay. By tapping into the experience and memories of sailors and traders, by scrutinising the available data, Clarkson had established a highly effective pattern of research, and had created an influential political tool for attacking the slave trade. Moreover, the voices of slave captains and surgeons, aligned with raw data from the slave ships (sickness, suffering and death of Africans – and sailors), proved both astonishing and unassailable. There were some surprises, notably the evidence of high mortality rates among the ships' crews. William Pitt was personally moved by evidence about sailors' deaths which Clarkson presented to him from ships' rosters. All this potent evidence, long hidden in the bellies of the slave ships, was now freely and widely available. It reached and persuaded armies of people previously ignorant about the slave trade. An irresistible feeling began to emerge, from within the Privy Council hearings, and at crowded public meetings across Britain, that the slave trade was an abomination. And it could be *proved* to be a dangerous and often fatal business.

Only five years had passed between Lord Mansfield hearing the *Zong* case in May 1783 and parliament's first serious scrutiny of the slave trade in May 1788, but in that time huge numbers of British people learned about the slave trade in very great detail. Now, just as when the story of the *Zong* was made public in 1783, the revelations about the slave ships possessed an *immediacy* which was lacking in earlier and more traditional ethical and religious condemnations of the slave trade, and this new critique – shaped by eye-witness accounts and statistical analysis – reached unprecedented numbers of British people. The thousands of abolition tracts, pamphlets, essays and articles, public lectures and – eventually – parliamentary scrutiny, were followed by a dramatic upsurge of popular abolition sentiment.

Thomas Clarkson's method of unearthing and publicising primary evidence also had a remarkable energising effect across the country, establishing a vogue for local investigations. Critics and intellectuals everywhere turned their attention to the slave trade. Data from the slave ships was seized upon, analysed, disputed and republished across Britain. In large part, the timing was fortuitous, for Clarkson's calculations paralleled the new vogue for statistical analysis among groups of educated people dotted around provincial Britain, many of whom were drawn to the scientific and mathematical societies which proliferated (often in unlikely places) in the late eighteenth century.[28] A Mr Clarke of Salford, for example ('universally known to rank among the first mathematicians of this kingdom'), responded to the mathematical challenge posed by Clarkson's data. He illustrated, statistically, the fatal and harmful consequences of the trade, and incorporated his own findings into an abolitionist pamphlet published in Warrington.[29] Here was one simple, local example, from the north-west of England, of a national pattern: provincial society responding to the abolitionist prompting from London. But it also illustrates the widespread appetite for the application of mathematical and statistical analysis to pressing social and political problems. Statistics were of course to become a dominant tool in nineteenth-century Britain, from counting the population (first done in 1801) through to analysing poverty and even illness. Statistics seemed to provide the means towards a greater understanding of an increasingly complex world at large, and the debate about the slave trade provided an early and effective example of how that might be done.

At the heart of all this evidence about the slave trade, about all the people involved (black and white), there was *one* unique event which stood out from the rest: the killings on the *Zong*, of which Clarkson gave a moving account in his 1788 *Essay*.

It was a deed, he wrote, 'Unparalleled in the memory of man, or in the history of former times, and of so black and complicated a nature, that were it to be perpetuated to future generations, and to rest on the testimony of an individual, it could not possibly be believed.' In conclusion, he wrote that 'hundreds can come and say, that they heard the melancholy evidence with tears'.[30]

But the abolition movement that Clarkson spearheaded could actually claim far larger audiences. In March 1783 an outraged Granville Sharp had resolved to tell the world about the murders on the *Zong* – and to demand an end to the slave trade. Four years later 60,000 people petitioned parliament with the same aim.[31] It was twenty more years before parliament decreed that 'from and after the 1st day of May, 1807, the African slave trade, and all manner of dealing and trading in the purchase, sale, barter or transfer of slaves . . . shall be . . . utterly abolished, prohibited and declared to be unlawful'.[32]

Although abolitionists had to wait two decades from the foundation of the Abolition Society for success, the wonder is that abolition passed through parliament at all. Those twenty years were characterised by political turmoil, revolution, warfare and slave revolts. The initial optimism and support for abolition (between 1787 and 1792) was simply ground down, by the mid-1790s, by a rising tide of reactionary alarm about the mounting unrest and dangers in Britain, Europe and in the slave colonies. Popular politics, of all kinds, withered. One of the founders of the Abolition Society, the Quaker Joseph Woods, admitted in 1796, 'I keep myself as quiet as I can in my own habitation.'[33]

In the world of slavery, the most daunting threat flowed from the volcanic slave revolt in St Domingue. The spark came from France, and its debates about social and political rights on the eve of its own Revolution, which inspired a massive slave uprising in August 1791 led by Toussaint L'Ouverture, the rise of a powerful slave army – and the ultimate defeat of French colonial authority. The slaves had overthrown the slave system. It sent shockwaves of discontent (and ideas about freedom) rippling through the slave quarters of the Americas. In November 1791 the Colonial Office received word from Jamaica that 'the ideas of liberty have sunk so deep in the minds of all Negroes, that wherever the greatest precaution are not taken they will rise'.[34]

Slaveholders everywhere had good reason to feel threatened. The contagion of liberty, unleashed first by France, then from St Domingue, made the dangers of tampering with slavery and the trade in slaves perfectly clear. Abolition supporters (including the normally irrepressible Wilberforce) languished, both in parliament and in Britain at large.

All this changed, however, and quickly, in the early years of the new century, when a changed political climate brought to power new ministers and new governments sympathetic to ending the slave trade. Parliament finally passed the necessary legislation, first in 1806 (in the form of the Foreign Slave Trade Act) and then, in 1807, the act for total British abolition – passed by 175 votes to 17 in the Commons, and then by the once-recalcitrant Lords – which also outlawed the use of British insurance to cover slaves or slave ships.[35] On 25 March 1807, the House of Commons rose to give a standing ovation – so rare that no one could remember the last time it had happened – for William Wilberforce, who quietly sat in his place, tears streaming down his face.[36] However much historians have argued about how the Abolition Act came into being, those most closely involved – the MPs who actually voted for abolition – were in no doubt that Wilberforce had been indispensable. A year later the US passed their own legislation abolishing the slave trade, which by that point had diminished in extent and importance; the North American enslaved population was growing rapidly of its own accord.

The British abolition of the slave trade in 1807 prompted great celebrations – and much self-congratulation: Bishop Beilby Porteus made the ecstatic claim that parliament and the British people should be praised for putting an end to 'the most execrable and inhuman traffic that ever disgraced the Christian world'.[37] Yet for all its achievements, it was soon apparent that the 1807 Act not only had serious limitations, but that there were plenty of slave traders keen to defy both the British and the Americans. It was clear that the Atlantic slave trade continued to thrive – despite the efforts of the British and American navies.

Stated bluntly, the Act of 1807 did *not* end the Atlantic slave trade. Nor did it stop *Zong*-like atrocities against Africans on ships. British abolitionists realised that they would have to keep up their guard after 1807. It was recognised that there were plenty of other Europeans – notably the French, Spanish and Portuguese (to say nothing of Brazilian and Cuban traders) – who were keen to continue slave trading in the Atlantic, whatever the risks. Brazil and Cuba were especially keen to welcome fresh boatloads of Africans to their burgeoning plantation economies. With this in mind, British governments sought to *extend* abolition by striking international abolitionist agreements, initially via the post-war Congress system, with other European maritime powers. Thomas Clarkson (once again) took up the cause at those gatherings around Europe's capitals, lobbying ministers and delegates to win them over to inter-national abolition (and greatly assisted by Lord Wellington allowing him to use the diplomatic bags[38]). Despite these efforts, and despite massive British public support for interna-tional abolition, Africans continued to be transported across the Atlantic in slave ships, mainly under Portuguese and Spanish flags.

International agreements allowed the British and American navies to stop and, when possible, impound suspected slave ships. Two thousand vessels were seized in this way, and though only one quarter of them was found to be carrying Africans, it meant that 125,000 Africans were released from captivity (and were resettled in Africa, the Caribbean and on the Atlantic islands).[39] These efforts, however, need to be set against the figures for the wider Atlantic slave trade: after 1807, 2.8 million Africans were loaded on to Atlantic slave ships, of whom 2.5 million survived to landfall in the Americas.[40] Though contemporaries did not have access to these precise figures, abolition must, at times, have felt like a losing battle. Charles Darwin – abolitionist to his boots – was working and travelling on the *Beagle* in 1831–2, and was incensed to see slave ships discharging their African victims at various points in South America.[41] This persistent trafficking in the South Atlantic raised serious doubts about the nature of the British effort (which was focused mainly on the African coast) to stop the trade. One historian has claimed that the entire project was 'a dumping ground for the worst ships in the Royal Navy'. There were too few ships, and most tended to be old and unsuitable: veterans of the recent wars, they were more sluggish than the faster slaving ships, and had to cover a vast stretch of coast and ocean. Slavers could make numerous

Atlantic crossings, packed with Africans, and never even encounter an abolitionist patrol.[42]

The captains of such 'illicit' slave ships naturally did their best to avoid capture by the British and American navies, which would mean the likely loss of their vessels and captive Africans. They tried to evade or outrun their pursuers. Sometimes, however, when they were in danger of being caught, slave captains decided to rid themselves of the evidence which would have condemned them: they simply jettisoned African captives overboard to their death. Though the *reason* was different, these killings from the decks of nineteenth-century slavers were a grim reprise of events on the *Zong* in 1781, and made for a troubling irony; the very instrument devised to impose effective abolition in the Atlantic may, unconsciously, have occasioned mass killings at sea.

News about these killings initially surfaced in Britain in parliamentary debates, and in reports in *The Times*. Later, the stories reappeared when they were used as evidence by abolitionists in their attacks on the continuing slave trade.[43] As early as 1814, a naval officer reported the capture of the Spanish slave ship the *Carlos*, but 'Eighty were thrown overboard before we captured her.'[44] The prohibition on the trade added an element of urgency, but, as in the past, unmarketable slaves were also regularly jettisoned. One of the reports from Royal naval officers declared:

> We do not know how common such killings were, though claims were made in Paris, but impossible to substantiate, That the slave captains throw into the sea, every year, about 3,000 negroes, men, women and children; of whom more than half are thus sacrificed, whilst yet alive, either to escape

from visits of cruisers, or because, worn down by their sufferings, they could not be sold to advantage.[45]

In 1819, the French slave ship the *Rodeur* suffered an epidemic of an eye-disease (described as 'ophthalmia') among the Africans (and the crew). A number of the Africans lost their sight, but before the ship reached Guadeloupe in the summer of 1819 'thirty of the slaves who were stated to have become blind were thrown into the sea and drowned.' In a grim reminder of the *Zong* story, it was also claimed that by throwing the Africans overboard, 'a ground was laid for a claim on the underwriters, by whom the cargo had been insured, and who are said to have allowed the claim, and made good the value of the slaves thus destroyed.'[46]

The case of the *Jeune Estelle*, a French slave ship intercepted by HMS *Tartar* that same year, 1819, was equally horrifying. The vessel was from Martinique and its master, Captain Sanguines, at first denied any involvement in slave trading. But the boarding party of British sailors remained suspicious, not least because the ship *smelled* like a slaver. Their attention was drawn to some barrels; 'a sailor who struck a cask, which was lightly closed, heard a faint voice issue from it, as of a creature expiring.' The cask contained two young girls aged twelve to fourteen.[47] The chilling truth dawned on the British: the casks jettisoned by the crew which they had seen floating past them as they had chased the *Jeune Estelle* had contained African slaves.[48]

Stories of cornered slave ships ditching large numbers of Africans over the side were a regular refrain in the reports about the continuing illicit slave trade. *The Times* in 1831 reported how two Spanish vessels, the *Rapido* and the *Regulo*, trapped by the Royal Navy (in another ship named the *Black Joke* – but this time HMS *Black Joke*) in the Bonny River, disposed of between 125 and 180 Africans in this way.[49] Late in 1835, when the *Charybdis*, under Lt Mercer, chased the Spanish brig *Argus*, ninety-seven Africans were thrown overboard.[50] The threat of being seized was not the only cause of such killings. In 1838 a smallpox epidemic broke out on the brig *Leao*, heading from Mozambique to Brazil: thirty Africans suffering from smallpox were pitched overboard.[51] It was also shocking to learn that the men who ordered such killings remained unrepentant: one captured Spanish captain declared 'he would never hesitate to throw the slaves overboard to prevent being taken'.[52] In 1820 the crew of the Spanish schooner *Vicua* were even preparing to blow up the entire ship and its African captives to avoid capture and prosecution. Such killings were in addition to other murderous incidents, when Africans were simply abandoned to their fate (chained and entombed in a sinking vessel, for example) when ships were seriously damaged by storm or shipwreck.[53]

These dismal accounts were widely circulated in the 1820s by the revived abolitionist campaign, now bolstered and greatly influenced by a remarkable female presence,[54] whose aim was both to end British colonial slavery *and* to stop the continuing Atlantic slave trade.[55] Led after 1824 by Thomas Fowell Buxton (who replaced the frail and ageing Wilberforce), the movement again bombarded a supportive British public with huge volumes of cheap literature. Thus, fifty years after the first wave of popular abolition, a new phase of popular agitation in the 1820s and 1830s focused on the inhumanities of the slave ships and of plantation slavery. Buxton, however, could not lead the campaign in parliament, having failed to be returned in

1837. Instead he turned his attention to the Atlantic slave trade, combing all the published evidence he could find for his book *The African Slave Trade and its Remedy* (1839). It concentrated on the continuing, post-1807 slave trade and was peppered with distressing details of mass killings on the Atlantic slave ships: page after dismal page of *Zong*-like inhumanities.

Such incidents from the 1820s and 1830s would have been familiar to anyone with experience of eighteenth-century slave ships. Indeed it all seemed to form a reprise of an old refrain, heard most memorably from the lips of the Lord Chief Justice in 1783: Africans were cargo, and, like other forms of cargo, might be disposed of when circumstances demanded. It was as if the spirit of the *Zong* lived on, long after the British had abolished their own slave trade in 1807.

Immediately after British emancipation in 1838, two publications sought to explain how the grand edifice of slavery had been destroyed. Robert Isaac and Samuel Wilberforce published a five-volume hagiography of their father in 1838.[56] A year later Thomas Clarkson reissued his history of abolition, first published in 1808, and now published as part of the political and highly personal battle conducted between Clarkson and Wilberforce's sons for the soul and for the historical memory of the abolition movement. The literary spat was, essentially, a dispute about who could claim credit for ending the slave trade: Thomas Clarkson (whose original account inevitably stressed his own contribution) or William Wilberforce (glorified, to the exclusion of others – notably Clarkson – by his sons).

That dispute aside, Thomas Clarkson's *History* reminded readers in 1839 of that extraordinary incident on board an

English slave ship fifty-eight years previously, and the political and legal argument which swirled around the case in 1783. But readers did not have to be reminded of the *Zong* to learn about the horrors committed on slave ships. Buxton's *History of the Slave Trade* (1838) offered a more immediate, and perhaps therefore more potent, reminder of the tradition of murdering Africans on slave ships. Anyone anxious to see the Atlantic trade ended had only to read Buxton to find recent illustrations of a violent saga which appeared to have reached its nadir on the *Zong* – but which in fact continued. It was precisely at this time that Turner was working on *The Slave Ship*. He may well have been aware of what had happened on the *Zong*, but he may also have been alert to the recently discussed killings of Africans on Atlantic slave ships.

When we consider the broad cultural response to the slave trade and slavery in the years 1838–40, the most memorable – the most powerful and devastating – was to be found, not in print, but in Turner's painting. It is a work which fairly bristles with outrage: about slave ships and about killings on those ships. Clearly, it represents Turner's personal revulsion about such events. But it also speaks to a mood of heightened contemporary agitation in Britain about the Atlantic slave trade and its attendant cruelties. Despite everything achieved by the British abolition movement over the previous half-century, cruelties and killings still haunted the Atlantic. Turner in *The Slave Ship*, like Thomas Fowell Buxton in his book, portrayed the Atlantic slave trade as a murderous venture. Whatever the commercial impulse behind it, and however intent its key players on turning African captives into profitable commerce, it was a trade which caused (indeed, at certain moments it seemed even to *require*) the killing of

Africans. It was as if, fifty years after the event itself, the dead souls from the *Zong* still hovered over the slave ships which continued to cross the Atlantic crowded with Africans. From among the galaxy of people – painters, writers, historians, poets – who responded to the slave trade, Turner's painting stands out as the one artistic device which has ensured that all the victims of the slave trade would not be forgotten. The Africans murdered on the *Zong* have become perhaps the best-remembered group of victims. But it speaks to the power of Turner's work that it points us, not so much to the *Zong* itself, as to the millions of other, nameless Africans devoured by the Atlantic slave ships.

CHAPTER II

Remembering the *Zong*

W HAT HAPPENED ON THE *ZONG* WAS AN EXCEPTIONAL
story of mass murder, but those killings have come to be seen
not merely as a single event (the story of one ship among thousands) but as a representation of the wider story of the slave
trade. It is, to repeat, the exception which became the rule – in
practice, in the decades before emancipation, as much as in
modern memory. In much the same vein, Turner's painting *The
Slave Ship* is an image which similarly addresses the entire
history of the slave trade – brilliant artistic shorthand for
the whole barbaric system. In the public mind – at least in
Britain – a close link has been forged between the *Zong*,
Turner's painting and the Atlantic slave trade in its entirety.

The bicentenary of the abolition of the slave trade in
2007 made these close associations palpable. *The Slave Ship*
appeared again and again, even adorning the cover of the
British government's elaborate brochure to commemorate the
anniversary.[1] That year's 'Understanding Slavery Initiative'
from the Department for Culture, Media and Sport included

a video, produced by the National Maritime Museum, depicting a courtroom scene from the *Zong* hearing; an actor portrayed John Lee, the Solicitor General in 1783, defending the killings on the *Zong*.[2] Another video was issued by the archive service of Gloucestershire County Council, this time with an actor playing Granville Sharp, reading letters about the *Zong* (to publicise the Sharp material in their collection).[3] Indeed, the commemorations of 2007 saw items about the *Zong* littering the web, and ranged from formal items by the BBC and the National Archives, through to a clip on YouTube. Most spectacular of all, a replica *Zong* sailed into the Port of London. A church ministry, the Centre for Contemporary Ministry, keen to promote awareness about the history of slavery and the slave trade, raised £300,000 for the lease of an old square rigger, the *Madagascar* – and temporarily renamed it the *Zong*. For a few weeks it was moored alongside HMS *Belfast* in London and hosted a series of commemorations of the *Zong* killings and the slave trade.[4]

Memories of the *Zong* were never far below the surface in Britain in 2007. But what happened on that ship is also an important aspect of the history of Jamaica. The 208 African survivors from that ship, the people who saw and heard the killings, landed in Jamaica in December 1781, and for many Jamaicans, 2007 was not so much the bicentenary of abolition as the 226th anniversary of the *Zong*'s arrival. Thanks to the efforts of the Jamaica National Bicentenary Committee, a permanent stone memorial was erected close to the *Zong*'s docking place at Black River. A major unveiling ceremony, with plentiful media coverage, was marked by speeches from politicians and academics, and with frequent mention of the killings. The atrocity was declared by Professor Verene

Shepherd, chairman of the Bicentenary Committee, to be 'an important part of St Elizabeth's [the local parish] and Jamaica's history which needs to be exposed and its victims need to be memorialised in some tangible way.' The *Jamaica Gleaner* recorded that the *Zong* incident 'serves as a gruelling reminder of the atrocities committed against our ancestors and the vagaries of a system that continued for too long.' Shepherd concluded her address with the chilling lyrics of a popular Jamaican song, 'Murderer, blood is on your shoulder'.[5]

On both sides of the Atlantic in 2007 it was clear that the story of the *Zong* had moved well beyond the esoteric world of historical scholarship, and had come to occupy a special niche in public and political imagination. The fact that the *Zong* has become so widely known, and is so frequently cited, used (and sometimes misused), speaks to its continuing power, and to its place in the popular imagination. It has become a name which is used to evoke guilt and shame on the one hand and, on the other, anger often laced with demands for recompense for historical sins. Demands for reparations, for example, were rarely below the surface when the *Zong* was discussed in public in 2007.[6] It is as if that one exceptional ship speaks not merely to the history of Atlantic slavery, but also invokes the wrongs done by the West to the peoples of Africa.

The *Zong* is an example of how men got away with murder, and seems to illustrate the rapacious history of the Western world: an example of the callousness displayed by the dominant and the powerful towards the lives of the oppressed and weak. To paraphrase the question of one outraged critic after 1783, did anyone on the ship consider drowning white men when the water began to run out? It is a story, now more than two centuries old, which plays to a range of modern preoccupations and worries. Yet even when we strip away all these modern associations and interpretations which have accumulated like barnacles on the *Zong*'s hull, we are left with a historical event which remains as deeply troubling as ever.

On 12 January 1782, a mere three weeks after the *Zong* docked at Black River, Gregson's agent in Jamaica, Coppells and Aguillar, wrote to Liverpool about 'the *Richard* alias the *Zong*'.[7] This change of name, so soon after arriving from its disastrous voyage from Africa, was clearly no accident or whim. Most likely it was a swift transformation designed to distance the vessel from what had happened on board only weeks before. It clearly did not work, and to this day, the ship named the *Zong* remains tarnished with the reputation as perhaps the most terrible of Atlantic slave ships: no mean achievement in the world of Atlantic slavery.

There are, of course, other infamous slave ships which have found a niche in the popular memory. Five years after the *Zong* case, in 1788, another Liverpool ship, the *Brookes*, secured its own lasting fame via those images of crowded humanity, circulated by the abolitionist movement and which became a key *motif* of the slave trade itself. Endlessly reproduced down to the present day, they remain among the most popular of all slave-ship images, of humanity packed like sardines for the Atlantic crossing.[8] But if any slave ship *deserves* to be remembered it is surely the *Zong*.

Even now, it is not easy to penetrate to the full truth of what happened on the *Zong*, for it is a story peppered with deceit and deception: who said what, who did what, and who was responsible? Despite everything that has been said and written about the *Zong*, an element of mysterious uncertainty pervades the entire story. The record of events was shaped by the word of an irrepressible liar. What we know of the crew itself remains patchy and unclear. Today the ship's chief owner, William Gregson, is remembered (if at all) not so much for his association with the *Zong* but as a major figure in the mercantile history of Liverpool, celebrated among the city's famous sons for his commercial success, his political position, and for founding a prosperous family dynasty – even though he lent his name to the pursuit of gain at the cost of 132 murdered Africans. The man who effectively decided that legal issue was Lord Mansfield, whose reputation as one of the giants of eighteenth-century English law has been badly damaged in the eyes of some modern critics by his role (and above all his words) in the *Zong* hearings in 1783.

The people about whom we know least of all are the African survivors from the *Zong*. Today, their descendants must surely be scattered among the people of modern Jamaica, and, perhaps, via the diaspora of Caribbean peoples, even further afield. What happened to their memories of that voyage? At what point did old Jamaican slaves stop reciting the nightmare stories of their crossing on the *Zong*, and when did the folk memory fade? Or were those stories too traumatic to repeat, remaining bottled up and hidden away within the *Zong*'s survivors?

There are, then, many unanswered questions about the *Zong*. But the events emanating from the killings helped to clarify issues for contemporary critics of slavery. It was instantly recognised, notably by Granville Sharp and his African friends, that what had happened on the ship had a significance which transcended the killings and the specific legal dispute in 1781–3. The *Zong* case offered a glimpse not merely into the violence of the slave ships, but into the brutal mentality of Atlantic slavery: ordinary men were persuaded to do terrible things in the name of 'necessity'. The *Zong* made clear an essential truth – there was a rotten moral core to the slave system – and the legal case exposed it, publicly, as never before. Thereafter, Sharp's task was to seek justice for the dead, and to generate vital support for his long-held and frequently expressed view that such outrages would continue as long as slavery and the slave trade survived. The answer was to abolish slavery.

The *Zong* affair was a single, unpredictable event which helped spark a seismic shift in public mood: a 'tipping point', to use modern parlance.[9] Here was the very moment, not so much when opinion began to shift, but when a new kind of opinion came into being. Before 1783, the slave trade had provoked a discussion which was, broadly speaking, devoid of an ethical dimension; after 1783, the slave trade stimulated a rising mood of deep-seated popular outrage. The *Zong* marked the point at which a new ethical dimension was intruded into what had been, overwhelmingly, a commercial and political debate.

The legal hearing about the *Zong* proved to be a major revelation, exposing the sufferings endured by millions of Africans on the slave ships. Previously, the flow of slave-grown produce from the plantations of the Americas had seemed relatively cost-free; after 1783, those goods were shown to have a very high price indeed. Moreover the real cost of slave-grown produce was to be calculated not simply in demographic or financial terms: it was not merely a matter of the staggeringly high numbers of dead (black and white) thrown overboard from the armada of Atlantic slave ships.

After 1783 there was an additional *moral* equation to be assessed.

It is impossible to know precisely how many people, before 1783, had ethical or religious concerns about slavery, but by 1788 they could actually be counted in their thousands. In the wake of the *Zong*, there emerged a widespread abolition sentiment: after 1787 it sprang up as if conjured forth by an abolitionist magician. Of course this widespread support for abolition did not emerge simply or uniquely from the *Zong* case. It had roots deep in trans-Atlantic debates about reform and about representation, notably in the language of democracy which lay at the heart of the North American conflict before and after 1776. American independence and the war had a major influence on British political life, and the story of the *Zong* was able to make its own distinctive impact *because* it was a story which unfolded under the shadow of the British defeat in North America. Britain's imperial bravado was successfully challenged by American rebel colonies, and at the very moment when the British lost their American empire, the story of the *Zong* seeped across the country, confirming Granville Sharp's long-argued case that slavery begat acts of great wickedness – and punishment was bound to follow. The evidence from the *Zong* offered proof that here was wrongdoing on a staggering scale. For those who looked for heavenly influence in the ways of man, the defeat in North America looked remarkably like divine punishment for the sins of slavery. Even before the revolution in France transformed the debate about human rights, evidence from the slave ships had exposed troublesome questions about 'rights', and after 1783 more and more people came to view slavery as a rotten canker at the heart of a Christian nation.

The irony is that it was the commercial avarice of William Gregson's syndicate which ensured that we learned about the *Zong* in the first place. What would we have known had Gregson and friends *not* demanded payment from the insurers, and had *not* sought legal redress to secure it? The story might have remained a fading memory among the small band of men involved, and the African survivors. In going to court, Gregson not only exposed the story to legal scrutiny, but in the process laid bare the entire slaving system to critical public gaze. Moreover the legal hearings did much more than reveal the details about the *Zong* killings: they also exposed the remarkable role played by English law itself in shaping and encouraging Britain's Atlantic slave system. For those of a critical bent, it became obvious in 1783 that to change slavery (or the slave trade) it was necessary to change the law – the very battle Granville Sharp had been fighting for almost twenty years. The instinctive and natural legal resistance to such changes (personified by Lord Mansfield) also served to expose the law's broader complicity with slavery. After all, both the Lord Chief Justice and the Solicitor General agreed with the slave traders that the killing of 132 Africans was *not* a matter of murder. Today, that legal complicity seems best expressed by Lord Mansfield's terse statements in 1783. Merely to recite some of Mansfield's words (and those of John Lee) is to convey an impression that English law and Liverpool slave traders were singing in unison from the same soiled hymn sheet.[10]

The widening debate about the slave trade which spread from the *Zong* courtroom after 1783 revealed the full complexity and extent of domestic British involvement in the Atlantic slave system. Since time out of mind, slavery had seemed far removed from British life. It seemed alien, associated more with Africa, with Atlantic shipping, and with the Americas, than with Britain itself. Now, slavery had an immediacy and a moral ambiguity, notably in the friction between successful slave-based commerce and traditional English liberties. The people most clearly exposed to those moral ambiguities in 1783 were the Liverpool slave traders and their insurers. But many other people were also dragged in. Where did collusion and responsibility end in the matter of the slave trade? Was it solely a matter for the major players – the Gregsons or the Gilberts? What about the little men, the bit-players, the ordinary men and women, the sailors, the thousands of working people in Liverpool – shipwrights building the 'Guineamen', the rope-makers, chandlers, gunsmiths and ironworkers? Armies of people were involved in the slave system in some fashion, from labouring people whose efforts sustained the ships and the plantations, through to the mightiest of West Indian planters. More indirectly, few communities, on both sides of the Atlantic, remained untouched by African slavery. Which British household was complete without its daily use of slave-grown sugar? And which circle of men, at leisure or when working, would be complete without the shared pleasure of tobacco, grown by slaves in the Chesapeake?[11] Such awkward matters – questions really about public involvement in slavery and its benefits – were raised as matters of pressing political consideration in the wake of the *Zong*. One simple, personal step – available to everyone – was to decide *not* to consume slave-grown produce (a tactic used to very great effect in the later abolition campaign).[12] Put simply, this meant that people had begun to make up their own minds about slavery and the slave trade. And that personal, individual choice was ultimately to coalesce into a massive public denunciation. When that happened, slavery was doomed.

John Ruskin was only one of millions troubled by the slave ships, though in his case it was ninety years after the *Zong* killings. For all its intensity and dazzle, Turner's painting proved too much for its first owner. As he grew older, Ruskin felt he could no longer live with the African ghosts that haunted the picture: he cleared his mind and conscience by selling the painting. But the *real* ghosts lingered on, and memories of the dead Africans from the slave ships survive right down to the present day, on both sides of the Atlantic: bleak reminders of the human disasters which the slave trade visited upon many millions of Africans.

Notes

Sources

Suggestions for further reading are given on pp. 236–9 below. This summary of the main sources I consulted for this book is arranged by their present location.

British Library

Minutes of the London Abolition Committee, 3 vols, Add. Ms 21,254–21,256.

Gloucestershire Archives

Granville Sharp's own papers are rich in evidence about the *Zong*. They are now deposited in the Gloucestershire Archives; I studied them when they were privately owned by the Lloyd-Baker family and held at Hardwicke Court, Gloucestershire. Some of those papers were reprinted, and are readily available, in Prince Hoare's *Memoirs of Granville Sharp*, London, 1820. Granville Sharp's published tracts can be found in the extraordinary pamphlet collection in the Goldsmiths' Library of Economic Literature, University of London Library, Senate House, London.

The Jamaica Archives

I consulted the Vice-Admiralty Court papers (High Court of Vice-Admiralty, Jamaica, Calendar of Records, 1776–1783) and related materials for the crew of the *Zong* (St Elizabeth Parish Records, Burials, 1707–1820) in the Jamaica Archives, Spanish Town, Jamaica.

Middle Temple Library

The Gibbs and Dampier Ms, Cases in the Kings Bench, 23 and 24 Geo. III, especially 'Gregson v. Gilbert', Dampier Ms, fols 33ff.

The National Archives, Kew (TNA)

For the ships *William* and *Richard*, see Muster Rolls, Liverpool, 1781–1782, BT98/42 and 43.

For the *Zong* being renamed the *Richard* (18 May 1782): 'Jamaica returns, 1782–3–4, List of ships cleared out of Kingston', CO142/1.

Answers of William Gregson (January 1784) and James Kelsall (November 1783); and Petitions to William Pitt: Documents in Exchequer, E112/1528.

Minutes of the Company of Merchants Trading to Africa, 1780–1787, T70/145, and Miscellaneous Letters to the African Committee, T70/1695, both for accounts of Robert Stubbs at Cape Castle and Anomabu.

Insurance policies on slave ships can be found in T70/1695 (for 1756–57) and in T70/1549 (for 1779).

The final legal act in the *Zong* case is to be found in Documents in Exchequer, E112/47, item no. 110, 3 May 1784.

National Maritime Museum, Greenwich (NMM)

The essential manuscript account of the history of the *Zong* is the one commissioned by Granville Sharp of the legal hearing held before Lord Mansfield in May 1783, now at the National Maritime Museum, Greenwich: Documents Relating to the Ship Zong, 1783, REC/19. Following the convention of James Oldham, this document is referred to here as the *Sharp Transcript*.

Chapter 1: A painting and a slave ship

1. Granville Sharp, 19 March 1783, 'Extracts from Diary, 1783–98', in Granville Sharp's Papers.
2. The case was reported in detail in the 18 March 1783 edition of the *Morning Chronicle and London Advertiser*, quoted at length in F.O. Shyllon, *Black Slaves in Britain*, London, 1974, pp. 187–8.
3. The ship was owned by William Gregson, James Gregson, John Gregson, Edward Wilson, George Case and James Aspinall: hereafter I abbreviate ownership to 'William Gregson'. The *Zong* was insured by Thomas Gilbert, John Dawson, William Bolder, John Thompson, John Parker, Edward Mason and Ellis Bent: hereafter I abbreviate the insurers to 'Gilbert'.
4. James Oldham, 'Insurance Litigation Involving the *Zong* and Other British Slave Ships, 1780–1807', *Journal of Legal History*, vol. 28, no. 3, December 2007.
5. Though known as *The Slave Ship*, its formal title is *Slavers Throwing Overboard the Dead and Dying, Typhoon Coming On*. For the best analysis of the painting see Marcus Wood, *Blind Memory. Visual Representations of Slavery in England and America, 1780–1865*, Manchester, 2000, pp. 41–64.

6. See ch. 10.
7. Seymour Drescher, *Abolition. A History of Slavery and Antislavery*, New York, 2009, pp. 267–8, and *The Mighty Experiment. Free Labor versus Slavery in British Emancipation*, Oxford, 2002, ch. 4.
8. 'Exhibition of the Royal Academy', *The Times*, 6 May 1840.
9. Quoted in Martin Butlin and Evelyn Joll, eds, *The Paintings of J.M.W. Turner (Text)*, London, 1984, p. 239.
10. Quoted in Wood, *Blind Memory*, p. 43.
11. Letter from Ruskin, 28 April 1872, in File 99.2, Museum of Fine Arts, Boston. I am indebted to Sabrina Abron for facilitating my access to the Turner files at the MFA.
12. Wood, *Blind Memory*, ch. 2.
13. Wood, *Blind Memory*, p. 41.
14. Butlin and Joll, eds, *The Paintings of J.M.W. Turner (Text)*, p. 237; James Sambrook, *James Thomson, 1700–1748. A Life*, Oxford, 1991, pp. 233–4; John Gage, *J.M.W. Turner. A Wonderful Range of Mind*, London and New Haven, 1987, pp. 193–4.
15. 'Summer', lines 1015–25, in *James Thomson, Poetical Works*, ed. J. Logie Robertson, London, 1908, p. 88; Andrew Wilton, *Turner and the Sublime*, London, 1980, pp. 22–3, 98.
16. Drescher, *Abolition*, ch. 5.
17. Robert Isaac Wilberforce and Samuel Wilberforce, *The Life of William Wilberforce*, 5 vols, London, 1838; Thomas Clarkson, *The History of the Rise, Progress, and Accomplishment of the Abolition of the African Slave-Trade . . .*, 2 vols, London, 1839 (throughout I use the 1788 edition).
18. James Walvin, *Black and White. The Negro and English Society, 1555–1945*, London, 1973, and *Britain's Slave Empire*, Stroud, 2007 edition.

Chapter 2: The city built on slavery

1. Jane Longmore, 'Civic Liverpool, 1680–1800', in *Liverpool 800. Culture, Character, History*, ed. John Belchem, Liverpool, 2008, p. 129.
2. The *Annual Register*, 1764, vol. 34, p. 278.
3. Longmore, 'Civic Liverpool', pp. 167, 169.
4. Edward Daniel Clarke, *A Tour through the South of England, Wales, and Part of Ireland, Made during the Summer of 1791*, London, 1793, pp. 353–4.
5. Longmore, 'Civic Liverpool', pp. 142–3.
6. William Moss, *The Liverpool Guide, including a sketch of the environs*, Liverpool, 1796, pp. 101–2.
7. Moss, *Liverpool Guide*, p. 86.
8. *The New Liverpool Songster, or Musical Companion*, Liverpool, 1789; David Russell, *Popular Music in England, 1840–1914, A Social History*, Manchester, 1987; Peter Bailey, *Leisure and Class in Victorian England*, London, 1978, ch. 7.
9. *Laws and Regulations of the Athenaeum in Liverpool*, Liverpool, 1799, pp. 7–8; Jane Longmore, ' "Cemented by the Blood of a Negro?" The Impact of the Slave Trade on Eighteenth Century Liverpool', in *Liverpool and Transatlantic Slavery*, ed. David Richardson, Suzanne Schwarz and Anthony Tibbles, Liverpool, 2007, pp. 228–9. For the

NOTES to pp. 15–23

eighteenth-century urban renaissance, see Peter Borsay, *The English Urban Renaissance. Culture and Society in the Provincial Town, 1660–1770*, Oxford, 1989.

10. T.H.B. Oldfield, *An Entire and Complete History, Political and Personal, of the Boroughs of Great Britain*, 2 vols, London, 1792, I, pp. 343–4; Longmore, 'Civic Liverpool', p. 148; Ian Baucom, *Specters of the Atlantic. Finance Capital, Slavery, and the Philosophy of History*, Durham, NC, 2005, p. 52.
11. Nigel Tattersfield, *The Forgotten Trade. Comprising the Log of the Daniel and Henry of 1700 and Accounts of the Slave Trade from the Minor Ports of England, 1698–1725*, London, 1991; Melinda Elder, *The Slave Trade and the Economic Development of Eighteenth-century Lancaster*, Halifax, 1992.
12. *The Liverpool Memorandum Book*, London, 1752, p. 12. British Library.
13. Thomas Bentley, *A View of the Advantages of Inland Navigation*, title page, London, 1765.
14. 'Index Map to the Canals, Rivers and Roads', in John Aiken, *A Description of the Country from Thirty to Forty Miles round Manchester*, London, 1795, p. 2.
15. M.J. Power, 'The Growth of Liverpool', in *Popular Politics, Riot and Labour. Essays in Liverpool History, 1790–1940*, ed. John Belchem, Liverpool, 1992, pp. 24–5.
16. Kenneth Morgan, 'Liverpool's Dominance in the British Slave Trade, 1740–1807', in Richardson *et al.*, *Liverpool and Transatlantic Slavery*, pp. 22–3.
17. Moss, *Liverpool Guide*, p. 98.
18. See 'Lancashire', in John Aiken, *England Delineated; or a Geographical Description of every County in England and Wales . . .*, London, 1800.
19. Longmore, 'Civic Liverpool', p. 135.
20. Longmore, 'Cemented by the Blood of a Negro?', pp. 230, 237, and *passim*.
21. Ramsay Muir, *Introduction to the History of Municipal Government in Liverpool*, Liverpool, 1906, p. 245; Power, 'The Growth of Liverpool', pp. 24–5.
22. Longmore, 'Civic Liverpool', p. 113.
23. Longmore, 'Civic Liverpool', pp. 118–23, 133, 134; David Pope, 'Liverpool's leading slave merchants, 1750–1790' (Appendix 1), in Richardson *et al.*, *Liverpool and Transatlantic Slavery*, pp. 194–207.
24. Oldfield, *An Entire and Complete History . . .*, vol. I, p. 343.
25. Longmore, 'Civic Liverpool', p. 232.
26. Moss, *Liverpool Guide*, p. 100.
27. *The Liverpool Memorandum Book*, London, 1753, p. 14; Baucom, *Specters of the Atlantic*, p. 50; Longmore, 'Civic Liverpool', p. 232.
28. Moss, *Liverpool Guide*, p. 99.
29. Longmore, 'Civic Liverpool', p. 132.
30. Kenneth Morgan, *Slavery and the British Empire*, Oxford, 2007, pp. 64–5.
31. Paul Lovejoy and David Richardson, 'African Agency and the Liverpool Slave Trade', in Richardson *et al.*, *Liverpool and Transatlantic Slavery*, ch. 2.
32. Longmore, 'Cemented by the Blood of a Negro?', p. 241.
33. Morgan, 'Liverpool's Dominance', p. 19.

34. Longmore, 'Cemented by the Blood of a Negro?', p. 243. For Bristol, see Madge Dresser, *Slavery Obscured. The Social History of the Slave Trade in an English Provincial Port*, London, 2001.
35. J.H. Elliott, *Empires of the Atlantic World. Britain and Spain in America 1492–1830*, New Haven and London, 2006, p. 100; Nuala Zahediah, 'Overseas Expansion and Trade in the Seventeenth Century', in *The Origins of Empire. The Oxford History of the British Empire*, ed. Nicholas Canny, vol. I, Oxford, 1998.
36. John Chamberlayne, *Magnae Britanniae notitia: or the present state of Great-Britain*, London, 1755, p. 132.
37. N.A.M. Rodger, *Wooden Worlds. An Anatomy of the Georgian Navy*, London, 1987; John Brewer, *Sinews of Power. War, Money and the English State, 1688–1783*, New York, 1989.
38. Daniel Fenning, *A New System of Geography: or, a General Description of the World*, 2 vols, London, 1778, I, p. 425.
39. For an account of Cape Coast Castle, see William St Clair, *The Grand Slave Emporium. Cape Coast Castle and the British Slave Trade*, London, 2006.
40. St Clair, *The Grand Slave Emporium*, pp. 186, 204–5.

Chapter 3: Crews and captives

1. Jane Webster, 'The *Zong* in the Context of the Eighteenth-century Slave Trade', *Journal of Legal History*, vol. 28, no. 3, December 2007, p. 289.
2. *The Brookes*, voyage number 80666 (1787), *Trans-Atlantic Slave Trade Database*, www.slavevoyages.org.
3. See Assessing the Slave Trade, Estimates, 1501–1866, *Trans-Atlantic Slave Trade Database*.
4. *The Importance of Effectually Supporting the Royal African Company of England*, London, 1745, p. 3. Beinecke Library, Yale University.
5. Malachi Postlethwayt, *The African Trade*, London, 1745, p. 6.
6. An African Merchant, *A Treatise upon the Trade from Great-Britain to Africa*, London, 1772, pp. 4–5.
7. William Wood, *A Survey of Trade. In Four Parts*, London, 1718, p. 179.
8. John Hippisley, *Essays. On the Populousness of Africa*, London, 1764, p. 17.
9. David Richardson, 'The British Empire and the Atlantic Slave Trade', in *The Oxford History of the British Empire*, vol. 2, *The Eighteenth Century*, ed. P.J. Marshall, Oxford, 1998; Lorena Walsh, 'Liverpool's Slave Trade to the Colonial Chesapeake: Slavery on the Periphery', in Richardson *et al.*, *Liverpool and Transatlantic Slavery*.
10. Philip Morgan, 'The Black Experience in the British Empire, 1680–1810', in P.J. Marshall, ed., *The Oxford History of the British Empire*, vol. 2.
11. William Pettigrew, 'Parliament and the Escalation of the Slave Trade, 1690–1714', in *The British Slave Trade. Abolition, Parliament and People*, ed. Stephen Farrell, Melanie Unwin and James Walvin, Edinburgh, 2007, pp. 12–26.
12. Richardson, 'The British Empire and the Atlantic Slave Trade', p. 440. See also Estimates, Timeline, *Trans-Atlantic Slave Trade Database*.

13. For the best and most vivid account of the slave ships, see Marcus Rediker, *The Slave Ship. A Human History*, London, 2007.
14. Rediker, *The Slave Ship*, pp. 53–4; M.K. Stammers, ' "Guineamen": Some Technical Aspects of Slave Ships', in *Transatlantic Slavery. Against Human Dignity*, ed. Anthony Tibbles, London, 1994, pp. 35–40; Jane Webster, 'The Material Culture of Slave Shipping', in *Representing Slavery*, ed. Douglas Hamilton and Robert J. Blyth, Aldershot, 2007, pp. 105–10.
15. John Atkins, *A Voyage to Guinea, Brasil, and the West Indies; in his Majesty's Ships, the Swallow and Weymouth . . .*, London, 1735, p. 198.
16. *The Journal of a Slave Trader*, ed. Barnard Martin and Martin Spurrel, London, 1962 (afterwards *Newton's Journal*), pp. 3–62.
17. Alexander Falconbridge, *An Account of the Slave Trade on the Coast of Africa*, London, 1788, p. 9.
18. Falconbridge, *Account of the Slave Trade*, p. 61.
19. Webster, 'The Material Culture of Slave Shipping', pp. 105–10.
20. Quoted in Rediker, *The Slave Ship*, p. 196. For precautions against possible revolt, see Eric Robert Taylor, *If We Must Die. Shipboard Insurrections in the Era of the Atlantic Slave Trade*, Baton Rouge, LA, 2006, pp. 82–3.
21. John Newton, *Thoughts upon the African Slave Trade*, London, 1788, p. 12.
22. Newton, *Thoughts upon the African Slave Trade*, pp. 15–16.
23. William Snelgrave, *A New Account of Some Parts of Guinea and the Slave Trade*, London, 1734, pp. 189–90.
24. Taylor, *If We Must Die*, pp. 82–3.
25. Stammers, 'Guineamen', p. 40.
26. Falconbridge, *Account of the Slave Trade*, p. 6.
27. Thomas Clarkson, *The History of the Rise, Progress and Accomplishment of the Abolition of the African Slave trade by the British Parliament*, 2 vols, London, 1808, II, p. 377 (afterwards *History of Abolition*).
28. Newton, *Thoughts upon the African Slave Trade*, p. 11.
29. John Atkins, *The Navy Surgeon; or, a Practical System of Surgery*, London, 1742, p. 370.
30. Ottobah Cugoano, *Thoughts and Sentiments on the Evil and Wicked Traffic of the Slavery and Commerce of the Human Species, Humbly Submitted to the Inhabitants of Great Britain*, London, 1787, p. 10.
31. David Eltis, *The Rise of African Slavery in the Americas*, Cambridge, 2000, p. 118; Stephanie Smallwood, *Saltwater Slavery. A Middle Passage from Africa to American Diaspora*, Cambridge, MA, 2008, p. 93.
32. Falconbridge, *Account of the Slave Trade*, pp. 27–9.
33. Mr Claxton, *An Abstract of the Evidence Delivered before a Select Committee of the House of Commons, in the years 1790 and 1791*, Edinburgh, 1791, p. 39.
34. Falconbridge, *Account of the Slave Trade*, pp. 25–6.
35. *Newton's Journal*, pp. 54–5.
36. *Abridgement of the Minutes of the Evidence, taken before a Committee of the whole House, to whom it was referred to consider of the Slave-trade, 1790*, London, 1790, p. 229.
37. Emma Christopher, *Slave Ship Sailors and their Captive Cargoes, 1730–1807*, Cambridge, 2006, p. 34.

38. John Newton, *Letters and Sermons*, 6 vols, Edinburgh, 1787, I, p. 53.
39. Newton, *Thoughts upon the African Slave Trade*, p. 4.
40. *Newton's Journal*, p. 71.
41. Newton, *Thoughts upon the African Slave Trade*, p. 14.
42. Thomas Clarkson, *An Essay on the Impolicy of the African Slave Trade*, London, 1788, p. 53. See also Herbert S. Klein, *The Atlantic Slave Trade*, Cambridge, 1999, p. 152.
43. Newton, *Thoughts upon the African Slave Trade*, p. 43.
44. Claxton, *Abstract of the Evidence*, p. 46.
45. Christopher, *Slave Ship Sailors*, ch. 2. See also W. Jeffrey Bolster, *Black Jacks. African American Seamen in the Age of Sail*, Cambridge, MA, 1997.
46. Assessing the Slave Trade, Estimates, Table, 1501–1866, *Trans-Atlantic Slave Trade Database*; Rediker, *The Slave Ship*, p. 225.
47. Christopher, *Slave Ship Sailors*, p. 28.
48. James Field Stanfield, *Observations on a Guinea Voyage. In a Series of Letters addressed to the Rev. Thomas Clarkson*, London, 1788, pp. 8–9.
49. *Newton's Journal*, p. 81.
50. Letter of 16 August 1700, in Ralph Davis, *The Rise of the English Shipping Industry in the Seventeenth and Eighteenth Centuries*, Newton Abbot, 1972, pp. 295–6.
51. *Newton's Journal*, p. 71.
52. Atkins, *A Voyage to Guinea*, p. 159.
53. *Newton's Journal*, pp. 85, 89, 91.
54. Christopher, *Slave Ship Sailors*, p. 38.
55. Stephen D. Behrendt, 'Human Capital in the British Slave Trade', in Richardson *et al.*, *Liverpool and Transatlantic Slavery*, ch. 3, pp. 66–97.
56. Evidence from slave-ship surgeons can be found in *An Abstract of the Evidence delivered before a Select Committee of the House of Commons, in the years 1790 and 1791*, Edinburgh, 1791, pp. 8–9.
57. Atkins, *A Voyage to Guinea*, pp. 179–80.
58. Christopher Bowes, *Medical Log of the 'Lord Stanley' 1792*, Library of the Royal College of Surgeons, Lincoln's Inn Fields, London.
59. Christopher, *Slave Ship Sailors*, p. 39.
60. Thomas Clarkson, *The Substance of the Evidence of Sundry Persons on the Slave Trade, Collected in the Course of a Tour made in the Autumn of the year 1788*, London, 1789, pp. 82–3.
61. 'A Muster Roll for the William, December 8 1781', Liverpool Muster Rolls, 1781, BT98/42, fol. 271. National Archives, Kew (afterwards TNA).
62. *An Abstract of the Evidence*, pp. 39–40; Falconbridge, *Account of the Slave Trade*, pp. 27–9; Klein, *Atlantic Slave Trade*, pp. 93–5.

Chapter 4: The making of the *Zong*

1. See Glossary, *Trans-Atlantic Slave Trade Database*.
2. *Carolina* (1745), voyage number 90011, and *Blackburn* (1747), voyage number 90086, *Trans-Atlantic Slave Trade Database*.
3. David Pope, 'The Wealth and Social Aspirations of Liverpool's Slave Merchants of the Second Half of the Eighteenth Century', in Richardson

et al., *Liverpool and Transatlantic Slavery*; Baucom, *Specters of the Atlantic*, pp. 48–9; Voyage Database, Vessel owner, William Gregson, *Trans-Atlantic Slave Trade Database*.

4. Morgan, 'Liverpool's Dominance in the British Slave Trade, 1740–1807', p. 20.
5. Names of slave-ship owners are derived from the *Trans-Atlantic Slave Trade Database*, cross-checked against David Pope, 'Liverpool's Leading Slave Merchants, 1750–1790' (Appendix 1), in Richardson *et al.*, *Liverpool and Transatlantic Slavery*, pp. 194–207.
6. *Fanny*, voyage number 91198, *John*, voyage number 92538, and *Viper*, voyage number 83974, *Trans-Atlantic Slave Trade Database*.
7. William Gregson Voyages, 1750–1800, *Trans-Atlantic Slave Trade Database*.
8. Pope, 'Liverpool's Leading Slave Merchants'.
9. Table, 1740–1800, Ships owned by William Gregson, Embarkation ports, *Trans-Atlantic Slave Trade Database*.
10. Morgan, 'Liverpool's Dominance in the British Slave Trade', pp. 28–9.
11. Table, 1740–1800, William Gregson, Specific disembarkation regions, *Trans-Atlantic Slave Trade Database*.
12. Table, *Gregson*, List of voyages, 1771–94, *Trans-Atlantic Slave Trade Database*.
13. Pope, 'Liverpool's Leading Slave Merchants', pp. 208–18.
14. Moss, *Liverpool Guide*, p. 104.
15. Aikin, *A Description of the Country*, p. 376.
16. Longmore, 'Civic Liverpool', pp. 137–8.
17. *Swallow* (1781), voyage number 83658, *Trans-Atlantic Slave Trade Database*.
18. List of Voyages, Richard Hanley, 1761–1781, *Trans-Atlantic Slave Trade Database*.
19. N.A.M. Rodger, *The Command of the Ocean. A Naval History of Britain, 1649–1815*, London, 2004, p. 331.
20. Wyndham Beawes, *Lex Mercatoria Rediviva: or, a Complete Code of Commercial Law*, 2 vols, Dublin, 1795, I, p. 223.
21. *Alert* (1782), voyage number 17905, *Trans-Atlantic Slave Trade Database*. The *Alert* had been built in Nantes, and had presumably been seized from the French.
22. *Zong* (1781), voyage number 84106, *Trans-Atlantic Slave Trade Database*. When she reached Jamaica, the name was changed again, to the *Richard*. See 'May 18 1782, Jamaica returns, 1782–3–4, List of Ships cleared out of Kingston', CO142/1; and Answer of William Gregson, January 1784, in Documents in Exchequer, E112/1528, TNA.
23. 'William, December 8 1781', Liverpool Muster Rolls, BT98/42, fol. 271.
24. John Lee, Solicitor General, in *Documents Relating to the Ship Zong*, 1783, National Maritime Museum, Greenwich (NMM), REC/19, p. 54. (Following the convention of James Oldham, henceforth I refer to this manuscript as the *Sharp Transcript*.)
25. 'Answer of Gregson and Company', Documents in Exchequer, E112/1528, TNA.

26. On the question of insurance, see Granville Sharp's Letter to William Pitt, 1783, in *Sharp Transcript*, p. 119.
27. The *William*, Liverpool Muster Rolls, 8 December 1781; *William* (1787), voyage number 80446, *Trans-Atlantic Slave Trade Database*.
28. For a description of sailing into São Tomé, with contemporary sketches of the main town and of the maritime approaches, see *Journal of the Diligent*, Beinecke Library, Yale University.
29. Table, List of voyages, 1750–1800, William Gregson, *Trans-Atlantic Slave Trade Database*. It is difficult to calculate the precise number of slave voyages William Gregson invested in; estimates vary from 143 to 174. See Jane Webster, 'The *Zong* in the Context of the Eighteenth-century Slave Trade', n. 9; Pope, 'Liverpool's Leading Slave Merchants' (Appendix 1), in Richardson *et al.*, *Liverpool and Transatlantic Slavery*.
30. Klein, *The Atlantic Slave Trade*, p. 150.
31. 'The Answer of Colonel James Kelsall', 12 November 1783, Documents in Exchequer, E112/1528, TNA.
32. *William* (1782), voyage number 84041, *Trans-Atlantic Slave Trade Database*.

Chapter 5: All at sea

1. *Black Joke* (1757), voyage number 77672, *Trans-Atlantic Slave Trade Database*.
2. *An Account of the Number of Negroes Delivered in to the Islands of Barbadoes, Jamaica and Antego, from the Year 1698 to 1708*. Beinecke Library, Yale University.
3. For contemporary economic arguments, see Charles Davenant, *A Clear Demonstration, from Points of Fact, that the Recovery, Preservation and Improvement of Britain's Share of the Trade to Africa, is Wholly Owing to the Industry, Care and Application of the Royal African Company*, London, 1709.
4. Morgan, *Slavery and the British Empire*, pp. 56–7; G.S.P. Freeman-Grenville, *The New Atlas of African History*, New York, 1991, p. 68; St Clair, *The Grand Slave Emporium*.
5. 'Minutes of the African Committee, 1780–1787', T70/145, TNA.
6. Table, William Gregson's voyages, Embarkation, 1750–1800, five year periods, *Trans-Atlantic Slave Trade Database*.
7. K.G. Davies, *The Royal African Company*, New York, 1970, pp. 247–8.
8. Mr Tweed, *Considerations and Remarks on the Present State of the Trade to Africa . . .*, London, 1771, p. 18.
9. *Extracts from an Account of the State of the British Forts on the Gold Coast of Africa*, London, 1778, pp. 5–6.
10. All these details about the behaviour of Robert Stubbs and John Robert are contained in the 'Interrogation' of witnesses, in T70/145, pp. 10–26, TNA.
11. Mr Miles, Interrogation, p. 16, T70/145, TNA.
12. Mr Ogilvie, Interrogation, pp. 10, 16, 20, T70/145, TNA.
13. Mr Miles, Interrogation, p. 14, T70/145, TNA.
14. Mr Ogilvie, Interrogation, pp. 10, 13–16, T70/145, TNA.
15. Mr Ogilvie, Interrogation, p. 16, T70/145, TNA.

16. Mr Weuves, Interrogation, p. 18, T70/145, TNA.
17. Mr Miles, Interrogation, p. 18, T70/145, TNA.
18. Mr Ogilvie, Mr Weuves, Mr Miles, Interrogation, pp. 26, 18–20, 25, T70/145, TNA.
19. *Minutes*, Committee Meeting, 22 December 1780, p. 1, T70/145, TNA.
20. *Minutes*, Committee Meeting, 26 July 1784, p. 234, T70/145, TNA.
21. Letter, 1781, in T70/146, TNA. I thank William St Clair for this reference.
22. Letter from Captain William Llewellin, Gold Coast, 13 January 1780, in 'Miscellaneous Letters to the African Committee', T70/1695, TNA. See also Andrew Lewis, 'Martin Dockray and the *Zong*: A Tribute in the Form of a Chronology', *Journal of Legal History*, vol. 28, no. 3, December 2007, p. 359.
23. *Richard*, 26 October 1782, Liverpool Muster Rolls, BT 98/42, p. 227. TNA.
24. Solicitor General, *Sharp Transcript*, p. 50.
25. The ship docked in Black River in the parish of St Elizabeth, but there is no trace of Collingwood's death or burial in the church records for that parish in 1782. See 'Burial of white persons, 1782', *St Elizabeth Parish Records, Burials, 1707–1820*, Jamaica Archives, 1B/11/8/61. James Kelsall reported that Collingwood died in Kingston: 'The Answer of Col. James Kelsall', Documents in Exchequer, E112/1528, TNA.
26. Stephen D. Behrendt, 'Crew Mortality in the Transatlantic Slave Trade in the Eighteenth Century', *Slavery and Abolition*, vol. 18, no. 1, April 1997; Thomas Clarkson, *History of Abolition*, I, ch. XIV.
27. *Journal de bord d'un Negrier, Guinee, 1731* (*Log of the Diligent, 1731*). Beinecke Library, Yale University.
28. Rediker, *The Slave Ship*, pp. 197–8.
29. *Newton's Journal*, 7 April–20 May 1754, pp. 93–4.
30. P.D. Curtin, *The Atlantic Slave Trade. A Census*, Madison, 1969, p. 278.
31. Information kindly provided by Dr Antonio de Almeida Mendes.
32. *Zong* (1781), voyage number 84106, *Trans-Atlantic Slave Trade Database*.
33. 'Gregson v. Gilbert', *Cases in the Kings Bench*, 23 and 24 Geo. III, fol. 33, Dampier MSS, Middle Temple Library.
34. Mr Davenport, *Sharp Transcript*, p. 4.
35. Robert Harms, *The Diligent. A Voyage through the Worlds of Slavery*, New York, 2002, pp. 308–9; Klein, *The Atlantic Slave Trade*, pp. 94–5.
36. Stanfield, *Observations on a Guinea Voyage*, p. 13.
37. Mr Pigot, *Sharp Transcript*, p. 25.
38. John Hamilton Moore, *The Practical Navigator and Seaman's Daily Assistant*, London, 1772, pp. 239, 162.
39. Rodger, *The Command of the Ocean*, pp. 382–3.
40. Dava Sobel, *Longitude. The True Story of a Lone Genius Who Solved the Greatest Scientific Problem of His Time*, New York, 1995.
41. Rodger, *The Command of the Ocean*, p. 382.
42. Moore, *The Practical Navigator*, p. 157.
43. Moore, *The Practical Navigator*, p. 170.
44. 'Gregson v. Gilbert', fol. 33.
45. 'Gregson v. Gilbert', fols. 33–40.
46. 'The Answer of Colonel James Kelsall', 12 November 1783, Documents in Exchequer, E112/1528, TNA.

47. 'Gregson v. Gilbert', fols 33–40; Lewis, 'Martin Dockray and the *Zong*', p. 364; *Sharp Transcript*, pp. 77–8; 'The Answer of Colonel James Kelsall'.
48. 'The Answer of Colonel James Kelsall'.
49. *Sharp Transcript*, p. 59.
50. Lewis, 'Martin Dockray and the *Zong*', pp. 363–4.
51. Evidence of Robert Stubbs, *Sharp Transcript*, pp. 79–80.
52. Lewis, 'Martin Dockray and the *Zong*', p. 364.
53. *Sharp Transcript*, pp. 40, 42, 50, 103.

Chapter 6: An open secret

1. *London Courant, Westminster Chronicle and Daily Advertiser*, 13 March 1782.
2. Letter, *Morning Chronicle and London Advertiser*, 18 March 1783, reprinted in Shyllon, *Black Slaves in Britain*, pp. 187–8.
3. For Equiano's own account, see Olaudah Equiano, *The Interesting Narrative of the Life of Olaudah Equiano, or Gustavus Vassa, the African. Written by Himself*, London, 2 vols, 1789. See also Vincent Carretta, *Equiano the African. Biography of a Self-Made Man*, Athens, GA, 2005; James Walvin, *An African's Life. The Life and Times of Olaudah Equiano, 1745–1797*, London, 1998.
4. *Gentleman's Magazine*, 1783, p. 228.
5. Abolition of the Slave Trade, first-class stamps, Royal Mail 2007.
6. Lord Mansfield presided at the original trial, although that crucial fact has only become apparent to historians in recent years. See Oldham, 'Insurance Litigation', p. 312.
7. Ottobah Cugoano, *Thoughts and Sentiments*, 1787, p. 112.
8. Francis Moore, *Travels into the Inland Parts of Africa: Containing a Description of the Several Nations up the River Gambia*, London, 1738, pp. 64, 156.
9. For a list of revolts, see Taylor, *If We Must Die*, pp. 179–213.
10. Harms, *The Diligent*, p. 270.
11. 'Letter of Philip Quaque, February 8th 1786', in Philip D. Curtin, *Africa Remembered. Narratives by West Africans from the Era of the Slave Trade*, Madison, WI, 1967, p. 133; Christopher, *Slave Ship Sailors*, p. 6.
12. *Lloyd's List*, London, 5 January 1745, NMM. See also *Scipio* (1749), voyage number 90227, *Trans-Atlantic Slave Trade Database*.
13. Atkins, *A Voyage to Guinea*, p. 73; Snelgrave, *A New Account*, pp. 183–4; Christopher, *Slave Ship Sailors*, p. 185.
14. Snelgrave, *A New Account*, pp. 183–4.
15. Vincent Brown, *The Reaper's Garden. Death and Power in the World of Atlantic Slavery*, Cambridge, MA, 2008, ch. 4.
16. Snelgrave, *A New Account*, pp. 183–4.
17. Christopher, *Slave Ship Sailors*, pp. 186–7.
18. Timothy Cunningham, *A New and Complete Law-dictionary, or General Abridgement of the Law*, 2 vols, London, 1771, I, 'Admiralty'.

19. Oldham, 'Insurance Litigation', p. 309; Shyllon, *Black Slaves*, pp. 202–4.
20. John Wesket, *A Complete Digest of the Theory Laws and Practice of Insurance*, London, 1781, p. 525, my italics.
21. Christopher, *Slave Ship Sailors*, p. 183, n. 64.
22. A copy of an original policy is reprinted in William D. Winter, *A Short Sketch of the History and Principles of Marine Insurance*, New York, 1935, pp. 24–5. For examples of insurance policies printed in London, but with handwritten details drafted on to the policy at Cape Coast, see policies for the ships *Unity*, *Scipio* and *Black Prince*, 1756–7, in T70/1695, TNA.
23. A recent commentator has remarked: 'if such a contract were to be drawn up for the first time today, it would be put down as the work of a lunatic endowed with a private sense of humour', quoted in Oldham, 'Insurance Litigation', p. 301.
24. Oldham, 'Insurance Litigation', pp. 301–2.
25. Oldham, 'Insurance Litigation', p. 307.

Chapter 7: In the eyes of the law

1. J.M. Baker, *An Introduction to English Legal History*, London, 1993, pp. 540–44. For Mansfield and slavery, see James Oldham, *English Common Law in the Age of Mansfield*, Chapel Hill, NC, 2004, ch. 17, 'Slavery'.
2. There is no recent biography of Granville Sharp. But for good portraits of him, see Steven M. Wise, *Though the Heavens May Fall. The Landmark Trial that Led to the End of Human Slavery*, Cambridge, MA, 2005; Christopher L. Brown, *Moral Capital. Foundations of British Abolitionism*, Chapel Hill, NC, 2006 and Shyllon, *Black Slaves in Britain*.
3. Prince Hoare, *Memoirs of Granville Sharp*, London, 1820, p. 33n.
4. Hoare, *Memoirs of Granville Sharp*, pp. 32–9.
5. The 'Yorke-Talbot opinion' is reprinted in Candidus, *A Letter to Philo Africanus*, London, 1788, pp. 33–4.
6. H.T. Catterall, ed., *Judicial Cases Concerning American Slavery and the Negro*, 5 vols, Washington, DC, 1926–37, I, pp. 9–12.
7. Hoare, *Memoirs of Granville Sharp*, p. 37.
8. Quoted in James Oldham, *The Mansfield Manuscripts and the Growth of English Law in the Eighteenth Century*, 2 vols, Chapel Hill, NC, 1992, II, pp. 1225–6.
9. For a remarkable study of Lord Mansfield, see Oldham, *The Mansfield Manuscripts*.
10. Wise, *Though the Heavens May Fall*, p. 71.
11. Oldham, *The Mansfield Manuscripts*, II, pp. 1222, 1226, 1243, ch. 21, 'Slavery'.
12. John Wentworth, 'Policies of Assurance', *A Complete System of Pleading*, Dublin, 1799, I; Sir James Allan Park, *Appendix to a System of the Law of Marine Insurance*, Boston, 1800 edition, ch. 3; William Tarn Pritchard, 'Marine Insurance', *Digest of Admiralty and Maritime Law*, 2 vols, London, 3rd edition, I; Oldham, *The Mansfield Manuscripts*, I, p. 197.

13. Jeremy Krikler, 'The *Zong* and the Lord Chief Justice', *History Workshop Journal*, 64, Autumn 2007, pp. 34–5. See also Wesket, *A Complete Digest*, pp. 11, 525.

14. James Allan Park, *A System of the Law of Insurances, with Three Chapters on Bottomry; on Insurance on Lives; and on Insurances against Fire*, London, 1789, p. iii. For Mansfield and insurance, see Oldham, *English Common Law*, ch. 5, 'Insurance'.

15. Hoare, *Memoirs of Granville Sharp*, pp. 39–42.

16. Sir John Fielding, *Extracts from such of the Penal Laws, as Particularly Relate to the Peace and Good Order of this Metropolis*, London, 1762, pp. 142–4.

17. Copy of advertisement, Letter Book of Granville Sharp, p. 3, York Minster Library.

18. Kathleen Chater, *Untold Stories. Black People in England and Wales, 1660–1812*, PhD thesis, University of London, 2007, pp. 136–9; Brown, *Moral Capital*, pp. 91–2; Clarkson, *History of Abolition*, I, p. 72.

19. Clarkson, *History of Abolition*, I, pp. 73–4; Shyllon, *Black Slaves*, pp. 43–6; Wise, *Though the Heavens May Fall*, p. 69.

20. Hoare, *Memoirs of Granville Sharp*, p. 52; Clarkson, *History of Abolition*, I, pp. 73–4.

21. Hoare, *Memoirs of Granville Sharp*, p. 48.

22. Francis Hargrave, *An Argument in the Case of James Somersett, A Negro*, London (Boston edition), 1774, p. 4. To complicate matters further, the two men, master and slave, had lived for four years in Massachusetts *before* sailing to England. The absence of slavery in that colony had important implications for the arguments about to unfold in an English court: Somerset had arrived in England *not* from a slave colony (Virginia) but from one which had a virtual 'common law' of abolition. Wise, *Though the Heavens May Fall*, pp. 130–1.

23. Hoare, *Memoirs of Granville Sharp*, p. 71.

24. Oldham, *Mansfield*, II, p. 1228.

25. Wise, *Though the Heavens May Fall*, p. 133.

26. Hoare, *Memoirs of Granville Sharp*, p. 75.

27. Oldham, *Mansfield*, II, p. 1228. For the latest study of the West India lobby, see David Ryden, *West India Slavery and British Abolition, 1783–1807*, Cambridge, 2009.

28. For the trial itself, see Edward Fiddes, 'Lord Mansfield and the Somersett Case', *Law Quarterly Review*, 1934, vol. L; Ruth Paley, 'After Somerset: Mansfield, Slavery and the Law in England, 1772–1830', in *Law, Crime and English Society, 1660–1830*, ed. Norma Landau, Cambridge, 2002, ch. 8; Shyllon, *Black Slaves in Britain*, chs 6–10.

29. Wise, *Though the Heavens May Fall*, pp. 150–53.

30. Oldham, *Mansfield*, II, pp. 1228–9.

31. Capel Lofft, Easter Term, 12 Geo. 3.1772. KB. *Report of Cases adjudged in the Court of King's Bench for Easter term 12 Geo. 3 to Michaelmas, 14 Geo. 3*, London, 1776.

32. Catterall, *Judicial Cases*, I, p. 2, n. 7.

33. Oldham, *Mansfield*, II, p. 1234.

34. *Scots Magazine*, vol. 34, 1772, p. 299.

35. Quoted in Shyllon, *Black Slaves in Britain*, pp. 110–11.
36. Oldham, *Mansfield*, II, p. 1238.
37. Edward Long, *Candid Reflections upon the Judgement lately awarded by the Court of King's Bench in Westminster Hall, on what is commonly called the Negroe-cause*, London, 1772, pp. ii–iii.
38. 'Knight v. Wedderburn, 1778', in Catterall, *Judicial Cases*, I, pp. 1–19; Iain Whyte, *Scotland and the Abolition of Black Slavery, 1756–1838*, Edinburgh, 2006, p. 18.
39. *Virginia Gazette*, 30 September 1773, p. 3.
40. Carretta, *Equiano*, p. 212.
41. Carretta, *Equiano*, pp. 208–9.
42. 25 November 1793, Letter Book of Granville Sharp, York Minster Library.
43. *The Interesting Narrative of the Life of Olaudah Equiano*, ed. Vincent Carretta, London, 1995, p. 181.
44. Hoare, *Memoirs of Granville Sharp*, p. 93n.

Chapter 8: A matter of necessity

1. See 'Interior of Westminster Hall', Exhibition Catalogue, no. 13, in *The British Slave Trade* ed. Farrell, Unwin and Walvin, pp. 290–1.
2. The case was not formally published until 1831. See 'Gregson v Gilbert', 3 Dougl 233 (1783) 99ER, 629–30. Available on *Commonwealth Legal Information Institute*, *English Reports*, www.commonliii.org.
3. For a good analysis of the documentation of the *Zong* case, see Oldham, 'Insurance Litigation'.
4. *Sharp Transcript*, p. 1.
5. Hoare, *Memoirs of Granville Sharp*, p. 236.
6. Oldham, 'Insurance Litigation', p. 312; 3 Dougl 233 (1783) 99ER 629–630, *Commonwealth Legal Information Institute*, *English Reports*.
7. Moore, *The Practical Navigator*, pp. 6, 157.
8. Petition to William Pitt, 1783, E112/1528/173, TNA. See also Letter to William Pitt, 1783, in *Sharp Transcript*, pp. 124–5.
9. Answer of William Gregson, January 1784, and 'Petition' for Thomas Gilbert, both in E112/1528, TNA.
10. *Sharp Transcript*, pp. 19, 125. See also Statements in E112/1528/173, TNA.
11. 'The Answer of Colonel James Kelsall', 12 November 1783, Documents in Exchequer, E112/1528, TNA.
12. Granville Sharp, Letter to Admiralty, *Sharp Transcript*, pp. 99–110. Also in Hoare, *Memoirs of Granville Sharp*, pp. 242–4.
13. *Sharp Transcript*, p. 1.
14. 'Minutes of the African Committee', 22 December 1780, T70/145, TNA.
15. 'Minutes of the African Committee', T70/145, p. 234.
16. *Sharp Transcript*, p. 2.
17. Mr Davenport, *Sharp Transcript*, p. 3.
18. Oldham, 'Insurance Litigation', pp. 307–10.
19. *Sharp Transcript*, p. 7.
20. *Sharp Transcript*, pp. 13–14.

21. Petition of Gilbert syndicate to William Pitt, *Documents in Exchequer*, E112/1528/173, TNA.

22. Hoare, *Memoirs of Granville Sharp*, pp. 236, 240. For a copy of a standard insurance policy – with gaps left for the names of the relevant parties to be written in – see Printed Insurance Form, 'Printed according to the Form revived and confirmed at New Lloyds, on the 12th of January 1779. Sold by W. Stephen, No. 2 Bartholomew Lane', T70/1549, TNA.

23. See Mr Heywood, *Sharp Transcript*, p. 39.

24. Solicitor General, *Sharp Transcript*, pp. 47–8.

25. Solicitor General, *Sharp Transcript*, p. 51.

26. Solicitor General, *Sharp Transcript*, pp. 52–3.

27. On the law of jettisoning, see Wyndham Beawes, *Lex Mercatoria Rediviva, or the Merchant's Directory*, London, 1761, 2nd edn, p. 130.

28. Mr Pigot, *Sharp Transcript*, p. 19.

29. Mr Heywood, *Sharp Transcript*, p. 32.

30. Mr Pigot was the fiercest of critics in court: see *Sharp Transcript*, pp. 19–30, and Hoare, *Memoirs of Granville Sharp*, p. 240.

31. All quotations are from *Sharp Transcript*, pp. 30–32.

32. *Sharp Transcript*, p. 20.

33. Hoare, *Memoirs of Granville Sharp*, pp. 236, 240.

34. Solicitor General and Mr Pigot, *Sharp Transcript*, p. 54.

35. *Sharp Transcript*, pp. 35–6.

36. *Sharp Transcript*, p. 50.

37. Mr Chambres, *Sharp Transcript*, p. 81.

38. Mr Chambres, *Sharp Transcript*, pp. 65–6.

39. Lord Mansfield, *Sharp Transcript*, p. 20.

40. Hoare, *Memoirs of Granville Sharp*, p. 241, my italics.

41. Lord Mansfield, *Sharp Transcript*, pp. 20–1.

42. See, for example, the public discussion in Jamaica about the *Zong* killings in 2007: *Jamaica Gleaner*, 1 July 2007.

43. Hoare, *Memoirs of Granville Sharp*, p. 243n.

44. *Sharp Transcript*, p. 47.

45. Hoare, *Memoirs of Granville Sharp*, pp. 239–40.

46. Letter to the Admiralty, *Sharp Transcript*, p. 104. Also in Prince Hoare, *Memoirs of Granville Sharp*, pp. 242–3.

47. Lord Mansfield, *Sharp Transcript*, pp. 60–61, 76.

48. Lord Mansfield, *Sharp Transcript*, pp. 89–90.

49. The final act in the legal proceedings took place when the injunction was formally dismissed in May 1784. See item no. 110, 3 May 1784, in E112/47, TNA.

50. 'The Answer of Colonel James Kelsall', Liverpool, 26 July 1783, E112/1528, TNA.

51. James Kelsall's evidence, quoted in court by the Solicitor General, *Sharp Transcript*, p. 57.

52. 'The Answer of Colonel James Kelsall', E112/1528, TNA.

53. July 1783, Granville Sharp to the Duke of Portland, *Sharp Transcript*, p. 113. Also in Hoare, *Memoirs of Granville Sharp*, p. 241.

Chapter 9: In the wake of the *Zong*

1. Table, William Gregson, Voyages, 1780–1800, *Trans-Atlantic Slave Trade Database*.
2. 'William Murray. Lord Mansfield, 1705–1793', entry by James Oldham in *The Oxford Dictionary of National Biography*, 2004.
3. Brown, *Moral Capital*, pp. 163–4.
4. Hoare, *Memoirs of Granville Sharp*, pp. 236–47.
5. Hoare, *Memoirs of Granville Sharp*, p. 236.
6. Hoare, *Memoirs of Granville Sharp*, part II, ch. 1.
7. E.C. Black, *The Association. British Extraparliamentary Political Organization, 1769–1793*, Cambridge, MA, 1963; Caroline Robbins, *The Eighteenth-century Commonwealth Man*, Cambridge, MA, 1968.
8. Brown, *Moral Capital*, p. 194.
9. Hoare, *Memoirs of Granville Sharp*, pp. 245–6.
10. Hoare, *Memoirs of Granville Sharp*, pp. 241–2.
11. *Sharp Transcript*, pp. 105, 108.
12. *Sharp Transcript*, p. 95; Hoare, *Memoirs of Granville Sharp*, pp. 242–4.
13. All these documents are in the National Maritime Museum, Greenwich: *Documents Relating to the Ship Zong*, 1783, REC/19 ('Sharp Transcript').
14. 'Answer of Colonel James Kelsall', E112/1528/173, TNA.
15. They are dated July 1783; the *Zong* hearing ended on 21 May 1783.
16. Much has been made of the arrangement: see Baucom, *Specters of the Atlantic*, pp. 123–6.
17. Hoare, *Memoirs of Granville Sharp*, p. 187.
18. 'Memorandum', 1779, p. 38. Gloucester County Archives.
19. Hoare, *Memoirs of Granville Sharp*, p. 187.
20. Brown, *Moral Capital*, p. 353.
21. Beilby Porteus, *A Sermon Preached before the Incorporated Society for the Propagation of the Gospel in Foreign Parts . . .*, 21 February 1783, London, 1783.
22. Hoare, *Memoirs of Granville Sharp*, p. 246.
23. Newton, *Thoughts upon the African Slave Trade*, pp. 18–19.
24. He thanked 'a Gentleman, whose unremitting endeavours in the cause of humanity demand the sincere thanks of every friend of liberty, justice and religion'. No one else other than Sharp fits that description in 1785. George Gregory, *Essays Historical and Moral*, London, 1785 edn, p. 304n.
25. Gregory, *Essays*, London, 1788 edn, pp. 355–7.
26. Gregory, 'Of the Justice and Humanity of the Slave Trade', *Essays*, pp. 357–8.
27. Gregory, 'Of the Justice and Humanity of the Slave Trade', p. 358.
28. Ottobah Cugoano, *Thoughts and Sentiments*. The best modern version is edited by Vincent Carretta, London, 1990, who describes *Thoughts and Sentiments* as 'the most overt and extended challenge to slavery ever made by a person of African descent', p. xx.
29. Cugoano, *Thoughts and Sentiments*, 1787, pp. 111–12.
30. Newton, *Thoughts upon the African Slave Trade*, pp. 18–19.

31. James Ramsay, *An Essay on the Treatment and Conversion of African Slaves in the British Sugar Colonies*, London, 1784; Brown, *Moral Capital*, pp. 228–9.
32. Shyllon, *Black Slaves in Britain*, p. 199, n. 2.
33. James Ramsay, *An Essay on the Treatment and Conversion of African Slaves*, p. 35n. See also F.O. Shyllon, *James Ramsay. The Unknown Abolitionist*, Edinburgh, 1977.
34. Thomas Cooper, *Letters on the Slave Trade*, Manchester, 1787, pp. 14–15.
35. Estimates, 5-year tables, 1780–1810, *Trans-Atlantic Slave Trade Database*.

Chapter 10: Abolition and after

1. For a study of the wider group of black writers, see *Unchained Voices. An Anthology of Black Authors in the English-Speaking World of the Eighteenth Century*, ed. Vincent Caretta, Lexington, KT, 1996.
2. Even women, traditionally excluded from public political debate, were secured a role in the politics of abolition: Clare Midgley, *Women Against Slavery. The British Campaign, 1780–1870*, London, 1992.
3. Colin Bonwick, *The American Revolution*, London, 2005; Edward Countryman, *The American Revolution*, London, 2003.
4. Laurent Dubois, *A Colony of Citizens. Revolution and Slave Emancipation in the French Caribbean, 1787–1804*, Chapel Hill, NC, 2004.
5. 'Peter Peckard, *c.*1718–97', entry by John Walsh in *The Oxford Dictionary of National Biography*, 2004; John Walsh and Ronald Hyam, *Peter Peckard. Liberal Churchman and Anti-Slave Trade Campaigner*, Magdalene College, Cambridge, Occasional papers, no. 6; James Elmes, *Thomas Clarkson. A Monograph*, London, 1854, pp. 8–11.
6. Walsh and Hyam, *Peter Peckard*; Elmes, *Thomas Clarkson*, pp. 8–11.
7. Clarkson, *History of Abolition*, I, pp. 207, 403.
8. Clarkson, *History of Abolition*, I, pp. 208–9.
9. Clarkson, *History of Abolition*, I, pp. 208–9.
10. Clarkson, *History of Abolition*, I, pp. 216–17; Judith Jennings, *The Business of Abolishing the British Slave Trade, 1783–1807*, London, 1997, ch. 3.
11. Clarkson, *History of Abolition*, I, pp. 214–16.
12. For the importance of Teston, see Brown, *Moral Capital*, pp. 341–53.
13. Clarkson, *History of Abolition*, I, p. 225.
14. Table, William Gregson, Voyages, 1785–90, *Trans-Atlantic Slave Trade Database*.
15. *Minutes of the London Abolition Committee*, 3 vols, Add. Ms 21, 254–21, 256, I, 22 May 1787, British Library; Clarkson, *History of Abolition*, I, pp. 277–8.
16. Granville Sharp to John Sharp, 19 July 1787, Granville Sharp Papers, Gloucester RO. In fact Quakers had petitioned parliament for abolition in 1783; Jennings, *The Business*, ch. 3.
17. For the story of popular literacy, see David Vincent, *Literacy and Popular Culture, England, 1750–1914*, Cambridge, 1993.

18. James Walvin, 'The Propaganda of Anti-Slavery', in *Slavery and British Society, 1776–1846*, ed. James Walvin, London, 1982, p. 52.
19. The popularity of abolition is explored in Seymour Drescher, *Capitalism and Antislavery: British Popular Mobilization in Comparative Perspective*, New York, 1987.
20. Ellen Wilson, *Thomas Clarkson. A Biography*, York, 1996, p. 42.
21. Clarkson, *History of Abolition*, I, p. 418.
22. *Hansard's Debates*, 1066–1918, vol. XXVII, 1788–1789, cols 396, 498, 501, 644. See also *Gentleman's Magazine*, 1788, pp. 610–13, 794–800.
23. *Hansard's Debates*, vol. XXVII, cols 495–501.
24. Betty Fladeland, ' "Our Cause being One and the Same": Abolitionists and Chartism', in *Slavery and British Society*, ed. Walvin, ch. 3; James Walvin, 'William Wilberforce, Yorkshire and the Anti-Slavery movement, 1787–1838', in *Richard Oastler and Yorkshire Slavery*, ed. John Hargreaves, Huddersfield, 2011.
25. Quoted in Seymour Drescher, 'Public Opinion and Parliament in the Abolition of the British Slave Trade', in Farrell *et al.*, eds, *The British Slave Trade*, p. 51.
26. *Hansard's Debates*, vol. XXVII, col. 644.
27. Wilson, *Thomas Clarkson*, pp. 43–4.
28. See Jenny Uglow, *The Lunar Men*, London, 2002.
29. *Supplement to Mr Cooper's Letters on the Slave Trade*, Warrington, 1788, p. 37.
30. Thomas Clarkson, *Essay on the Slavery and Commerce of the Human Species*, London, 1788, p. 99.
31. Drescher, 'Public Opinion and Parliament', pp. 48–51.
32. The Act is reproduced in *English Historical Documents*, ed. A. Aspinall and E. Anthony Smith, London, 1959, pp. 803–4.
33. Quoted in Jennings, *The Business*, p. 89.
34. Anonymous letter, 18 November 1791, in CO 137/89, TNA.
35. *Abstract of the Acts of parliament for abolishing the Slave Trade and of the Order, in Council Founded on them*, London, 1810, p. 23. The best account of the politics of abolition remains Roger Anstey, *The British Slave Trade and British Abolition*, London, 1975.
36. Robin Furneaux, *William Wilberforce*, London, 1974, p. 253; William Hague, *William Wilberforce*, London, 2007, p. 354.
37. Hague, *Wilberforce*, pp. 354–5.
38. Thomas Clarkson, 'The Account of Efforts, 1807–1824', pp. 12, 16–17, *Thomas Clarkson Papers*, Huntington Library, San Marino, CA.
39. David Eltis, 'A Brief Overview of the Trans-Atlantic Slave Trade', *Trans-Atlantic Slave Trade Database*.
40. Table of embarkations/disembarkation, 25-year periods, *Trans-Atlantic Slave Trade Database*.
41. Adrian Desmond and James Moore, *Darwin's Sacred Cause. Race, Slavery and the Quest for Human Origins*, London, 2010, ch. 4.
42. Leslie Bethell, *The Abolition of the Brazilian Slave Trade. Britain, Brazil and the Slave Trade Question, 1807, 1869*, Cambridge, 1970, p. 123.

43. Such cases were reported in the African Institute's *Annual Report* in 1821, 1823, 1825 and 1826. They also appeared in *Parliamentary Papers* in 1826 and in the *Edinburgh Review* in 1826. They were reported in the *United Services Journal* for 1833, and in Robert Walsh's *Notices of Brazil in 1828 and 1829*, London, 1830.
44. Thomas Fowell Buxton, *The African Slave Trade*, 1839, p. 109.
45. Quoted in Buxton, *The African Slave Trade*, p. 118. First reported in the *African Institution Report*, 1826, pp. 62–3, British Library.
46. *Foreign Slave Trade. Abstract of the Information recently Laid on the Table of the House of Commons on the Subject of the Slave Trade*, London, 1821, pp. 83–5. Buxton, *The African Slave Trade*, pp. 110–12.
47. *Foreign Slave Trade, Abstract*, pp. 104–6.
48. The case is discussed in Sian Rees, *Sweet Water and Bitter. The Ships that Stopped the Slave Trade*, London, 2009, pp. 58–60. Buxton, *The African Slave Trade*, p. 114.
49. *The Times*, 26 December 1831, p. 2; 27 March 1832, p. 2. Desmond and Moore, *Darwin's Sacred Cause*, p. 73. See also Buxton, *The African Slave Trade*, p. 129.
50. Buxton, *The African Slave Trade*, p. 130.
51. Buxton, *The African Slave Trade*, p. 135.
52. Buxton, *The African Slave Trade*, p. 130.
53. Buxton, *The African Slave Trade*, pp. 138–41.
54. James Walvin, 'The Propaganda of Anti-Slavery'; Midgley, *Women Against Slavery*; David Turley, *The Culture of English Antislavery, 1780–1860*, London, 1991.
55. When British slaves were emancipated, in 1838, the British parliament set aside a massive £20 million (raised by the Rothschilds) as compensation – for the slave-owners, not the slaves. See the current research project, 'Legacies of British Slave Ownership', www.ucl.ac.uk/lbs.
56. Robert Isaac Wilberforce and Samuel Wilberforce, *The Life of William Wilberforce*, 5 vols, London, 1838.

Chapter 11: Remembering the *Zong*

1. See HM Government, *Bicentenary of the Abolition of the Slave Trade Act, 1807–2007*, published by the Department for Communities and Local Government, March 2007.
2. See www.understandingslavery.com.
3. See www.gloucestershire.gov.uk/index.
4. Clifford Hill, *The Zong Report*, published by the Centre for Contemporary Ministry, Moggerhanger Park, Bedfordshire, 2007.
5. *Jamaica Gleaner*, 1 July and 31 December 2007.
6. 'Remembering Slave Trade Abolitions: Reflections on 2007 in International Perspective', Diana Paton and Jane Webster, guest editors, *Slavery and Abolition*, vol. 30, no. 2, June 2009.
7. Answer of William Gregson, January 1784, E112/1528, TNA.
8. Wood, *Blind Memory*, pp. 25–9. The *Amistad*, though not of course an *Atlantic* slave ship, carried slaves alongside other cargo, and became globally famous via the film by Stephen Spielberg. For drawings of the

Amistad Africans, see William H. Townsend, *Sketches of the Amistad Captives*, c. 1839–40, Beinecke Library, Yale University.

9. Malcolm Gladwell, *The Tipping Point*, London, 2001.
10. *Jamaica Gleaner*, 1 July 2007.
11. James Walvin, *Fruits of Empire. Exotic Produce and British Taste, 1660–1800*, London, 1997.
12. Midgley, *Women Against Slavery*, p. 35.

Further Reading

General

Anyone interested in the Atlantic slave trade should begin their enquiries online, by using the magnificent *Trans-Atlantic Slave Trade Database* at www.slavevoyages.org. The introductory essays written by the editors and contributors to that project provide an excellent starting point. Alternatively, the *Atlas of the Transatlantic Slave Trade*, edited by David Eltis and David Richardson, New Haven, 2010, is the best up-to-date study in print format. For the broader histories of slavery, consult D.B. Davis, *Inhuman Bondage. The Rise and Fall of Slavery in the New World*, New York, 2006, and Seymour Drescher, *Abolition. A History of Slavery and Antislavery*, New York, 2009.

The story of the *Zong* is the focus of Ian Baucom, *Specters of the Atlantic. Finance Capital, Slavery, and the Philosophy of History*, Durham, NC, 2005. An important collection of essays on the *Zong* can be found in the *Journal of Legal History*, vol. 28, no. 3, December 2007. The legal complexities posed by the *Zong* case can best be understood via the remarkable scholarship of James Oldham: *English Common Law in the Age of Mansfield*, Chapel Hill, NC, 2004, and *The Mansfield Manuscripts and the Growth of English Law in the Eighteenth Century*, Chapel Hill, NC, 2 vols, 1992. Finally, there is much to be learned from F.O. Shyllon's pioneering study, *Black Slaves in Britain*, London, 1974.

Chapter 1

On Turner's painting *The Slave Ship*, see the original in the Museum of Fine Arts, Boston, available on line at www.mfa.org. For commentary on that painting, see Marcus Wood, *Blind Memory. Visual Representations of Slavery in England and America, 1780–1865*, Manchester, 2000, and Martin Butlin and

Evelyn Joll, eds, *The Paintings of J.M.W. Turner*, London, 1984. For the influence of James Thomson on Turner, see James Sambrook, *James Thomson, 1700–1748. A Life*, Oxford, 1991.

Chapter 2

The history of Liverpool is fully covered in the essays in *Liverpool 800*, ed. John Belchem, Liverpool, 2008. Other themes in Liverpool's history are explored in John Belchem, ed., *Popular Politics, Riot and Labour. Essays in Liverpool History 1790–1940*, Liverpool, 1992.

For Liverpool and the slave trade, see the essays in *Liverpool and Transatlantic Slavery*, ed. David Richardson, Suzanne Schwarz and Anthony Tibbles, Liverpool, 2007. The slave trade at other English ports can be approached via Nigel Tattersfield, *The Forgotten Trade*, London, 1991; Melinda Elder, *The Slave Trade and the Economic Development of Eighteenth-Century Lancaster*, Halifax, 1992; and (for Bristol) Madge Dresser, *Slavery Obscured. The Social History of the Slave Trade in a Provincial Port*, London, 2001.

On the broader history of Liverpool, see the essays in *The Empire in One City?: Liverpool's Inconvenient Imperial Past*, ed. Sheryllynne Haggerty, Anthony Webster and Nicholas J. White, Manchester, 2008; and Sheryllynne Haggerty, *The British-Atlantic Trading Community, 1760–1810*, Leiden, 2006.

Chapter 3

For an evocative social history of the slave ship, see Marcus Rediker, *The Slave Ship. A Human History*, London, 2007. See also Emma Christopher, *Slave Ship Sailors and their Captive Cargoes, 1730–1807*, Cambridge, 2006. The early English slave trade is the concern of Stephanie Smallwood, *Saltwater Slavery. A Middle Passage from Africa to American Diaspora*, Cambridge, MA, 2008. The history of Atlantic slavery is best approached via David Eltis, *The Rise of African Slavery in the Americas*, Cambridge, 2000. Robert Harms, *The Diligent: a Voyage through the Worlds of Slavery*, New York, 2002, offers a remarkable case study of one French slave ship.

Many of the wider issues in this chapter are discussed in the essays in P.J. Marshall, ed., *The Oxford History of the British Empire*, vol. 2, *The Eighteenth Century*, Oxford, 1998. See also Anthony Tibbles, ed., *Transatlantic Slavery. Against Human Dignity*, London, 1994, and Douglas Hamilton and Robert J. Blyth, eds, *Representing Slavery*, Aldershot, 2007.

Chapter 4

The details of William Gregson's slave-trading career can be traced in the *Trans-Atlantic Slave Trade Database*. But see also David Pope, 'Wealth and Social Aspirations of Liverpool's Slave Merchants', in *Liverpool and Transatlantic Slavery*, ed. David Richardson *et al.*, Liverpool, 2007. The wider story of naval history is brilliantly captured in N.A.M. Rodger, *The Command of the Ocean. A Naval History of Britain, 1649–1815*, London, 2004.

Chapter 5

For the Royal African Company and its descendants, see K.G. Davies, *The Royal African Company*, New York, 1970, and William St Clair, *The Grand Slave Emporium. Cape Coast Castle and the British Slave Trade*, London, 2006. For the African slaving forts, see G.S.P. Freeman-Grenville, *The New Atlas of African History*, New York, 1991. Kenneth Morgan, *Slavery and the British Empire*, Oxford, 2007, places slavery succinctly in its broader imperial setting.

Chapter 6

By far the best study of Equiano is Vincent Carretta, *Equiano the African. Biography of a Self-Made Man*, Athens, GA, 2005. Violence on the slave ships is analysed in Eric Robert Taylor, *If We Must Die. Shipboard Insurrections in the Era of the Atlantic Slave Trade*, Baton Rouge, LA, 2006. The broader culture of violence in the world of Atlantic slavery can be studied in Vincent Brown, *The Reaper's Garden. Death and Power in the World of Atlantic Slavery*, Cambridge, MA, 2008.

Chapters 7 and 8

A good introduction to the story of English law and slavery is provided by J.M. Baker, *An Introduction to English Legal History*, London, 1993. Steven M. Wise, *Though the Heavens May Fall. The Landmark Trial that Led to the End of Human Slavery*, Cambridge, MA, 2005, is a recent account of the Somerset case of 1772. The intellectual and moral origins of abolition have recently been analysed in Christopher L. Brown, *Moral Capital. Foundations of British Abolitionism*, Chapel Hill, NC, 2006. The story of British black history has been studied most recently in Kathleen Chater, *Untold Stories: Black People in England and Wales during the Period of the British Slave Trade, 1660–1807*, Manchester, 2009.

Chapters 9, 10 and 11

For the broader story of abolition, see Seymour Drescher, *Abolition. A History of Slavery and Antislavery*, New York, 2009. For black writers of the eighteenth century, see Vincent Carretta, ed., *Unchained Voices. An Anthology of Black Authors in the English-Speaking World of the Eighteenth Century*, Lexington, Kentucky, 1996. The female campaign against slavery can be found in Clare Midgley, *Women Against Slavery. The British Campaign, 1780–1870*, London, 1992. For the seismic impact of the Haitian revolution, consult Laurent Dubois, *A Colony of Citizens. Revolution and Slave Emancipation in the French Caribbean, 1787–1804*, Chapel Hill, NC, 2004. Judith Jennings provides a detailed account of the organisation of abolition in *The Business of Abolishing the British Slave Trade, 1783–1807*, London, 1997. The best description of Thomas Clarkson is to be found in Ellen Wilson, *Thomas Clarkson. A Biography*, York, 1996. The most recent study of Wilberforce is William Hague's *William Wilberforce*, London, 2007.

For essays about abolition in 1807 (and its commemoration in 2007), see Stephen Farrell, Melanie Unwin and James Walvin, eds., *The British Slave Trade: Abolition, Parliament and People*, Edinburgh, 2007. The commemorations are also analysed in J.R. Oldfield, *'Chords of Freedom'. Commemoration, Ritual and British Transatlantic Slavery*, Manchester, 2007, and in the essays in the special edition of *Slavery and Abolition*, vol. 30, no. 2, June 2009. Finally, it is important to return to the classic account of abolition in Roger Anstey, *The British Slave Trade and British Abolition*, London, 1975.

Index